FEDERAL LAND,
WESTERN ANGER

DEVELOPMENT OF WESTERN RESOURCES

The Development of Western Resources is an interdisciplinary series focusing on the use and misuse of resources in the American West. Written for a broad readership of humanists, social scientists, and resource specialists, the books in this series emphasize both historical and contemporary perspectives as they explore the interplay between resource exploitation and economic, social, and political experiences.

John G. Clark, University of Kansas, General Editor

FEDERAL LAND, WESTERN ANGER

The Sagebrush Rebellion and Environmental Politics

R. McGreggor Cawley

 University Press of Kansas

© 1993 by the University Press of Kansas

Published by the University Press of Kansas (Lawrence, Kansas 66049), which was organized by the Kansas Board of Regents and is operated and funded by Emporia State University, Fort Hays State University, Kansas State University, Pittsburg State University, the University of Kansas, and Wichita State University

Library of Congress Cataloging-in-Publication Data

Cawley, R. McGreggor.
    Federal land, western anger : the Sagebrush Rebellion and environmental politics / R. McGreggor Cawley.
        p.   cm.
    Includes index.
    ISBN 0-7006-0613-0 (alk. paper)
    1. Public lands—United States—Management—Case studies.   2. Land use—Government policy—United States—Case studies.   3. Land use—West (U.S.)—Case studies.   4. Federal-state controversies—United States—Case studies.   5. Environmental policy—United States—Case studies.   I. Title.
HD216.C34   1993
333.1'0973—dc20   93-10690

British Library Cataloguing in Publication Data is available.

Printed in the United States of America
10 9 8 7 6 5 4 3 2 1

To Sondra, Aaron, and Leif
for their ongoing understanding and support

In recent years a concept of multiple land use has been growing. By the administration, at least, the grazing districts are no longer considered as grazing reserves only. It seems probable that this trend may continue.
—Phillip O. Foss, Politics and Grass, 1960

CONTENTS

PREFACE

In 1979 the State of Nevada enacted a law asserting a claim to title of lands within the state's boundaries administered by the Bureau of Land Management. This act marked the beginning of a movement—called the Sagebrush Rebellion—that ushered in one of the more turbulent episodes in the history of U.S. federal lands policy. It was a time, as former Colorado Senator Tim Wirth suggests, in which the West was "at war with itself" and public land policy was "paralyzed with animosity."[1] My primary intent in this book is to trace the contours of the controversy surrounding the Sagebrush Rebellion.

The question of what the Sagebrush Rebellion was is relatively easy to answer. It was a protest against the growth of environmental regulations throughout the 1960s and 1970s, orchestrated by various western public land users interested in pursuing commodity development activities such as grazing and mining. The question of why the Sagebrush Rebellion erupted is a bit more complicated.

To the extent that commodity interests believed environmental regulations restricted their use of the public lands, the Sagebrush Rebellion can be interpreted as an outburst motivated by economic self-interest. It is my contention, however, that approaching the Sagebrush Rebellion only in terms of self-interest is not as useful as it might appear. For example, it fails to explain the emotional energy expended by the Sagebrush Rebels and their opponents during the conflict. Nor does it explain how the complaints of disgruntled public land users became a national controversy that paralyzed the policy process. It is an answer to these questions that I have tried to construct in this book.

In pursuing this study, I have adopted some approaches that warrant brief comment. First, I chose to develop my study from the perspective of the Sagebrush Rebels. While this move runs the risk of having my book classified as an apology for the Sagebrush Rebellion, such was not my intent. I offer further explanation on my reasons for adopting this tack in Chapter 1.

Second, despite the recurring assertion that a primary job of policy analysis is to separate rhetoric from reality, I remain convinced that politics is first and foremost an artifact of language. Ideas structure our political world, and language is the medium in which ideas are developed. As my research progressed, it became increasingly clear that an implicit

ix

issue in dispute in this controversy was the meaning of conservation. In consequence, I have used the changing meaning of conservation as a background factor for developing my interpretation of the Sagebrush Rebellion.

Finally, this study is primarily concerned with the time span from the 1960s to the early 1990s. Although I have included historical background where it seemed necessary and appropriate, I elected not to offer a detailed history of public land policy. For those readers wanting a more thorough treatment of federal land history, I recommend Samuel Trask Dana's original *Forest and Range Policy* and Sally Fairfax's more recent updating of that text as useful starting places.

This book began as a dissertation completed in 1981. At the time, I understood that the Sagebrush Rebellion story had not yet ended. Nevertheless, expediency demanded that I conclude my study. In 1985, John Clark at University Press of Kansas expressed interest in both my dissertation and my desire to expand upon it. Thus began the journey that has culminated in this book. Were it not for the patience and encouragement of John Clark and Cynthia Miller at Kansas, the journey would never have been completed.

The writing of a book is always a joint process, and merely acknowledging the help of others never seems to offer just compensation. Nevertheless, there are many people who contributed directly and indirectly to this project to whom I owe a great debt of gratitude. Phillip O. Foss (my dissertation director), Henry Caulfield, Jr., and Robert Lawrence ushered me through my rather turbulent graduate studies at Colorado State University. I hope my work here demonstrates that their efforts were not wasted.

I am also grateful for the support offered by my colleagues at the University of Montana and the University of Wyoming. They remained continually cognizant of the formidable task posed by trying to write a book while fulfilling my normal academic duties. I particularly want to acknowledge my friend and colleague Bill Chaloupka. Bill not only introduced me to a new way of understanding politics, which helped organize my thinking for this book, but continues to serve as a seemingly inexhaustible source of insights and inspiration.

Sally Fairfax and John Freemuth kindly agreed to review my manuscript. Their insightful suggestions led to several changes that improved the manuscript. I doubt, however, that these changes will resolve the ongoing discussions between Sally and me over various aspects of public land policy.

I am also indebted to the many students in my environmental politics classes who were never afraid to point out the holes and flaws in my arguments. One of these students deserves special mention. Peter Zmyj showed up at my doorstep during a crucial period in this project, and through our many conversations, as well as his own very sound academic study, I became convinced that the book would be finished.

Despite the help of these people, and others too numerous to mention, responsibility for the interpretations (and misinterpretations) presented in the following pages remains mine, and mine alone.

CHAPTER ONE

Introduction

To the States . . . *Resist much, obey little*

—Walt Whitman[1]

In Federalist no. 16, Alexander Hamilton considered the question of whether state concurrence should be required before federal laws became binding. If such concurrence was required, he argued, the states would be able to paralyze the national government simply through inaction. On the other hand, if concurrence was not required the efforts of the states to overturn federal laws "would require not merely a factious majority in the legislature [of the states], but the concurrence of the courts of justice and the body of the people." Hamilton went on to suggest: "Attempts of this kind would not often be made with levity or rashness, because they could seldom be made without danger to the authors, unless in the case of tyrannical exercise of federal authority."[2] Nearly two hundred years later, a group of people in the western United States who believed that the exercise of federal authority had indeed become tyrannical embarked on the path outlined by Hamilton.

The Nevada legislature led the way with the passage of Assembly Bill 413 in 1979. Its legislative directive stated: "An act relating to public lands; creating a board of review; providing for state control of certain lands within the state boundaries; providing penalties; making an appropriation; and providing other matters properly relating thereto." The lands over which AB 413 asserted state control were the national public lands under the administration of the Bureau of Land Management (BLM). There were 48 million acres of BLM lands in Nevada, roughly 79 percent of the state. So began what has come to be called the Sagebrush Rebellion.

"Sagebrush" refers to the aridity and low productivity characteristic of the lands in question. The "Rebellion" was directed against an "Ordinance" attached to the Nevada constitution that reads in part: "That the people inhabiting said territory (Nevada) do agree and declare that they forever disclaim all right and title to the unappropriated public lands lying within said territory, and that the same shall be and remain at the sole and entire disposition of the United States." Originally required by the U.S. Congress as a condition for Nevada's admission to the Union, this provision remained in effect at the time AB 413 was passed. More important, the language of the ordinance was intended to affirm Article IV, Section 3 of the U.S. Constitution, which states: "The Congress shall have power to dispose of and make all needful rules and regulations respecting the territory or other property belonging to the United States." Thus, in asserting a claim to BLM lands, the Nevada legislature issued an overt challenge to a constitutional principle established two hundred years earlier.

At one level, Nevada's action was intended to draw attention to the sheer magnitude of the federal estate within its boundaries and throughout the West. In fact, about 93 percent of the total federal estate and 99 percent of the BLM lands are located in twelve western states: Alaska, Arizona, California, Colorado, Idaho, Montana, Nevada, New Mexico, Oregon, Utah, Washington, and Wyoming. Furthermore, all these western states were required to adopt a "disclaimer clause" similar to Nevada's ordinance. It is not surprising, therefore, that other western states joined the rebellion.

Arizona, New Mexico, Utah, and Wyoming enacted legislation patterned after Nevada's law. Moreover, Wyoming expanded the scope of the Sagebrush Rebellion by including claims to U.S. Forest Service lands as well as BLM lands. Governor Bruce Babbit of Arizona vetoed that state's bill, but the legislature overrode the veto—the only veto override sustained that session. In addition, the states of Alaska, California, Colorado, Montana, Nevada, New Mexico, Utah, and Wyoming provided funds for a multistate study of the Sagebrush Rebellion and related public land issues. Hawaii and North Dakota passed resolutions in support of the Sagebrush Rebellion without enlisting themselves in the movement.

Rebellions always have casualties, and this one was no exception. Sagebrush Rebellion measures were defeated by either legislative or executive action in California, Colorado, Idaho, Montana, Oregon, and South Dakota. The Washington state legislature passed a Sagebrush measure stipulating that it would not be enacted until an amendment to the state constitution eliminating that state's disclaimer clause was passed. The amendment met defeat during the 1980 general elections.

During the 1982 elections, Sagebrush initiatives appeared on the ballots in Alaska and Arizona. Voters in Alaska supported the "Tundra Rebellion" by an overwhelming 72.5 percent and thereby asserted a claim to 56 percent of BLM-administered lands. An Arizona initiative spearheaded by Governor Babbit that sought to repeal that state's measure was defeated, however.

The fires of rebellion were not limited to the state legislatures of the West. Although bills introduced by Senator Orrin G. Hatch (R-Utah) and

Representative James Santini (D-Nev.) that would have provided a mechanism for the transfer of federal lands to state ownership died in committee during the Ninety-sixth Congress and again in the Ninety-seventh, the movement received important support when 1980 presidential candidate Ronald Reagan proclaimed: "Count me in as a [sagebrush] rebel!" Subsequently, President-elect Reagan sent a telegram to a national Sagebrush Rebellion conference in which he declared: "I renew my pledge to work toward a Sagebrush solution." Reagan's pledge became reality in 1981 when James G. Watt, a self-proclaimed Sagebrush Rebel, assumed the post of secretary of Interior.

Yet the Reagan administration also introduced important shifts in the dialogue. On the one hand, Watt argued that "arrogant" federal managers, rather than federal ownership, represented the root cause of the controversy—a situation he promised to remedy by instituting a "Good Neighbor" policy. On the other hand, a group of libertarian political economists within the administration argued that the Sagebrush Rebellion was symptomatic of a more fundamental "problem"—public ownership of land. Their solution was privatization—the elimination of the federal estate by converting it into private property. And when Reagan suggested in his FY 1982 budget message that selling portions of the federal estate offered a way to help retire the national debt, it seemed that privatization, not the good neighbor policy, had become the administration's agenda.

The privatization proposal provoked opposition from both Sagebrush Rebels and environmentalists. Moreover, after a brief attempt to redirect privatization into a more moderate "asset management program," Watt also expressed opposition to the proposal. Frustrated by the lack of support for their plan, privatization advocates left the administration. And in 1983, Watt finally pushed his confrontational style too far, leading to his resignation. By the mid 1980s, then, a relative calm had returned to the public land policy arena.

The apparent calm did not mean that the arguments had been resolved. William Clark, who replaced Watt during the final months of Reagan's first term, adopted a less confrontational style but did not alter the administration's basic policy stance. After his 1984 victory, Reagan picked Donald Hodel to replace Clark. During the first term, Hodel served as a top deputy to Watt before becoming secretary of energy. As Watt's lieutenant, Hodel led the campaign for accelerated energy development on the public lands--an integral component of Reagan's "Sagebrush solution." Upon assuming Watt's job, Hodel clearly indicated that his appointment should not be interpreted as a change in the administration's prodevelopment goals. The environmental community's general reaction to Hodel was expressed by a *Washington Post* headline: 'Styles Change, But James Watt's Policies Linger."

At the same time, arguments began developing within the environmental community. Several of the national groups in the vanguard of opposition to the Sagebrush Rebellion and Watt announced major leadership and organizational changes during 1985. The expressed theme of these changes was a need to enhance the professional management and moderate image of the environmental movement.[3] However, other elements within the environmental community formed localized, frequently radical, groups that used tactics reminiscent of 1960s antiwar protests in attempts to block development activities on the federal lands. At least one of the groups in the forefront of this grassroots movement, Earth First!, represented an explicit protest against both the Sagebrush Rebellion and the moderating posture of national environmental groups.

It would appear, then, that the Sagebrush Rebellion did in fact leave an imprint on the policy arena. It seems appropriate to ask whether or not the Sagebrush Rebellion actually succeeded even though the public lands remain in federal ownership. The answer to this question, as to most political questions, lies largely in the realm of perceptions. A logical starting point, therefore, is with a consideration of the perceptions expressed by Sagebrush Rebels.

"APPREHENSIONS AND FEARS"

At the heart of the Sagebrush Rebellion was a belief that the ascendancy of the environmental movement throughout the 1970s produced an unacceptable burden of regulations. As Nevada Assemblyman Dean Rhoads, who sponsored the bill that launched the Sagebrush Rebellion, explained to a congressional committee: "Not only do we have to contend with present management policies that restrict production, we must look ahead apprehensively to wilderness review, grazing environmental impact statements and more rules, regulations and restrictions. It is these apprehensions and fears of what's coming next that has contributed to a mood and movement in the West that has been called the sagebrush rebellion."[4] The underlying theme in Rhoads's comment is not simply opposition to environmentally oriented policy. There is that, of course, but he also suggests a broader concern regarding the structure of the public land policy arena. His use of terms like "apprehensions" and "fears of what's coming next" implies a belief that environmentalists had secured an advantageous voice in the federal agenda discussion and were rapidly institutionalizing their position.

What makes this view intriguing is its apparent incongruence with the political dialogue of the "Environmental Decade." Throughout the 1970s, environmentalists portrayed themselves as champions of a national public interest struggling for recognition within a decision process dominated by the very groups allied in the Sagebrush Rebellion. The discrepancy between the claims made by Rhoads and those of the environmentalists opens an avenue for understanding the structure of the conflict. Rather than the central point of contention, the argument over title to the public lands was a kind of shorthand for a more complicated struggle about influence in the policy arena. The linkage between the title issue and arena influence emerged from a shared belief that federal managers were more sympathetic to environmental interests and state managers more sympathetic to the Sagebrush Rebels. This belief was certainly central to an incident in the Sagebrush Rebellion that occurred in Moab, Utah, on July 4, 1980.[5]

Moab, the county seat for Grand County, is located in arid east-central Utah. Of the 8,241 county residents, 5,333 live in Moab. In 1980, roughly 33 percent of Grand County's labor force was employed in agriculture and mining. And importantly, most of Grand County is federal land. In short, Moab and Grand County represent a microcosm of the Sagebrush Rebellion battlefield.

Generalizations about western political patterns are usually tenuous at best. However, one measure of Grand County politics is that in the six presidential elections between 1960 and 1980, excluding 1964, the Republican candidate received an average of 65 percent of the vote. In 1964, Johnson carried the county by a slim 50.3 percent. On this basis, at least, Grand County seems an unlikely place to discover officially sanctioned radicalism.

Nevertheless, on July 4, 1980, three hundred people gathered outside Moab to participate in just that kind of activity. In many respects, the assembly resembled a traditional Independence Day celebration. The local chapter of the American Legion presented the colors while the national anthem echoed across the desert. Local politicians used the opportunity to practice the rhetoric of their trade. But one feature of the scene suggested that this was to be an atypical ceremony. Rather than a flag-draped platform, the political speeches were delivered from the back of a Caterpillar bulldozer. Mounted on the bulldozer were several bumper stickers that read simply: "SAGEBRUSH REBEL."

Harvey Merrell, chairman of the Grand County Commission, warned the crowd of the "cancerous" growth of the federal bureaucracy—a bureaucracy that continually failed to listen to the "people." He went on to declare: "We will take control of our destiny in Southeastern Utah and not delegate it to a bureaucracy." Commissioners Larry Jacobs and Ray Tibbets echoed this sentiment by complaining that local concerns over Bureau of Land Management (BLM) decisions in the area had apparently fallen on deaf ears. Jacobs added that the Federal Land Policy and Management Act (FLPMA) was "devastating to our country." Ron Steele, a candidate for the commission, told the group they were "doing the right thing" because their actions served to preserve freedoms guaranteed by the U.S. Constitution for future generations.

The speeches ended and the bulldozer roared to life. The intent of this gathering was to scrape a road into a BLM wilderness study area that blocked access to a parcel of state land believed to have mineral potential. Such an action violated the terms of FLPMA, which required protection of the area until a decision was made about whether or not it should be formallly designated as wilderness. One lone protester stood in the path of the machine. A Grand County deputy asked him to step aside. He complied with the request after throwing a rock at the dozer's blade. With its path clear, the bulldozer proceeded to scrape the ground following the remnants of an abandoned mining road. When the bulldozer stopped, Tibbets announced: "You are now standing in a wilderness study area."

As it turned out, there was a second protester that day. Bruce Hucko, head of a local environmental group, thought he was sitting at the boundary of the proposed wilderness area. He was understandably surprised when the bulldozer stopped before reaching his position. The following Monday, BLM District Manager S. Gene Day explained to an emergency session of the Grand County Commission that someone had indeed misread the map, as the road fell about a quarter of a mile short of its goal. The commissioners responded by sending a county grader out to complete the road.

The BLM's official response to the situation came from Ronald L. Rencher, U.S. Attorney for the District of Utah. In a certified letter to the Grand County Commission, Rencher stated that restoration of the area to its "pre-July 4, 1980, condition must be accomplished within ten calendar days." Should the commissioners fail to take action, the letter continued, "the Bureau of Land Management will restore the land . . . and you will be billed for the amount of the cost expended therefor." Anticipating that the commissioners might refuse to pay this bill, Rencher warned that the amount could be deducted from "funds due Grand County under one of the federal programs in the area." He then concluded the letter with a brief civics lecture: "I trust that officials of Grand County recognize and will comply with the laws of the United States in the future and understand that Congress makes the laws, and the various agencies, including this office, will insure that the public lands of the United States are protected in a manner directed by statute."

One month later, John L. Harmer, chief executive officer for the

League for the Advancement of States' Equal Rights (LASER), editorially addressed the Moab incident.

> In this so-called confrontation we are given a classical example of the abuse and oppression that the federal government ever stands ready to inflict upon state and local officials who should have the temerity to think they had any rights. In its own modest way this situation vividly demonstrates the federal government's contempt for local authority and interests and their determination to eliminate any vestige of local control over the public domain.[6]

Though Harmer's view of the situation is perhaps overstated, it does echo Hamilton's earlier comment about the "tyrannical exercise of federal authority." In any event, the Grand County commissioners ultimately capitulated to federal authority. Confronted with litigation, they agreed to restore the area in an out-of-court settlement.

Constructing a political explanation of the Moab incident presents an interesting task. If we follow the dictates of traditional pluralist analysis, our interpretation would focus on the role self-interest played in structuring the confrontation. Given the importance of mining to the Grand County economy, we might conclude that the wilderness study area represented a threat because it blocked access to state land with mineral potential. Moreover, the rhetoric employed by the Moab rebels could be dismissed as simply an attempt to camouflage the vested self-interest at the heart of the dispute.

Yet the character of the Moab incident raises another issue. *Black's Law Dictionary* defines civil disobedience as "a form of lawbreaking employed to demonstrate the injustice and unfairness of a particular law and indulged in deliberately to focus attention on the allegedly undesirable law."[7] The Moab incident seems to fit this definition. Scraping a road into the wilderness study area was a deliberate violation of the Federal Land Policy and Management Act, a law that Commissioner Jacobs characterized as "devastating to our country." And though Harmer did not mention FLPMA specifically, his comment was apparently intended to focus attention on the injustice and unfairness of the situation. Finally, and perhaps most important, Rencher's letter is far less concerned about the "violation" of a potential wilderness area than the overt violation of a duly constituted federal law.

A complete explanation of the event requires a frame of reference capable of incorporating both pluralist analysis and civil disobedience. Cobb and Elder provide a useful observation in their work on agenda-building:

> There is a strong status quo bias in any existing system, and the legal machinery of that system is designed and operates to reinforce and defend that bias. . . . Understandably, then, established interests may be willing to change and to consider previously excluded issues and demands only under the threat of severe disruption of the status quo. To make such a threat both credible and visible, underrepresented or unrepresented groups may have to demonstrate willingness to use extralegal or even illegal means, such as resorting to violence.[8]

We can reconstruct the Moab incident following the lines suggested by Cobb and Elder.

The Moab rebels were obviously opposed to wilderness and in favor of economic development. Hovever, their rhetorical attacks on FLPMA and the federal bureaucracy expressed a view of themselves as "underrepresented or unrepresented groups" within the existing policy arena, a view reinforced by their act of civil disobedience and consequent disruption of the status quo. Rencher's response, in turn, looks very much like "legal machinery" attempting to "reinforce and defend" the status quo. Furthermore, that the commissioners ultimately relented turns out to be less significant than might otherwise be suspected. The purpose of the incident was to draw attention to the Moab rebels' complaints. In this regard, the rebels succeeded, even though the area was eventually restored.

This framework appears to be applicable to Rhoads's description of the broader Sagebrush Rebellion. Once again, part of the complaint was situated in vested self-interest—a protest against restrictions on resource production activities. Another part, however, was a belief that existing restrictions reflected the environmental movement's success in redefining the patterns of influence and representation within the established policy arena. And though AB 413 was an act of the Nevada state legislature, it generally fits the definition of civil disobedience. It seems possible, then, that the Sagebrush Rebellion, like the Moab incident, was intended primarily as a move to disrupt the established policy arena.

Whether or not this interpretation actually captures the original intent of the Sagebrush Rebellion is, of course, open to dispute. Nevertheless, it does serve to incorporate the various events of the controversy. The Sagebrush Rebellion did disrupt the policy arena in ways that focused attention on the Sagebrush Rebels' complaints. Indeed, it gained the attention of candidate Reagan, and led to his promise to address the complaints if elected. Reagan's election and his subsequent appointment of Watt clearly signaled that policies enacted during the previous decade would be open to new interpretations and renegotiation. And while the duality of the Reagan administration's initial response—Watt's good neighbor policy versus privatization—created confusion, both postures were portrayed as possible solutions to the Sagebrush Rebellion.

In short, the Sagebrush Rebels succeeded in posing a credible threat and thereby forced a reconsideration of the existing structure of the policy arena. One indication of this success is the continuing, though more moderate, advocacy of prodevelopment goals by Watt's successors in the Interior Department. Other, and perhaps more telling, indicators are the organizational changes and conflicts within the environmental community. Although the result of several forces, these factors suggest a movement seeking to reclaim and stabilize its position in an arena undergoing transformation. However, before making a final assessment about the possible success of the Sagebrush Rebellion, we must first explore the various twists and turns of the controversy.

PLAN OF STUDY

The central premise of this study is that the Sagebrush Rebellion was a protest originating from three interrelated perceptions: first, that environmentalists had succeeded in gaining a dominant position in federal land policy discussions; second, that the environmental community's influence had created an underlying bias in favor of preservation over development in federal land management decisions throughout the 1970s; and third, that the only way to counteract the increasingly restrictive character of federal land management decisions was to precipitate an open confrontation.

There are at least two general directions a study of the Sagebrush Rebellion might follow. One approach would be an attempt to assess the legitimacy of the Sagebrush Rebels' complaints by comparing their claims to the facts of the situation. The other approach would be to reconstruct the issues and events identified by the Sagebrush Rebels, as *they* perceived them, in an effort to understand *their* motivations.

Several factors argue in favor of the second path. First, most of the central issues in federal land policy are value questions, and endeavoring to evaluate the legitimacy of various claims is, at best, a treacherous venture. For example, there is evidence that federal land management decisions throughout the 1970s did tend to emphasize preservation at the expense of development activities. However, whether or not that evidence justifies the Sagebrush Rebellion is largely a question of interpretation. As is often the case with interpretation, conclusions are largely dependent upon initial premises. If, for example, we begin with the premise that environmental protection should be the primary goal of management, then the direction of federal land decisions appears both reasonable and appropriate. If, on the other hand, we begin with the premise that resource production should be the primary goal, then federal land decisions appear misdirected.

Second, despite their oppositional character, environmental protection and resource development are equally important management goals. There is a sense, then, in which all claims raised by actors in the federal land policy arena are legitimate. Environmentalists are correct in asserting the need for policies to preserve ecological values, even if they restrict or exclude development activities. Conversely, development advocates are also correct in pointing out that preservation policies may lock up resources needed by society. In consequence, the true measure of effective federal land decisions is the extent to which they succeed in eliciting acquiescence, if not agreement, among federal land users.

Herein lies a third factor. Whatever else might be said of the Sagebrush Rebellion, it clearly indicated that federal land use decisions could no longer sustain either the agreement or acquiescence of the commodity producers by the late 1970s. Indeed, the Sagebrush Rebels' willingness to use civil disobedience in pressing their claims suggests that the disagreement turned on issues more fundamental than restrictions on specific development activities. At dispute here were the justifications for those restrictions. Approaching the argument from the perspective of legitimacy, therefore, simply misses the point. The important question is why the Sagebrush Rebels *believed* that the established decision process was no longer responsive to their interests.

There is a final factor. Although the Sagebrush Rebellion centered on federal land policy, it was also a conscious political strategy. Thus a study of the Sagebrush Rebellion affords the opportunity to examine the dynamics of the political system. More specifically, it provides a case study that demonstrates the advantages and disadvantages associated with the use of confrontational politics as a vehicle for pursuing policy goals. Once again, to fully appreciate the political character of the Sagebrush Rebellion, it is necessary to view the events from the perspective of the rebels.

What I have attempted to do, then, is to construct an explanation of the Sagebrush Rebellion by investigating the themes and issues identified by the movement's participants. It is my belief that this explanation helps shed light on the forces that gave rise to the Sagebrush Rebellion. However, I leave the question of whether or not the Sagebrush Rebellion was warranted to the judgments of readers.

In form, this book is perhaps better classified as a policy "story" than policy analysis. But as Deborah Stone argues, stories have their place in analysis:

Definitions of policy problems usually have narrative structure; that is, they are stories with a beginning, a middle, and an end, involving some change or transformation. They have heroes and villains and innocent victims, and they pit the forces of evil against the forces of good. The story line in policy writing is often hidden, but one should not be thwarted by the surface details from searching for the underlying story. Often what appears as conflict over details is really disagreement about the fundamental story.[9]

The Sagebrush Rebellion was, first and foremost, a disagreement about the underlying story in federal land policy.

Since the beginning of the twentieth century, "conservation" has served as the basic story line in natural resource policy. It has been the crucial referent for determining legitimate policy initiatives and for sorting out the heroes from the villains. Although preservation demands have always had a place in natural resource policy, before the 1960s conservation was generally understood as a doctrine that emphasized the development of natural resources following the principles of wise use and sustained yield management. During the 1960s, however, Secretary of Interior Stewart Udall led a concerted and successful effort to redefine conservation in a way that emphasized preservation over use.

The argument explored in Chapter 2 is that, given the importance of conservation in justifying policy initiatives, this redefinition served to alter the patterns of influence within the federal land policy arena. In short, the new conservation story line tended to make preservation advocates (environmentalists) "insiders" and development advocates "outsiders" within federal land policy discussions throughout the 1970s.

In Chapter 3 I examine the consequences of this new story line within five major public land policy areas: wilderness, grazing, mining, recreation, and urban/suburban growth. While these were certainly not the only areas of conflict during the 1970s, they were the areas consistently identified by the Sagebrush Rebels in explaining the sources of their frustrations. And true to the Sagebrush Rebels' claims, each area exhibited a pattern of increasing emphasis on environmental values. Thus evidence suggested that federal managers were more attentive to preservation than development demands.

Taken together, chapters 2 and 3 establish a background for understanding the root cause of the Sagebrush Rebellion. In chapters 4 and 5 the focus shifts to exploring the strategic considerations underlying the design of the Sagebrush Rebellion.

The Sagebrush Rebellion was, in many important respects, the same strategy employed by western stockgrowers during controversies in the 1920s and the 1940s. Yet the Sagebrush Rebels, unlike their predecessors, had to contend with the organized and influential opposition of the environmental movement. The question posed in Chapter 4, then, is what led the Sagebrush Rebels to believe that a replay of this familiar strategy might succeed in the changed policy arena? The argument advanced is that several factors created a national political climate that allowed the Sagebrush Rebels to portray their complaints about federal land policy as symptomatic of broader concerns.

The 1970s were a time of rapidly expanding federal regulations. Not surprisingly, the increase in federal regulations set off a growing public protest that, by 1979, had become what President Jimmy Carter termed a "crisis of confidence" in government. Moreover, economic conditions during the 1970s created regional tensions that often seemed to pit eastern states against the West. Finally, relations between the federal government and the western states, though never especially congenial, deteriorated into open, heated confrontations. In short, these factors suggested a national audience sympathetic both to the Sagebrush Rebels' protests against heavy-handed federal bureaucracy and to their calls for increased state involvement in the political process.

Chapter 5 completes the strategic considerations by tracing the evolving issues and tactics that animated the Sagebrush Rebellion. It begins with an analysis of the issues developed in the rebellion's formative stage and then moves to the changes brought about by the 1980 elections. Particularly important in this regard was the tenure of James Watt as secretary of Interior. A self-proclaimed Sagebrush Rebel, Watt promised to "defuse" the rebellion through his good neighbor policy. While clearly a shift from the Sagebrush Rebels' initial strategy, Watt's initiative was nonetheless consistent with the overall goals of the movement. Indeed, Watt's tenure may have been the single most important development in the Sagebrush Rebellion.

In openly advocating development goals, Watt clearly signaled that environmentalists would no longer occupy an influential position in the policy dialogue. More important, Watt situated his defense of development within the earlier, use-intensive definition of conservation. In so doing, he further weakened environmentalist influence by making their claim to the conservation legacy problematical. As such, Watt offered promise for a new era in public land management that addressed the Sagebrush Rebels' complaints and thereby precluded the need for further discussions about transferring federal lands to state ownership.

The optimism Watt generated for the Sagebrush Rebels' cause was quickly counterbalanced by the privatization initiative. At the time, the privatization proposal was portrayed as an extension of both the Sagebrush Rebellion and Watt's good neighbor policy. However, in Chapter 6 the roots of the privatization initiative are traced to a group of political economists who drew inspiration from Garrett Hardin's 1968 essay, "The Tragedy of the Commons," and libertarian economic theory. Indeed, the first call for privatization of the federal estate was issued in 1973, well in advance of the Sagebrush Rebellion. Nevertheless, the intrusion by privatization advocates ushered in the final episode of the dispute that began with the Nevada Legislature's 1979 action.

Although relative calm seemed to have returned to the federal land policy arena by the mid 1980s, the argument advanced in Chapter 7 is that many of the underlying issues were still undergoing negotiation. Indeed, changes in the Reagan administration after the demise of the privatization initiative and Watt's resignation, as well as developments within the environmental community, sketch a portrait of protagonists seeking to establish new postures in a changed policy arena. On this basis, there is evidence to support the claim that the Sagebrush Rebellion produced lasting consequences. Those consequences are outlined in the concluding section of the chapter.

Throughout this discussion I have used phrases that are fairly standard in natural resource policy but may be confusing to some readers. The first is *public lands*. While all lands owned by government (federal, state and local) are technically public lands, I have adopted the convention established by the Federal Land Policy and Management Act of 1976, which defines public lands as those lands under the administration of the Bureau of Land Management. Therefore references to the public lands should be interpreted as specific to the BLM lands. Where the need arises to discuss non-BLM lands, I use the administrative category as a referent (forest service lands, national parks). Following from this, I use the term *federal lands* or *federal estate* to include all lands owned by the federal government.

A second phrase is *commodity users* (or *development interests*). In general, these terms apply to groups and individuals primarily interested in the economic development of public land resources. For example, the major commodity group in the BLM's administrative realm is the western livestock industry. One of the more powerful political manifestations of the stockgrowers, in turn, is the National Cattlemen's Association. Other commodity groups include mining interests, oil and gas interests, and to some extent, timber interests. Although there are multiple points of potential conflict among commodity users—it's difficult to graze cattle in a surface mine, for instance—historically these groups have all supported economic production as the dominant policy emphasis for the public lands.

Opponents of the commodity point of view will be referred to by the term *environmentalists* and related derivatives (e.g. *environmental interests*, *environmental community*). In many respects, the environmental community contains a more diverse set of interests than the commodity users, but in major policy discussions these interests agree on the need to emphasize protection of environmental values over economic development. Examples of the groups in the environmental community include the Sierra Club, the National Wildlife Federation, the Wilderness Society, Friends of the Earth, and the Natural Resources Defense Council.

The most important term in this study—Sagebrush Rebels—defies convenient definition. The term *Sagebrush Rebellion* was originally coined by journalists in Nevada and intended to carry a derogatory connotation. However, proponents of the Nevada Legislature's action quickly adopted it as their rallying cry. Moreover, there was no formal leadership or structure for the Sagebrush Rebellion, and in consequence, no membership roster. In fact, the only national meeting of the Sagebrush Rebels occurred in 1980 at a conference sponsored by the League for the Advancement of States' Equal Rights (LASER). Nevertheless, there were points of agreement throughout the public statements made by people who claimed to be Sagebrush Rebels. From these common themes I have gathered insights regarding the philosophy and membership of the movement. In general, Sagebrush Rebels were advocates of commodity production and related uses, such as off-road-vehicle use of the public lands. And though the Sagebrush Rebels were connected with organized groups, they seldom represented themselves as spokespersons for those groups. The Sagebrush Rebellion appears to have been an authentic political movement, deriving support from a diverse group of people who believed that federal land management policies had become overly responsive to environmental preservation values.

We are now ready to begin the story of the Sagebrush Rebellion. Our starting point will be a discussion of the changing meaning of the word conservation. Although the meaning of words may seem immaterial to the actual outcome of political decisions, I hope to demonstrate that the word "conservation" represents a kind of shorthand for a bundle of attitudes regarding the proper use of public lands, and that the particular meaning attached to it empowers some claims and excludes other claims. Thus, by tracing the changing meaning of conservation we can begin to uncover the roots of the Sagebrush Rebellion.

CHAPTER TWO

Conservation:
The Changing Story

Yet if I were to single out the one major issue that is most likely to dominate the nation's political attention in the 1970s, it would be environmental protection. . . . What good is a booming economy if the air is too foul to breathe, the water too polluted to drink and our cities too cluttered with ugly examples of environmental neglect to provide comfortable living?

—*Governor Ronald Reagan, 1970*[1]

I suspect that the politicians and businessmen who are jumping on the environmental bandwagon don't have the slightest idea what they are getting into.

—*Denis Hayes, 1970*[2]

No special expertise in federal land issues is required to recognize the central role played by the word "conservation" in the policy dialogue. It appears in virtually every story reported by the popular press, and the context of those stories makes it abundantly clear that conservation carries an implicit judgmental character—the "good guys" are always conservationists. And yet, if we pay close attention to popular accounts, it quickly becomes obvious that a certain amount of confusion exists over the meaning of conservation. Everyone claims to be a conservationist, no matter what kind of policies he or she advocates.

In this chapter we will explore two meanings that have been attached to conservation in federal land policy discussions. The first is the meaning developed during the early 1900s, and the second is a meaning developed during the 1960s. The point of this discussion is not to determine which meaning is "correct," but to demonstrate that the definition of conservation has always been linked to specific policy goals. Thus the meaning assigned to conservation in policy discussions provides a measure of the patterns of influence in defining the character of federal land policy decisions.

The importance of this aspect of the story of the Sagebrush Rebellion is twofold. First, the successful redefinition of conservation in the 1960s helped establish the foundation for environmentalist influence on federal land policy throughout the 1970s. Second, understanding these differing meanings of conservation will provide a context for explaining the subtext of the complaints raised by the Sagebrush Rebels.

TRADITIONAL CONSERVATION

Conservation first entered our policy lexicon at the dawn of the twentieth century in the context of western reclamation efforts,[3] but it quickly became the banner of a movement seeking to effect radical change in federal land policy. It would be useful, then, to summarize briefly the nature of land policy prior to the conservation movement.

Three factors characterized federal land policy throughout the nineteenth century. First, land was understood to include the "resources" riparian to the soil (trees, minerals, and the like). Second, though there were exceptions, the dominant policy goal was "disposal": that is, the conversion of the federal estate into state or private property through sales and grants. Third, the rate and scope of land disposals were primarily the result of interstate bargains negotiated in Congress.[4]

The advent of conservation brought changes to all three areas. Because it was first a part of the Progressive movement, conservation reflected the underlying principles of scientific management. These principles require two basic steps: breaking down complex systems into their constituent parts, then training people in the most efficient techniques for managing each part. When applied to the federal estate, scientific management dictated that "land" be divided into various resource categories (timber, water, grazing forage, minerals). The resource categories, in turn, became management areas to be placed under the direction of trained professionals. As Hays notes: "Foresters should determine the desirable annual timber cut; hydraulic engineers should establish the feasible extent of multiple purpose river development and the specific location of reservoirs; agronomists should decide which forages areas could remain open for grazing without undue damage to water supplies."[5] It then followed that other changes needed to be made. Since resource management needed a subject, land disposal policies were replaced with policies that retained the federal estate in federal ownership. Moreover, the emphasis on management by expertise expanded the role of the bureaucracy in the decisional arena.

These changes did not occur overnight, of course, nor did they go unchallenged. Nevertheless, the conservation movement did succeed in making these changes, and primary among the factors accounting for its success was the definition of conservation popularized by Gifford Pinchot, the founder of the U.S. Forest Service. Animated by the belief that the "first duty of the human race is to control the earth it lives upon," Pinchot argued that conservation embodied three principles.

> The first principle of conservation is development, the use of the natural resources now existing on this continent for the benefit of the people who live here now. . . . In the second place conservation stands for the prevention of waste. . . . In addition to the principles of development and preservation [prevention of waste] of our resources there is a third principle. . . . The natural resources must be developed and preserved for the benefit of the many, and not merely for the profit of the few.[6]

Viewed in this way, the "outgrowth of conservation, the inevitable result, is national efficiency." For Pinchot, national efficiency was the "deciding factor" in the "great commercial struggle between nations which is eventually to determine the welfare of all."[7]

In short, Pinchot linked technical prescriptions of scientific management with the social goals of economic prosperity and national efficiency to create a powerful justification for the planned, orderly development of federally controlled natural resources. Others in the early conservation movement—most notably Sierra Club founder John Muir—were openly hostile to Pinchot's vision. As Roderick Nash explains, a schism developed within the movement "between those who defined conservation as the wise use or planned development of resources and those who have been termed preservationists, with their rejection of utilitarianism and advocacy of nature unaltered by man."[8]

Although a complete discussion of the struggle between these competing views falls beyond the scope of this project, one event during the early 1900s is widely recognized as a crucial turning point—the battle over Hetch Hetchy Dam in California. At dispute was a proposal by San Francisco city officials to construct a dam on the Tuolumne River. The primary obstacle to this proposal was that the dam site—the Hetch Hetchy Valley—had been made a part of Yosemite National Park in 1890. However, the 1906 earthquake and fire that destroyed much of San Francisco strengthened the city's case, and in 1908, Interior Secretary James Garfield approved the request. That action set the stage for a major national controversy.[9]

As the battle was joined it became apparent that the Hetch Hetchy Dam was a symbol for both conservationists and preservationists. Conservationists viewed it as an example of the wise use of natural resources for the betterment of society, and preservationists viewed it as an example of unwarranted intrusions by humans into the beauty of nature. But the more important point for this discussion is that the dispute clearly delineated the inherent differences between preservationists and conservationists.

Despite mobilizing widespread public support, preservationists ultimately lost the battle when Congress authorized construction of Hetch Hetchy Dam in the Raker Act of 1913. Nevertheless, the controversy did establish important precedents. On the one hand, it heightened public awareness of and concern about the national parks, leading to the enactment of the National Park Service Act in 1916. And though preservationists had various disagreements with the National Park Service, most commodity development activity was excluded from the parks.[10] On the other hand, as Henry Caulfield has suggested, the Hetch Hetchy battle also confirmed that Pinchot's definition of conservation would dominate the "mainstream of federal natural resource policies that were established up to the early 1960s."[11]

Throughout the first half of the twentieth century, then, federal land policy operated under the assumption that planned, orderly resource development was the primary management mission. Thus the structure of the policy arena tended to afford commodity users an influential position in management discussions. Federal managers and commodity users had their disagreements, of course, but since they shared the goal of resource development, most of their arguments centered on questions about the rate and scope at which development activity should proceed. Though they continued to press their claims, preservation interests discovered that in a policy arena emphasizing development and use, their demands received little substantive attention.

But two factors in the political climate after World War II created new possibilities for preservation interests. First, a general increase in the American public's disposable income, mobility, and leisure time heightened interest in a variety of outdoor recreation activities. Second, outdoor recreation provided preservation interests with a "public use" that required management policies that would protect nature in its undisturbed state. It seemed likely, therefore, that preservation interests were in a position to expand their influence over the federal land policy agenda.

Several events during the 1950s suggested that a shift in the patterns of influence within the natural resource policy arena was indeed at hand. The decade began with a major controversy over the U.S. Bureau of Reclamation's proposed Colorado River Storage Project. Because part of the project called for construction of Echo Park Dam within Dinosaur National Monument, it precipitated a battle reminiscent of the Hetch Hetchy controversy. In this case, however, preservation interests prevailed. The project's final authorization, adopted in 1956, specifically prohibited the construction of dams in national parks and monuments.[12]

The Echo Park victory, in turn, strengthened the preservationists' hand in negotiations over two major federal land proposals introduced during 1956. The first granted statutory authority for the Forest Service's traditional practice of multiple use management; the second called for creation of a national wilderness system. Moreover, in 1958 Congress established the Outdoor Recreation Resources Review Commission (ORRRC) to study the nation's recreation needs and prepare recommendations for meeting those needs.

Though these events were important in their own right, taken together they signaled a period of agenda instability in which claims that had been at the periphery of federal land policy moved to the center of attention. As Grant McConnell observed, in the political climate of the 1950s, the "clarity of the vision seen and proclaimed by Gifford Pinchot has diminished to the point at which it is difficult to say whether conservation still carries any of the meaning which he gave it."[13] The unravelling of the traditional definition of conservation became manifest in the attempt to establish multiple use management on the federal lands.

MULTIPLE USE

On June 12, 1960, President Dwight Eisenhower signed the Multiple Use–Sustained Yield Act (MUSY) into law, thereby completing a legislative effort begun in 1956. The primary purpose of MUSY was to establish statutory authority for the management approach developed by the Forest Service throughout the first half of the twentieth century. Indeed, the original impetus for MUSY had been the Forest Service's desire to clarify its management mission in the face of growing criticism. Since the basic concept of the act had been endorsed by a wide array of federal land users,[14] MUSY offered promise that future management decisions could strike a balance among the competing demands raised by forest users.

The act's major directive required management of the National Forests for "outdoor recreation, range, timber, watershed, and wildlife and fish purposes . . . in the combination that will best serve the needs of the American people." It also identified the "establishment and maintenance of areas of wilderness" as consistent with the other uses.[15] Furthermore, MUSY recognized the need for "periodic adjustments in use" resulting from "changing needs and demands;" and that "some land" would be "used for less than all the resources." Finally, MUSY acknowledged that forest management would not always produce the "greatest dollar return or the greatest unit output."[16]

It is not surprising, then, that MUSY was generally hailed as a major milestone in federal land policy. In prescribing a dynamic management mission among equal uses, MUSY sought to allay apprehensions within the forest user community. It would not end arguments, since each user group would want to expand access at the expense of others, but it did provide a framework that included all user groups in the decision process.

Furthermore, MUSY gave the Forest Service a specific management mandate, which nonetheless left the agency with considerable discretion. That kind of mandate, as Chief Forester Richard McArdle had explained during the final hearings on MUSY, was the only way to insure the "continued management of the national forests for 'the greatest good of the greatest number in the long run.'"[17] That phrase, "the greatest good of the greatest number in the long run," was a slogan developed by Pinchot and his followers to describe the underlying philosophy of conservation. As it turned out, the specter of traditional conservation made some preservationists uneasy about the actual intent of MUSY. In a 1961 analysis, for example, Michael McCloskey demonstrated that, historically, the Forest Service had practiced a "dominant with compatible use" approach to multiple use management. Generally speaking, this approach emphasized management for a primary use and any secondary uses that did not interfere with it. The more important point was that commodity production activities were more frequently identified as primary uses than recreation and wildlife—a pattern, McCloskey argued, that Gifford Pinchot had originated in the early days of the conservation movement.[18]

For McCloskey and other preservationists,[19] then, the issue was whether MUSY actually represented a new management philosophy or merely a repackaging of the Forest Service's traditional approach. This was not a trivial issue. If MUSY did in fact represent a shift, then preservation interests would enjoy greater influence in forest management decisions. If it was simply a continuation of traditional practices, then preservation values would remain a secondary consideration in forest management. What made this issue especially important was the effort to establish a national wilderness system.

Unlike MUSY, the wilderness bill had encountered widespread opposition. Development interests were opposed, of course, but the Forest Service and the Park Service also expressed misgivings about the proposal. Preservation interests were concerned, therefore, about the possibility that the inclusion of wilderness in MUSY would be interpreted as precluding the need for a separate wilderness bill. Thus, in demonstrating the Forest Service's traditional commitment to commodity production, preservation interests hoped to reinforce their wilderness effort.

The multiple use discussion developed yet another twist in February 1961, when President Kennedy sent a "Special Message to Congress on

Natural Resources" directing, in part, that the secretary of Interior "develop a program of balanced usage [for the BLM lands] designed to reconcile the conflicting uses—grazing, forestry, recreation, wildlife, urban development, and minerals."[20] Although portrayed by Kennedy as a parallel effort to MUSY, converting the BLM into a multiple use agency presented a fundamentally different task.

The Taylor Grazing Act of 1934, which brought the final remnants of the public domain under federal management, specifically identified livestock grazing as the dominant use. And though the merger of the Grazing Service with the General Land Office in 1946, creating the BLM, broadened the agency's management responsibilities, livestock interests continued to exert significant policy influence. As Marion Clawson (BLM Director, 1948–1953) noted in 1949: "It is doubtful if today any public land policy could be adopted which was unitedly and strongly opposed by the range livestock industry."[21] Moreover, the power of the livestock industry had not decreased by the 1960s. Consequently, convincing the livestock industry of the need for multiple use management represented a crucial step in the process of changing BLM's mission.

That task began in March 1961, when Interior Secretary Stewart Udall and BLM Director Karl Landstrom amplified the implications of Kennedy's directive at the twenty-first Annual Meeting of the BLM National Advisory Board Council (NABC). Referencing Kennedy's message, Udall suggested: "The public lands in grazing districts no longer have value only for livestock and wildlife grazing. Now in many areas of the West—and the number will surely grow in the future—other multiple-uses are growing in importance. Modern day land management programs must take full account of all these values."[22] Meeting these challenges, in turn, required adopting "new approaches and methods" to public land management. One new approach was that Udall appointed himself, "effective immediately," as cochairman of the NABC; another was that the advisory boards were to be given a multiple use character by expanding their membership to include representatives from the full spectrum of public land user groups.

In defending the latter proposal, Landstrom argued: "I do not see this as diminishing the privilege afforded to livestock representatives to express themselves on land use questions. . . . I do think that such broadening would enlarge the stature of the boards and tend to restore the confidence of the public."[23] Landstrom's reference to public confidence reflects a political undertow apparent throughout the discussion. Although the expanded membership proposal was consistently justified on the basis of changing use demands, Landstrom frequently alluded to growing public criticism of the boards as yet another reason for change. The specific source of this criticism was never identified, but Landstrom did make passing reference to the recently published book, *Politics and Grass*. This is indeed interesting because Foss's now classic study offers a detailed account of how the western stockgrowers "captured" the BLM through the use of a three-tiered advisory board structure.

Foss characterized these boards as a "kind of private government" with the ability to "formulate the broad policy, make the rules, and superintend the execution of these rules and policies."[24] The NABC was the top tier in this structure, with a membership consisting of twenty livestock representatives and three wildlife representatives. Moreover, the rules of the NABC required that a livestock representative be a BLM-grazing permit holder as well as a member of both state and district advisory boards. These representatives were usually members, and often past officers, of the major livestock associations as well. Finally, Foss even anticipated the course adopted by the Kennedy administration when he observed:

> In recent years a concept of multiple land use has been growing. By the administration, at least, the grazing districts are no longer considered as grazing reserves only. It seems probable that this trend may continue. If this happens there will be increasing pressures to broaden or diversify representation on the advisory boards. Diversified advisory board representation could mean a return to competitive politics and a diminution of the strength of the stockman.[25]

Understanding the proposal's significance, Judge Dan Hughes, chairman of the NABC and a Colorado sheepman, countered on behalf of the stockgrowers: "When you say we are here to represent livestock, I think that is narrowing the thinking of your advisory committee. We are here to represent what in our humble judgement is the best community interest of the areas from which we come."[26] Chairman Hughes's comments were not representative of the entire NABC membership, however. Three members represented wildlife interests and their position was summarized by Thomas Kimball, Executive Director of the National Wildlife Federation:

> No longer can we see these lands as designed primarily for one specific use. In certain areas that may be true, but in other areas it may be some other use that is of primary importance and in the public interest. . . . It is our distinct feeling that representation on local, state, and national advisory boards should be broadened to include all of the other uses.[27]

Kimball would subsequently emerge as a leading opponent of the Sagebrush Rebellion.

In the end, the stockgrowers acquiesced to the expanded member-ship proposal. At one level the political implications of this confrontation seemed clear: A restructured NABC meant an end to the livestock indus-try's institutionalized dominance in the BLM policy arena. It also set the stage for transformation of the BLM into a full-fledged multiple use man-agement agency. However, the BLM still lacked statutory authority for multiple use management. The effort to secure such a legislative man-date was part of another political storm brewing over the federal lands: a storm that formed around such issues as the meaning of conservation, and consequently, the future direction of public land management.

FROM TRADITIONAL TO NEW CONSERVATION

Although it was articulated in terms of equity among user groups and management policies based on compromise, the drive for multiple use was clearly an attempt by federal officials to exert greater influence over the federal land agenda. The question, then, was whether federal man-agers actually sought to establish an arena in which the agenda would emerge from negotiations among user groups, or rather, to establish an agenda that determined the mix of uses permitted on the federal lands. In the public land arena, at least, it seemed that the latter was the case.

At a NABC meeting, Udall explained: "Words which my associates and I use seem to get twisted and we are pictured as relegating grazing to an inferior place. This is not the case. . . . Under multiple use each use is on par with others—over the entire system. But each either singly or in combination with others is in its proper place."[28] It is not difficult to understand why stockgrowers were skeptical. Udall offered a multiple use formula that promised equity but assumed that each use had a "proper place." Such a formula could produce balanced management policies; however, it could also become a justification for reducing graz-ing by classifying larger areas of the public lands as simply improper for that use. There were, however, other events that fueled the stockgrowers' suspicions about the actual intent of multiple use management.

In January 1962, ORRRC published its final report, documenting that recreation represented a significant demand for federal lands. Al-though it contained no specific recommendations for the BLM, it did note that there was an "immense potential" for recreation activities on public lands.[29] Moreover, ORRRC recommended enactment of legislation establishing wilderness areas in "portions of national forests, parks, monuments, wildlife refuges, game ranges, and the unreserved public domain."[30] And since a key management principle for wilderness was to preserve its primitive condition, "any economic use of the area, such as the grazing of livestock, that may exist at the time of its establishment should be discontinued as soon as practicable and equitable, and no further commercial utilization of the resources should be allowed."[31] Viewed in this light, wilderness did not seem to fit into a multiple use management program.

Indeed, as McCloskey noted in his assessment of MUSY, a multiple use framework based on the traditional conservation philosophy was not well suited for the kinds of preservation demands being raised in the 1960s. Gifford Pinchot had incorporated preservation as part of the original conservation doctrine, but his meaning for the term was the "prevention of waste." In fact, Pinchot went so far as to suggest that preservation in a wilderness sense came dangerously close to violating the intent of conservation. "There may be just as much waste," he surmised, "in neglecting the development and use of certain natural resources as there is in their destruction."[32] Udall was fully aware of this disjuncture: "Pinchot had his shortcomings," he wrote. "He always had a blind spot to wildlife and wilderness values: to him, untrammeled wilderness was a form of waste."[33]

Thus fitting preservation and recreation demands within the multiple use framework required a transformation in the meaning of conservation. For Udall, at least, such a redefinition seemed justified. At the 1962 White House Conference on Conservation, he argued: "[Conservation] is a concept that grows. Each generation has to redefine it because it has new meaning."[34] The following year Udall outlined the new meaning of conservation in his book *The Quiet Crisis*. The crisis, Udall explained, is that "we live in a land of vanishing beauty, of increasing ugliness, of shrinking open space, and of an over-all environment that is diminished daily by pollution and noise and blight."[35] Very little word twisting was needed to understand that a crisis thus defined led in the direction of a policy agenda preoccupied with preservation efforts. Indeed, Udall went on to argue: "Only prompt action will save prime park, forest, and shore line and other recreational lands before they are preempted for other uses or priced beyond the public purse. . . . The task must begin immediately and be completed within the next three decades."[36] There is little wonder, then, why the stockgrowers refused to accept Udall's explanation of multiple use at face value.

Not only were the stockgrowers unconvinced of the need to redefine conservation, but Wayne Aspinall (D-Colo.), chairman of the important House Interior and Insular Affairs Committee, made it clear that the policy dialogue would not be easily finessed. As he explained at a 1962 NABC meeting: "In recent months, I have taken every opportunity to espouse the doctrine of traditional conservation."[37] At the White House Conference, Aspinall defined traditional conservation as: "Accepting all the material resources that nature is capable of providing, taking those natural resources where they are, and as they are, and developing them for the best use of the people as a whole. Conservation means that we do not waste; however, it does not mean that we save merely for the sake of saving."[38] He then added further distance between his position and the effort to redefine conservation: "I do not know when, where or how, the purist preservationist group assumed the mantle of the conservationists."[39]

Reaffirming traditional conservation was only one part of the overall posture Aspinall sought to establish. The other part centered on reminding the administration of Congress's role in defining the character of public land management. At the White House conference, for example, Aspinall asserted: "Congress will continue to equate conservation with wise use; [and] will not put out of reach resources that may be required for our national continuance."[40] Aspinall did not speak for all members of Congress, of course, but as chairman of the Interior Committee, he was in a position to delay or block public land initiatives. His comment about not putting resources out of reach seemed to be a reference to the Wilderness Act.

In an October 1962 letter to Kennedy, Aspinall made his position explicit. The key problem, he argued, was the need to delineate the "degree of responsibility and authority to be exercised by the legislative and executive branches" in federal land policy. In this matter, Aspinall had a specific plan: "I think we should, in the interest of orderliness, take up the matter of congressional-executive relationships first; when that question has been settled through the enactment of legislation setting up a pattern for future guidelines we can immediately turn our attention to wilderness preservation."[41] The implication was clear—if the administration wanted the wilderness bill passed, it would have to make concessions to Aspinall's demands.

In January 1963, Kennedy responded with a carefully crafted letter that recognized the "constitutional prerogative of the Congress to make rules for the management and disposal of the public lands." He also noted that "Congress has not fully discharged its responsibilities but has, in effect, abdicated some of its prerogatives to administration discretion," and that "many of the great issues in public land policy have come about as the result of action by progressive-minded Presidents. . . . On occasion these choices may have seemed to outdistance express statutory authority, but the policies which have governed the choices have been under constant congressional scrutiny." Thus, while agreeing with Aspinall that the federal land law "system warrants comprehensive revision," Kennedy indicated that his administration would continue its proactive stance.[42]

By the mid 1960s, then, political battle lines had been drawn. On one side stood Udall, with his insistence that a clear, albeit quiet, crisis demanded a new, preservation-oriented conservation; on the other was

Aspinall, with his position that conservation and preservation represented different, perhaps incompatible, policy goals. These positions set the stage for a complicated matrix of compromises contained in four acts adopted by Congress during September 1964.

Preservationists realized their goal with the enactment of the Wilderness Act.[43] The victory was not without cost, however. Although the act defined wilderness as "an area of undeveloped Federal land retaining its primeval character and influence," it allowed limited commodity use, including mining, within the wilderness system. The inclusion of commodity activity was both a concession to traditional conservation advocates and, as we will see, a source of conflict throughout the 1970s.

Aspinall's goal was also realized with an act establishing the Public Land Law Review Commission (PLLRC).[44] Reflecting the exchange between Aspinall and Kennedy regarding the appropriate roles of the executive and legislative branches, the PLLRC was to be composed of nineteen members: twelve selected from the House and Senate Interior committees, six appointed by the President, and a chairman elected by the commission members. According to its mandate, the PLLRC was to undertake a comprehensive study of federal land policies "to determine whether and to what extent revisions thereof are necessary" in order to meet the "demands on the public lands which now exist and which are likely to exist within the foreseeable future."

The issue of converting BLM into a multiple use management agency was also addressed by Congress. The Classification and Multiple Use Act[45] directed the BLM to inventory lands under its administration in order to determine which lands were suitable for sale and which were suitable for retention. The BLM was directed to recommend appropriate uses for the retained lands under the principle of multiple use management. Authority for disposal of those lands classified as suitable for sale "because they are required for the growth of a community or because their chief value is for residential, commercial, agricultural, or industrial use" was provided by the Sales of Public Lands Act.[46] Although both of these acts were intended to provide temporary authority while the PLLRC completed its study, the train of events seemed clear—BLM was well on its way to becoming a multiple use management agency.

FROM NEW CONSERVATION TO
ENVIRONMENTALISM

Although these four acts represented gains for preservation interests, Aspinall's effective advocacy of traditional conservation and the concessions he'd won during the wilderness battle darkened the prospects for future preservation efforts, especially if Aspinall emerged as the PLLRC chairman. Even if Aspinall did not direct the effort, the commission's long-term study would allow development interests to argue that enactment of new initiatives should be postponed until the PLLRC completed its work. Such delays, in turn, would not only undermine the sense of urgency cultivated by preservationists but would also allow commodity interests time to solidify their power base.

What preservation interests needed, then, was a means to sustain the momentum they had developed throughout the late 1950s and early 1960s. In February 1965 President Johnson provided such a means in his "Special Message to Congress on Conservation and Restoration of Natural Beauty." Johnson explained that population growth, urbanization, and technology had created "new problems" that required a "new conservation." This new conservation, he continued, "must be not just the classic conservation of protection and development, but a creative conservation of restoration and innovation. Its concern is not with nature alone, but with the total relation between man and the world around him."[47] His message affirmed a continuation of the agenda advanced by Kennedy. More important, the tone of mobilization adopted by Johnson gave clear warning that preservation and recreation claims would continue to be pressed, regardless of the PLLRC effort.

At one level, Johnson's message contained familiar but troublesome themes for commodity users. For instance, although Johnson made it clear that preservation and restoration of natural beauty were to be priority agenda items, he remained ambiguous in defining beauty. "Certainly no one would hazard a national definition of beauty. But we do know that nature is nearly always beautiful. We do, for the most part, know what is ugly."[48] The dual implications that undisturbed nature constituted beauty and that any disruptive activity equaled ugliness were obviously objectionable to the commodity users. In a dialogue thus structured it is indeed difficult to defend proposals for timbering, surface mining, oil drilling, dam building, or even grazing. Because these activities are inherently disruptive, the argument runs, they are therefore perpetrators of ugliness.

But Johnson's message went beyond advocacy of preservation and recreation values within federal land policy. The umbrella of beauty allowed him to move among a diverse set of issues and incorporate them as merely different facets of new conservation. Under the umbrella concept of beauty, the preservation of rural landscapes is allied with providing urban parks and open spaces. Within the cities new conservation "requires attention to the architecture of building, the structure of our roads, preservation of historical buildings and monuments, careful planning of new suburbs."[49] The new conservation argument, broadly conceived, begins by protecting beauty from development activity and leads to preventing pollution, which is not only ugly but a menace to health as well. In short, Johnson's message foreshadowed the matrix of issues that would emerge as the environmental agenda of the 1970s.[50]

Affirmation that the PLLRC would serve as a forum for traditional conservation also came in 1965 with the election of Aspinall as chairman. With the battle lines thus drawn, the struggle for control of the national agenda for federal land use moved into a new phase. Rather than the open confrontation that had characterized the first half of the 1960s, a largely disjointed pattern emerged in the latter half of the decade as the competing interests pursued their opposing agendas more or less independently.

Many of the PLLRC's activities were conducted by consultants hired to produce studies on various aspects of federal land policy. However, the PLLRC did hold a series of public hearings from 1966 to 1968, which served to reinforce its prodevelopment orientation. Reporting on the initial hearings, Tom Kimball warned that "commercial user interests have far outnumbered conservationists and there is a real danger that many of the lands may be turned over to state or local governments or sold to private individuals and groups."[51] Little had changed by the final hearings, as demonstrated by this report in *Audubon*: "Of the 62 persons who sought to advise the commission on how best to modify the laws that govern the use of public lands, 55 asked for relaxation of the regulations or an outright giveaway of the federal lands to the states or existing users."[52]

Despite this ongoing concern regarding the PLLRC, other events suggested that new conservation was actually making inroads into agenda control. By 1968, most of the policies and programs Johnson had called for in his 1965 message had received congressional approval, as is apparent from the following list of legislation:

The Highway Beautification Act of 1965
The Water Quality Control Act of 1965
The National Historic Preservation Act of 1966
The Air Quality Act of 1967
The National Trails System Act of 1968
The Wild and Scenic Rivers Act of 1968

In addition, 2.4 million acres were added to the national park system between 1965 and 1968, compared to the 30,000 acres added during the 1950s, and the wilderness system was expanded by 800,000 acres. Moreover, the BLM had inventoried roughly 147 million acres under the auspices of the Classification and Multiple Use Act, recommending that 145 million acres should be retained in federal ownership.[53] There seemed to be little reason, then, to believe that the PLLRC's report, scheduled for completion in 1970, would have any meaningful impact.

However, events took an unexpected turn when Johnson announced that he would not seek reelection. Throughout the 1960s arguments over federal land policy had exhibited only limited partisan overtones—Udall and Aspinall were both Democrats, after all. Yet when president-elect Richard Nixon nominated Walter Hickel, a self-proclaimed development advocate, for the post of secretary of Interior, it did not seem that the Republican administration was committed to the drive for preservation. The controversy surrounding Hickel's confirmation foreshadowed the fiercer battle that would erupt a decade later over the confirmation of Reagan's Interior secretary, James Watt. The similarities were not merely coincidental—James Watt was the person selected to prepare Hickel for his confirmation hearings.

Watt entered the Washington political arena in 1962 as a staff member for Wyoming's Senator Milward Simpson. For the next four years, as the battle between new conservation and classic conservation took shape, Watt's primary assignment was with the Senate Interior and Insular Affairs Committee. Upon Simpson's retirement in 1966, Watt moved to the Natural Resources Committee of the United States Chamber of Commerce. Throughout the next two years he articulated, as a lobbyist, the same basic ideas that would characterize his posture as secretary of Interior. For example, in a letter submitted as testimony during 1968 hearings on a bill to regulate surface mining, Watt argued that the measure should be rejected

> for three basic reasons: (1) local and state governments are constitutionally responsible for regulating land use, not the Federal Government; (2) the facts indicate that there is no need for the Federal Government to preempt the field of land conservation and reclamation; and (3) there is reason to believe that the proposed formula for federal-state cooperation, although reasonable, would be improperly administered by the Department of Interior.[54]

It might be noted that surface mining regulation became one of the major controversies during Watt's tenure as secretary of Interior.

But by Watt's own account, the most important formative event for him during this time was the controversy surrounding Hickel. Watt's experiences with the Senate Interior Committee and the Chamber of Commerce had given him important insights into the nature of the brewing controversy. In consequence, he attempted to steel Hickel against the attacks that would be leveled at him. Hickel, however, chose another path, as recounted by Watt:

> Wally Hickel was so brutalized by the environmentalists that he must have said to himself, "I'm going to prove to these guys that I'm an environmentalist, too." Once he was confirmed, Wally tried to outrun them to the left. He was no longer a States' Righter. He was no longer a hard-liner. He was no longer pro-development. He wasn't experienced enough in the Washington scene to realize that you can't outrun an environmentalist to the left, that they will always stay ahead of you and demand more from you.[55]

Although this retrospective observation sheds considerable light on the question of why Watt chose an openly confrontational style as secretary of Interior, it does not demonstrate a grasp of the political climate confronting Hickel in 1969. Eight days after his confirmation hearings, an oil well in the Santa Barbara Channel ruptured and ran uncontrolled for ten days. This event, in the words of Ross MacDonald, "triggered a social movement and helped create a new politics, the politics of ecology."[56] It seems unlikely, therefore, that even as forceful an advocate as James Watt would have been able to sustain an antienvironmental stance in the face of the gathering momentum.

The more important point, however, is that Hickel's "defection" to the environmental cause was perfectly consistent with the policies of the Nixon administration. An early indication that the struggle between new conservation and classic conservation was nearing resolution came in February 1969, when Nixon identified one of the "tough problems" facing the Department of Interior as "making the decision between whether you develop resources or conserve them."[57] In this context, "conserve" clearly implies preservation, not the planned development advocated by Pinchot and Aspinall. The following May, Nixon fulfilled a promise he had made after viewing the consequences of the Santa Barbara oil spill by creating an Environmental Quality Council. This council would serve as a "Cabinet-level advisory group which will provide the focal point for this administration's efforts to protect all of our natural resources."[58] Another indicator of the policy shift taking shape was Nixon's "Special Message on Population Growth," delivered in July 1969, a message David Brower called "the boldest statement any President ever made on population."[59] Significant as these actions were, they merely foreshadowed the level of commitment to environmentalism that emerged in 1970. Signing the National Environmental Policy Act (NEPA) into law on January 1, Nixon observed that the event marked the beginning of a new agenda for the decade. In February he offered a first glimpse of this agenda by proposing a "37–point program, embracing 23 major legislative proposals and 14 new measures being taken by administrative action of Executive Order."[60] And in an obvious, though unacknowledged, reference to Johnson's new conservation, Nixon explained: "At the turn of the century, our chief environmental concern was to conserve what we had—and out of this concern grew the often embattled but always determined 'conservation' movement. Today, 'conservation' is as important as ever—but no longer is it enough to conserve what we have; we must also restore what we have lost. We have to go beyond conservation to embrace restoration."[61] One month after Nixon's speech, environmentalists christened their new movement with the first national Earth Day celebration.

CONCLUSIONS

Writing in *Ecotactics: The Sierra Club Handbook for Environmental Activists*, one of the many publications produced for Earth Day 1970, Paul Brooks argued: "The conservation movement has in fact become a revolution. . . . Through long and often tedious experience, we are learning to meet the exploiters on their own ground. And we are also finding that the public—particularly the young—are prepared to accept a whole new set of values, a quite different concept of man's relation to earth."[62] Although it was certainly not unique in the rhetoric surrounding Earth Day, this comment demonstrates some of the continuities and disjunctures between the environmental movement and the conservation movement. For example, Brooks's assertion that the conservation movement had become a revolution may have seemed accurate in the heady days of the early 1970s, but it did not prove historically accurate. The conservation movement of the early 1900s was certainly a revolution in that it transformed federal land policy. Moreover, the early conservation movement was also predicated on a new set of values and a different concept of man's relation to earth.

These new values were encapsulated in the principles of scientific management which, as Hays notes, had implications beyond the management of natural resources: "The broader significance of the conservation movement stemmed from the role it played in the transformation of a decentralized, nontechnical, loosely organized society, where waste and inefficiency ran rampant, into a highly organized, technical, and centrally planned and directed social organization which could meet a complex world with efficiency and purpose."[63] Furthermore, the conservation movement sought to replace the dominant view of unlimited resources, which drove earlier exploitative attitudes, with the realization that the nation's resource base was limited and therefore needed careful husbandry. In that sense, the movement did establish a different conception of man's relation to earth.

When viewed in the context of their times, then, both traditional conservation and new conservation promised a radical change from the past. In addition, both movements employed the same basic political script: Each documented a pending "crisis" created by past abuses but argued that the crisis could be averted if the policy prescriptions advocated by the movement were implemented. It is at this point, of course, that the disjunctures between the movements become apparent.

Despite the radical changes proposed by the conservation movement, its ultimate goal—resource development—was consistent with the demands of the dominant federal land users. Although the initial alliance between conservationists and preservationists had created some confusion, the resolution of the Hetch Hetchy controversy had affirmed Pinchot's position: that the first principle of conservation was development. Thus traditional conservation did furnish commodity users with a prima facie claim to legitimacy in the natural resource policy arena.

In contrast, the goal of new conservation was to furnish preservation interests with an equally legitimate claim in the policy arena. In several respects, new conservationists faced a more formidable task in this regard than did the traditional conservationists. New conservation, after all, was not really new. The claims raised by preservation interests in the 1960s and 1950s were essentially identical to the claims that had been raised by preservationists in the early 1900s. Moreover, the controversies in the early 1900s had clearly established the distinction between preservation and conservation. Equally important, the dominance of traditional conservation throughout the first half of the twentieth century had allowed commodity interests to institutionalize their influence in the policy arena.

Nevertheless, growing demands for outdoor recreation, along with increasing concern about the condition of the environment, provided new conservationists with an avenue for intervention. The situations that confronted society required new definitions, even if those new definitions disrupted existing influence patterns. And though there were reasons to doubt the efficacy of this contention in the early 1960s, new conservation had become an established force on the political landscape by the end of the decade. In fact, the need to maintain a distinction between new and traditional conservation diminished as the policy dialogue increasingly used conservation and environmentalism as synonymous terms.

But the redefinition of conservation was not yet complete. In 1970, the PLLRC published its final report, *One Third of the Nation's Land*. Given Aspinall's role as chairman, it came as no surprise that the report offered perhaps the best-articulated, most sophisticated defense of traditional conservation prepared during the twentieth century. The environmental community's response was also predictable. In their view, the report was "anti-environmental, blatantly in favor of exploitative development of resources, and antithetical to social interests."[64] Thus, in the first year of the environmental decade, battle lines were clearly delineated.

In the next chapter, we will explore how this confrontation played out in public land policy during the 1970s. Before doing so, however, there are some connections between the events of the 1960s and the Sagebrush Rebellion that warrant attention. First, the redefinition of conservation and ascendancy of the environmental movement sounded a clear warning that preservation values would receive greater attention in management decisions. Though this possibility raised apprehensions among all commodity users, it was particularly troublesome for the livestock interests. Prior to the 1960s, the livestock industry had enjoyed considerable influence over BLM management decisions. By the 1970s, the question for livestock interests was not whether their influence would decline, but rather, how much of their influence they could retain as the changes took shape.

There is another factor that links the controversies of the 1960s to the Sagebrush Rebellion directly. Many of the people involved in these earlier disputes were also prominent in the argument over the Sagebrush Rebellion. For example, Thomas Kimball of the National Wildlife Federation was a member of the NABC when Udall expanded the board's membership, and he would emerge as a major critic of the Sagebrush Rebellion. Michael McCloskey, who wrote the above-noted analysis of MUSY, became executive director of the Sierra Club in the late 1960s—a position he occupied until the mid 1980s. And then there was the ubiquitous James Watt.

Clearly, the Sagebrush Rebellion was in many respects a continuation of the controversies of the 1960s. If so, why didn't it happen sooner? Part of the answer to this question is offered in the next chapter, as we trace the implications of new conservation and the environmental movement for public land management in the 1970s. The other part is discussed in Chapter 4, where we will consider broader controversies that created a political climate in which a renegotiation of the patterns of influence within the public land policy arena seemed possible.

CHAPTER THREE

Multiple Use—
Multiple Frustration

You want to know why I believe that we have got to resort to more dramatic and emphatic statements such as the Sagebrush? It is the perverse and distorted way that the Department of Interior took a sincere, from my perspective at least, legislative product and tried to use it to arrive at tortured, twisted and preconceived bureaucratic desires and designs.

—*James Santini, 1980*[1]

The [Sagebrush] "rebellion's" weapons were hysteria and slander supported neither by history nor by facts, but by a thin tissue of lies. It was fueled by greed. Every "rebel" leader was tied to public-land exploitation.

—*Bernard Shanks, 1984*[2]

According to a 1979 press release prepared by the Select Committee on Public Lands of the Nevada Legislature, the Sagebrush Rebellion represented "both a general attitude and a specific set of actions." The purpose of this chapter is to begin dissecting the attitude of the Sagebrush Rebellion by considering a collection of federal land policy issues from the 1970s. The list of issues considered here certainly does not include all federal land management disputes of the environmental decade, but focuses instead on those issues that consistently appeared in the public statements made by people who claimed to speak for the Sagebrush Rebellion.

I begin this chapter with a brief overview of the evolution of the Federal Land Policy and Management Act of 1976 (FLPMA). Frequently called the BLM Organic Act, FLPMA represented the culmination of the effort begun in the 1960s to establish a multiple use management mandate for the Bureau of Land Management (BLM). Although an important background issue, FLPMA was not the only source of frustration that would eventually find voice in the Sagebrush Rebellion. Throughout public statements made by various Sagebrush Rebels complaints recur about five major public land policy areas: wilderness, grazing, mining, recreation, and urban/suburban growth. The remainder of this chapter, then, offers what might be called "mini" case studies of these five areas.

NEW CONSERVATION AND FLPMA

The Public Land Law Review Commission undertook one of the most comprehensive analyses of public land policy ever attempted in this country. Its final report, *One Third of the Nation's Land*, published in 1970, contained 137 major recommendations and literally hundreds of subrecommendations and specific suggestions. However, three general themes advanced in the report best capture the underlying philosophy adopted by the commission. The first is contained in the initial recommendation: "The policy of large-scale disposal of public land reflected by the majority of statutes in force today be revised and that future disposal should be only of those lands that will achieve maximum benefit for the general public in nonfederal ownership, while retaining in federal ownership those lands whose values may be preserved so that they may be used and enjoyed by all Americans."[3] At one level, this statement seems to represent a call for the end of disposals. Indeed, the commission went on to suggest that "at this time most public lands would not serve the maximum public interest in private ownership." Yet the full set of recommendations leads to a different interpretation.

First, PLLRC called for the enactment of legislation to enable the sale "at full value" of those lands deemed suitable only for mining, livestock grazing, dryland farming, and commercial, residential, or industrial purposes. Second, the commission also recommended legislation to "provide a framework within which large units of land may be made available for the expansion of existing communities or the development of new cities."[4] Finally, it advocated the transfer of lands "at less than full value" to state and local governments on the condition that the lands remain in public ownership. Taken together, these positions define a disposal process for lands with an identifiable single or dominant use and a means for insuring that the retained lands were truly public in character.

The disposal theme, in turn, anticipated the PLLRC's posture regarding future management of retained lands. While recognizing that the federal lands could serve various purposes, the commission expressed serious reservations about the efficacy of multiple use management. " 'Multiple use' is not a precise concept. It is given different meanings by different people, as well as different meanings in different situations. We have listened to statements from diverse interests who all commended the idea of multiple use, but it was apparent that they were supporting different basic positions. This confusion permeates public land policy."[5] A more useful approach, PLLRC argued, would be the adoption of a "dominant use" philosophy. Under this procedure, federal lands with a clearly identifiable "highest primary use" were to be managed for that use and any "secondary uses that are compatible with the primary purpose." The remaining areas, then, would be managed so that "all uses are considered equal until such time as a dominant use becomes apparent."

The third general theme advanced by PLLRC was the need to clarify and consolidate the multiple, often conflicting, directives contained in the body of public land law. Although the commission offered numerous suggestions in this regard, its recommendations for the BLM are especially noteworthy. Affirming the multiple use trend prevalent throughout the 1960s, PLLRC urged enactment of legislation mandating permanent multiple use management on BLM lands. It should be noted, however, that this mandate was for multiple use as defined by the commission report.

Rather than a manifesto for open exploitation, the PLLRC offered a carefully crafted set of recommendations attuned to both traditional conservation and new conservation. Indeed, some aspects of the report made important and surprising concessions to preservation demands. Despite Aspinall's obstructionist posture during the Wilderness Act battle, for example, the commission actually recommended an expansion of the wilderness system. "There is nothing in the Wilderness Act to preclude additions to the National Wilderness Preservation System of lands not previously identified for review. Accordingly, while maintaining the priority of review for areas designated in the Wilderness Act, we believe that the initial inventory and review of other areas should be started as soon as possible."[6]

Nevertheless, the environmental community expressed serious reservations about the underlying philosophy of the PLLRC report. Particularly troublesome in their view was the concept of dominant use. Michael Frome argued:

> The dominant use principle, which stands out as a basic objective of the PLLRC report, is hopelessly lopsided and totally irreconcilable with environmental protection. . . . [It] is predicated upon measurement of land values, in narrow economic terms, . . . [that] deny the ecological interrelationship of life-forms and thus sanctions the elimination of elements in the land which lack commercial value, but which are essential to its well being.[7]

Frome was not alone; virtually every critic of the report expressed similar skepticism. What made this criticism curious, however, was that designating wilderness, recreation, wildlife, and other ecological values as the highest primary use was certainly compatible with a dominant use scheme. Indeed, there was very little difference between the PLLRC's approach and Udall's earlier assertion that "under multiple use each use is on par with others—over the entire system. But each either singly or in combination with others is in its proper place." Both approaches sought to strengthen the hand of federal land managers by freeing them, in the words of the PLLRC, from the "barrage of claims from all sides that a particular use ought to be permitted or barred, all in the name of 'multiple use'."[8]

It seems plausible, therefore, that environmentalist criticism of the PLLRC was based on something other than complaints about dominant use. When Sierra Club President Phillip Berry suggested that the "assumptions of the Report are fundamentally at odds with modern conservation thinking,"[9] the actual complaint became clear. The threat posed by the PLLRC report was its potential to rekindle support for traditional conservation as the guiding principle in federal land management. Thus, in seeking to discredit the PLLRC report, environmentalists wanted to insure that future policy initiatives would be founded upon new conservation. Primary among the policy initiatives of concern to environmentalists were congressional deliberations to create a formal multiple use management mandate for the BLM.

The first versions of what would become the Federal Land Policy and Management Act were introduced in early 1971. On February 23, Senator Henry Jackson (D-Wash.) introduced the Public Domain Lands Organic Act (S. 921). Jackson had been a member of the PLLRC, but he also played a key role in the creation of the National Environmental Policy Act and had initiated an effort to establish a national land use planning mechanism. Thus S. 921 can be viewed as an attempt to implement the PLLRC recommendations as interpreted by the environmental community.

Jackson's bill, for example, called for multiple use management with no mention of dominant use. It also contained a provision indicating that any land classifications in "effect on the date of enactment" were subject to "review for possible reclassification."[10] Immediately following this provision was another directing the secretary of Interior to undertake a wilderness review of BLM lands. Finally, the general tenor of S. 921 was clearly to strengthen the federal government's control over the public lands, culminating in a provision that granted BLM employees authority to "make arrests for the violation of the laws and regulations" established pursuant to the act.[11]

On April 6, Aspinall introduced the counterpoint to Jackson's bill in the form of the Public Land Policy Act (H.R. 7211). As expected, Aspinall's bill called for dominant use management where appropriate and multiple use management everywhere else. It also proposed the creation of a citizen advisory board structure with unmistakable parallels to the controversial BLM boards. In addition, though clearly intended to affirm federal management, Aspinall's bill was equally clear in granting states a major role in the overall process. For example, H.R. 7211 directed "each public land management agency [to] pursue a systematic program of land use planning." However, the plans established by federal agencies were to be "consistent with State and local government programs to the extent possible and no public land shall be designated for a use inconsistent with state or local zoning unless . . . there is an overriding national need therefor."[12] Finally, the only mention of wilderness expansion contained in H.R. 7211 was an exception from dominant/multiple use classification for "primitive areas," those areas designated for further study by the Wilderness Act.

Given the differences between these bills, crafting a new management mission for the BLM would not be an easy task, yet the protagonists understood that the outcome would be worth the effort. In a very real sense, the battle over FLPMA was as much about realigning patterns of influence within the policy arena as it was about defining BLM management policy.

In this regard, the commodity users' cause suffered a serious setback when Aspinall's twenty-four year congressional career came to an abrupt end in the 1972 primaries. At the time, Aspinall blamed his defeat on "environmental extremists." There is some truth to this claim. Alan Merson, Aspinall's opponent, was an avowed environmentalist, though probably not an extremist, and 1972 was a watershed year for environmental politics in Colorado. However, redistricting added a portion of the Denver metropolitan area to Aspinall's traditionally rural constituency. This change in combination with public cynicism precipitated by the Watergate Affair were probably more influential factors leading to Aspinall's defeat.

There is no way to know, of course, what might have happened had Aspinall remained in the struggle. However, it is safe to say that Aspinall's defeat significantly altered the congressional battle lines. James Haley (D-Fl.) replaced Aspinall as chairman of the House Interior Committee. Although Haley was in his eleventh term, he had no discernible ties with western commodity users and therefore no reason to continue Aspinall's agenda.

Yet, the FLPMA odyssey continued, and hearings in 1973 and 1974 offered the first glimpse of the complaints that would be raised in the Sagebrush Rebellion. Testifying on behalf of the Nevada Cattlemen's Association and the Nevada Woolgrowers' Association, Dean Rhoads provided fifteen specific objections to the version of FLPMA under consideration. The basic theme, however, was that the proposed legislation vested "too much broad discretionary authority and power in the Secretary of Interior, and [did] not follow the recommendations of the Public

Land Law Review Commission."[13] Particularly troublesome in this regard, Rhoads testified, was the planning process: "In Nevada eighty-seven per cent of our lands are Public Lands and a land use plan and inventory will have significant impact upon the State and local government and the residents of the State. This proposed act is a broad sweeping grant to the Secretary of Interior of the power to plan our state of Nevada."[14]

Calvin Black, then a member of the Utah legislature but subsequently a spokesman for the Sagebrush Rebellion, offered a similar, but more emotional statement:

> We plead with you to leave the public land laws as they are and rather than pass this proposed Organic Act which in my opinion is the desire of the bureaucracy and not the people, reestablish the original intent of these old, proven public land laws, overrule the administrative repeal of the same by the administrative agencies, and allow the private citizens the opportunity to acquire a more reasonable percentage in their rightful inheritance in their State and counties than they now have.[15]

Finally, Representative Steve Symms (R-Idaho), who would become a senator in the 1980 general election, asserted: "My people in Idaho view the act as devastating."[16]

It is important to remember that the bill that elicited these comments was not the final version. Several of the provisions criticized by commodity users during these hearings were deleted before the bill was signed into law by President Ford on October 21, 1976. Indeed, passage of FLPMA seemed to indicate that a compromise between new and traditional conservation could be constructed. On the one hand, FLPMA directed that the "public lands be managed in a manner that will protect the quality of scientific, scenic, historical, ecological, environmental, air and atmospheric, water resources, and archeological values."[17] On the other hand, it also directed that "the public lands be managed in a manner which recognizes the Nation's need for domestic sources of minerals, food, timber, and fiber from the public lands including implementation of the Mining and Minerals Policy Act of 1970 as it pertains to the public lands."[18]

Nevertheless, the compromise promised by FLPMA failed to materialize. In fact, Senator Orrin Hatch (R-Utah) described FLPMA's symbolic role in the Sagebrush Rebellion as similar to that played by the Bastille during the French Revolution. It was FLPMA that former Nevada Congressman James Santini described as the "sincere legislative product" gone awry. And it was FLPMA that was portrayed as "devastating to our country" by the Moab County Commissioners.

It could be, of course, that critics were correct in portraying the Sagebrush Rebels as obstructionists unwilling to set aside their "greed" and abide by the terms of FLPMA. The Sagebrush Rebels never denied their pursuit of self-interest, and the rebellion did seem designed to be purposely disruptive. After all, the Grand County Commissioners had coupled their rhetorical attack with the bulldozing of a wilderness study area. Hatch and Santini raised the possibility of dismantling the "Bastille" and the bureaucracy that occupied it through bills calling for the transfer of federal lands to the states. These actions do not seem directed at discovering the basis for a compromise capable of resolving the dispute.

But dismissing the Sagebrush Rebellion as merely an expression of occlusive self-interest begs the question. The Sagebrush Rebels' pursuit of commodity use, though objectionable to environmental interests, was clearly sanctioned by FLPMA. However, their disruptive style was at odds with the traditional process for resolving political disagreements. As Robert Dahl suggests: "Because constant negotiations among different centers of power are necessary in order to make decisions, citizens and leaders will perfect the precious art of dealing peacefully with their conflicts, and not merely to the benefit of one partisan but to the mutual benefit of all the parties to a conflict."[19]

However, Dahl's view presupposes that all groups share a common goal of arriving at some decision. Cobb and Elder have suggested another possibility. Asserting that participation in pluralist politics is restricted to "only those (groups) that have already gained access to the political arena," they argue that groups excluded from the arena may be forced into "extralegal action or behavior that is outside the legitimate 'rules of the game.'"[20] Obstructionist behavior serves two purposes for excluded groups: first, to call attention to claims falling outside the recognized arena; and second, to disrupt decisions that otherwise might be made without consideration of their claims.

There is a sense in which these observations shed light on the meaning of the Sagebrush Rebellion, yet other issues intervene. The groups allied in the Sagebrush Rebellion, for instance, were commonly assumed to be recognized participants in the public lands policy arena. Moreover, environmental and preservation interests had effectively appropriated the posture of excluded groups. Finally, the tenets of conservation and multiple use undermine efforts to sustain an "insider-outsider" dialogue by including commodity use and environmental protection as components of legitimate policy initiatives. Therefore, portraying the Sagebrush Rebellion as a manifestation of protest politics would require reversing the roles of commodity users and environmental interests, while at the same time denying the apparently inclusive nature of multiple use management.

Despite the evident disjuncture such an interpretation creates with traditional renditions of natural resource policy, there is evidence that speaks to its utility. For example, Marion Clawson offered a rather curious assessment of FLPMA. Acknowledging that FLPMA appeared to be an "armistice in the long policy debates over the public lands," Clawson argued:

> A great deal will depend, I think, on how the general public, or at least the public user of the federal lands, views the new law. Will those who want to drive their off-road vehicles anywhere and everywhere they choose pay any attention to the new law? Will ranchers, mining interests, the timber industry, and other firms interested in acquiring raw materials from the federal lands really endorse the new law and seek to work cooperatively with each other, with other users, and with the BLM and other public officials?[21]

Clawson's use of the term armistice here is particularly interesting. In its usual sense, armistice means a cessation of hostilities by mutual consent. Yet his statement has a decidedly one-sided tone to it: future political harmony in the public lands arena is dependent upon the willingness of interests associated with environmentally disruptive uses to moderate their demands. Missing from Clawson's statement is the possibility that environmentalists might be less than cooperative in working with commodity users.

Furthermore, although Ford signed FLPMA into law, its implementation fell to the Carter administration, specifically to Interior Secretary Cecil Andrus. As a former governor of Idaho, Andrus understood the tensions underlying public lands management. Testifying during his confirmation hearings, Andrus offered an optimistic view: "I am hopeful that we are now entering an era when the concept of multiple use will be better understood. . . . The problem is that multiple use does not mean that every acre should be logged, mined, or grazed. Some areas are best used for one purpose, some for another."[22] Andrus was more troublesome from the commodity users' perspective. For instance, David Speights suggested in a profile for *Congressional Quarterly Weekly Reports*: "Andrus is a conservationist who is a sure bet to please environmentalists and displease mining, logging and other development interests."[23]

What begins to emerge, then, is an alternate explanation of the events during the 1970s. At the root of the Sagebrush Rebellion were two interrelated complaints. The first, and most obvious, protest centered on the shift from traditional conservation to new conservation, and in consequence, represented an expression of vested self-interest. Stated differently, the Sagebrush Rebels simply objected to restrictions on their use of the public lands and their declining influence within the policy arena. The second, and perhaps more important, protest focused on what appeared to the Sagebrush Rebels as a violation of the expressed intent of federal land policy. More specifically, the Sagebrush Rebels viewed events throughout the 1970s as a concerted effort to exclude development activity from the public lands, even though the declared policy intent was to strike a balance between development and preservation. For example, the basic complaint raised by Sagebrush Rebels regarding FLPMA was that the compromise promised by the language of the law did not materialize because federal managers emphasized environmental values over development values in its implementation.

In order to gain a full understanding of this second complaint, we will now turn to a brief discussion of the events in five public land policy areas: wilderness, grazing, mining, recreation, and urban/suburban growth. These areas were selected because they were consistently identified as the sources of the frustration that motivated the Sagebrush Rebellion.

We begin with a discussion of wilderness for two reasons. First, wilderness disputes, by definition, produce a highly polarized debate between development advocates and preservation advocates. Second, although public land disputes did not begin with the adoption of the Wilderness Act in 1964, the character of those conflicts was significantly altered by the advent of legally mandated attention to wilderness in federal land management decisions. In short, the wilderness debate helped establish background tension between commodity users and environmentalists, which affected the dialogue across the spectrum of public land policy issues.

WILDERNESS

Throughout roughly eighty years of formal policy debate, wilderness has had two meanings. It is first a place, and therefore it constitutes a resource use pattern categorically similar to grazing districts. Wilderness is a geographical area managed to protect its natural condition; grazing districts are geographical areas managed to protect forage condition. Moreover, the aura of exclusivity associated with wilderness does not make it unique on the menu of public land uses. Surface mining, after all, excludes other uses perhaps more completely than wilderness.

Even if this were the only meaning attached to wilderness, it would produce conflict. The conflict would be structured, however, around the question of the appropriate amount of acreage designated for wilderness in relation to other demands. Though part of the controversy does center on this issue, there is another part that exhibits an intensity unfamiliar to the traditional multiple use dialogue. It is this aspect, in turn, that points to a second meaning associated with wilderness.

The first sentence of the Wilderness Act portrays the preservation of wilderness as an effort to "assure that an increasing population, accompanied by expanding settlement and growing mechanization, does not occupy and modify all areas within the United States." Aside from displaying a lyrical quality uncommon to federal legislation, this language moves wilderness from the resource-attentive, multiple use dialogue into a discourse with a distinct flavor of social criticism. It implies that the designation of a wilderness area should be understood as both a resource allocation decision and a protest against industrial society. Equally important, it forces advocates of development activity to respond in kind, defending their use as a legitimate contender in the resource matrix and as a manifestation of a legitimate social order. There is little wonder, then, that wilderness invokes emotional confrontations animated by suspicions and charges of hidden intent.

The interplay between these two meanings was clearly evident during the 1960s. In Chapter 2 we saw that Udall and other preservation advocates used wilderness as the unifying theme for a new conservation agenda while simultaneously arguing that it was simply one of diverse resources provided by the federal lands. Troublesome as these apparently conflicting signals were, it could be argued that had the wilderness system remained at the limited size discussed in 1964, there would have been less cause for conflict. However, by 1980 the wilderness system had grown from the original 9.1 million acres to encompass about 80 million acres.[24]

Some growth was to be expected, of course, as the Wilderness Act mandated a review of Forest Service primitive areas and roadless areas of five thousand or more contiguous acres within the national park and wildlife refuge systems administered by the Department of Interior. Yet the expansion of the wilderness system offers an excellent example of the role perception plays in assessing federal land disputes. On the one hand, 80 million acres represents only about 11 percent of the federal estate. Moreover, it was not always clear that wilderness designation actually reduced commodity use. For example, a significant portion of the wilderness system is located in remote areas of Alaska. From this perspective it is difficult to view the wilderness movement as a serious threat.

On the other hand, the wilderness system had grown by 779 percent. Equally important, expansion in the wilderness system occurred during a time of increasing demands for restrictions on and reductions in commodity use. In consequence, the symbolic image of wilderness as the antithesis of development provided a convenient target for commodity-user frustrations. Indeed, rather than merely a competing claim on the multiple use menu, wilderness preservation increasingly appeared to be, in the words of William Tucker, a "all-purpose tool for stopping economic activity."[25]

The primary configuration of the wilderness battle is perhaps best demonstrated by the issues of "release lands" and "de facto wilderness" as they have played out in the context of the national forests. The designation process defined by the Wilderness Act contained two phases. First, several areas were defined by the act for immediate inclusion in the national wilderness system (hence, "instant wilderness"). Second, the Forest Service was directed to review areas within the national forests that had been designated as "primitive" under earlier administrative regulations to determine their "suitability or nonsuitability for preservation as wilderness." Those areas found suitable would then become subjects of congressional deliberation, and those found unsuitable would be "released" for continued multiple use management.

This process seemed to frame a workable approach, yet wilderness advocates remained suspicious about the Forest Service's actual commitment to wilderness. These suspicions fueled the controversy that led to the *Parker v. United States* case.[26] At dispute was the Forest Service's announced plan to conduct a timber sale in an area adjacent to a primitive area. Wilderness advocates challenged the sale on the grounds that it would preclude the area from consideration as a potential wilderness area. Wilderness advocates won in the district court, the Forest Service appealed, but the ruling was upheld.[27]

The *Parker* ruling was a major victory for wilderness advocates. It confirmed that the decision to release lands from the wilderness designation process was a matter of congressional determination. In consequence, the Forest Service had to manage areas in question as wilderness until congressional deliberations were completed. It also confirmed the fears of wilderness opponents. In blocking the proposed timber sale, the *Parker* ruling offered a graphic example of the extent to which wilderness designation could be used as a "tool for stopping economic activity."

Another consequence of the *Parker* ruling became one of the factors that caused the Forest Service to reconsider its position on the "de facto wilderness" issue.[28] De facto wilderness is a term coined by environmentalists for roadless areas within the national forests that were neither primitive areas nor contiguous to primitive areas. As Robinson suggests, one reason wilderness advocates wanted to extend the wilderness designation process to de facto wilderness is that it offered a way to considerably increase the size of the wilderness system. In 1967 there were roughly 15 million acres of national forests designated as wilderness or primitive areas. De facto wilderness comprised another 56 million acres.[29]

The problem, however, was that while the Wilderness Act recognized that lands contiguous to primitive areas might be included in the designation process (the basis for the *Parker* ruling), it made no reference to de facto wilderness areas. Thus the Wilderness Act did not provide a basis for extending the wilderness review process. Nevertheless, based on the "judgement of agency personnel that the [Wilderness Act] did not prevent" a review of de facto wilderness, and that "conservationists would soon be demanding classification of additional wilderness lands not specified in the act,"[30] the Forest Service inaugurated the Roadless Area Review and Evaluation (RARE) study.

Although the RARE study seemed to be a major concession to wilderness advocates, it has been a source of ongoing antagonism between wilderness advocates and the Forest Service. In 1974, for example, the Forest Service released the results of its initial assessment (RARE I), which recommended wilderness designation for 12 million acres of 56 million studied. The Sierra Club challenged RARE I in the courts, charging that there had been inadequate public participation in the process and that the study constituted a major federal action under the terms of the National Environmental Policy Act (NEPA), thereby requiring the Forest Service to prepare an environmental impact statement (EIS). An out-of-court settlement was reached when the Forest Service agreed to prepare the EIS. The Carter Administration, however, subsequently rejected RARE I in total and ordered the Forest Service to conduct a new study. The RARE II results, released in 1979, recommended 15.6 million acres for wilderness designation, 10.6 million for further study, and the remainder for release. Environmentalists filed suit once again, this time attacking the adequacy of the EIS.[31]

It is not difficult to understand why commodity users grew increasingly suspicious of the wilderness advocates' intent. Whatever complaints wilderness advocates had with the RARE process, the fact remained that as long as the RARE controversy dragged on, it curtailed, if not eliminated, development activity on the lands under study. Thus, from the wilderness opponents' perspective, the RARE process had the effect of creating additional wilderness acreage without formal congressional designation.

Prior to 1976 the wilderness controversy centered almost exclusively on the national forest system. At first glance, this situation seems easy to explain: BLM lands were not included in the Wilderness Act. However, the question of why BLM lands were excluded leads in interesting directions.

Sally Fairfax argues that the omission of BLM lands "was not the result of special pleadings or policy but simply an oversight."[32] Such may in fact have been the case since the early leaders of the wilderness movement—Aldo Leopold, Arthur Carthart, Bob Marshall—were Forest Service employees, and early Forest Service regulations had established a wilderness system administratively. And yet, the events of the 1960s and 1970s cast doubts on this interpretation.

As noted earlier, the Forest Service provided a model for the drive to establish multiple use management on BLM lands throughout the 1960s. Moreover, the Multiple Use–Sustained Yield Act of 1960, which formally established a multiple use mandate for the Forest Service, identified wilderness as a component of the management mission. It was unlikely, therefore, that wilderness would be completely ignored in regard to BLM lands. And as it turns out, BLM wilderness potential was not ignored. At one point during 1962 hearings on the Wilderness Act, Representative Ralph Rivers (D-Alaska) asked Interior Secretary Udall if any BLM lands "would be put into a wilderness system." Udall responded: "The public domain administered by the Bureau of Land Management is not involved in any way. I do not think it should be. I do not know anyone that intends that it should."[33]

The emphatic tenor of Udall's answer, which appears oddly out of context in the hearing record, may provide a clue as to why BLM lands were excluded from the wilderness process. Given Aspinall's open opposition to wilderness, as well as his crusade to reclaim traditional conservation, it seems likely that wilderness advocates would want to minimize the areas of potential confrontation with him. Seeking to dispel the recurring argument that wilderness would "lock up" valuable resources, for instance, wilderness advocates amassed evidence demonstrating that the areas in concern had very little commercial value. In so doing, they established a position from which wilderness could be portrayed as both an important national heritage and an appropriate use for lands no one else wanted.

The BLM lands, however, are commercially valuable. Though primarily dedicated to grazing, they also contain considerable mineral wealth and small but valuable timber resources. Thus including BLM lands in the effort would not only risk intensifying Aspinall's opposition but also undermine the wilderness advocates' contention that little commercial value was at stake.

Whatever the explanation for excluding BLM lands from the Wilderness Act, wilderness advocates subsequently changed their position. In

1969, a coalition of national conservation groups, which included the Sierra Club and the Wilderness Society, submitted a list of policy positions to the PLLRC. One of these positions was to extend the Wilderness Act to BLM lands.[34] The PLLRC report did not mention the BLM specifically, but its call for wilderness expansion clearly implied a review of BLM lands. It came as no surprise, therefore, that Jackson's original version of FLPMA would contain a wilderness provision. Aspinall's version did not, of course. Wilderness advocates prevailed, and BLM joined the Forest Service in the vortex of the wilderness controversy when Section 603 of FLPMA required that "roadless areas of five thousand acres or more and roadless islands" within the public lands be reviewed for possible designation as wilderness areas under the criteria of the Wilderness Act.[35]

In one sense Section 603 of FLPMA reflected an attempt to avoid the kinds of confrontations that had developed over the forests. Although calling for a review following the criteria established by the Wilderness Act, Section 603 contained two provisions that specifically addressed the problematic issue of study area management. The "non-impairment" clause required management of review areas so as to prevent degradation of their wilderness qualities. This clause was consistent with the precedent established in the *Parker* case. However, Section 603 also contained a grandfather clause that allowed any grazing, mining and mineral leasing activities authorized before the passage of FLPMA to continue, even though it might threaten the wilderness character of the areas in question.

These directives confused the situation as much as they clarified it. On the one hand, they were a recognition of the fact that the BLM, unlike the Forest Service, did not have a lengthy history of administratively based wilderness management.[36] In consequence, attempts to establish BLM wilderness would be far more susceptible to the charge of excluding commodity use than forest wilderness. On the other hand, the mandates were simply contradictory, guaranteed to make the BLM a target of criticism from both sides. And as we will see below, the BLM's regulatory efforts to harmonize these clauses became a recurring source of conflict.

Although this brief summary does not map all the complexities of the wilderness struggle, it does provide some initial clues regarding the sources of the attitude that motivated the Sagebrush Rebellion. While much of the conflict over wilderness was situational—confrontations over designation of specific areas—the review processes imparted a tentative and unsettled character to land management decisions. In such a political climate, it is difficult to predict actual outcomes, and consequently, suspicions about motives and potential repercussions move to the forefront. And as we have seen, a primary component of the Sagebrush Rebellion attitude came from fears and apprehensions about future land management decisions.

Wilderness controversies frequently intersected with other public land disputes. In the next section, we consider the consequences of wilderness and other environmental regulations on the traditional area of livestock grazing. Since many of the leading spokespersons for the Sagebrush Rebellion were associated with the livestock industry, this section will help shed light on a major complaint raised by the Rebels.

GRAZING

The Taylor Grazing Act of 1934 mandated a federal regulatory program to "stop injury to the public grazing lands by preventing overgrazing and soil deterioration." Overgrazing is not necessarily the only activity that has caused injury to the public range. Foss suggests, for instance, that as much as 25 million acres were damaged by homesteaders who plowed the vegetative cover under and then abandoned the land.[37] In fact, any activity that removes the vegetative cover from the land in the arid West can lead to injury through erosion. Thus the list of potentially damaging activities includes not only sodbusting and grazing but also surface mining, clearcutting, dam building, road building, motorized recreation, and even hiking and camping. However, grazing has been the historical center of public land controversies, and given the stockgrowers' vanguard position in the Sagebrush Rebellion, it seems the contemporary conflict fits the previous pattern.

With the advent of the environmental decade, attention once again focused on the condition of the public range and, by implication, on the effectiveness of federal regulation. It quickly became apparent that assessing range conditions was an issue heavily affected by perception (see Table 3.1). Range classified by the BLM as "static" or "declining" is range in unsatisfactory condition. Thus some 81 percent of the public range was considered unsatisfactory in 1974, which did not bode well for range management efforts. A similarly pessimistic conclusion can be drawn by focusing on the trend in the "improving" category—forty years of management efforts have resulted in only an 18-percent increase. If the trend assessment focuses on the "declining" category, however, a somewhat more optimistic conclusion results. In this case, BLM management efforts have succeeded in improving 77 percent of the range from a deteriorating condition.

That these varying interpretations had political implications is suggested by the following observation from a BLM report:

TABLE 3.1. Range Trends in Percent of Public Range

	1935	1964	1974
Improving	1	17	19
Static	6	69	65
Declining	93	14	16

Source: General Accounting Office, *Public Rangelands Continue to Deteriorate* (Washington, D.C.: Government Printing Office, 1977), p. 4.

Among livestock interests in all States, assessments of the range were frequently made by comparing current conditions to those prior to the Taylor Grazing Act with the consensus that the lands have improved since then. . . . Environmentalists and wildlife interests much more frequently described the range as poor and in some instances deplorable. These groups cited overgrazing as well as other man-caused abuses as responsible for the condition of the range.[38]

In 1974 this difference of opinion found its way into federal district court in the form of *Natural Resources Defense Council (NRDC) v. Morton.*[39]

At issue was whether or not the Department of Interior, through the BLM, had satisfied the requirements of the National Environmental Policy Act (NEPA) in regard to its grazing permit program. In 1973 the BLM published a draft "programmatic" environmental impact statement on the grazing program. A programmatic impact statement treats a program as a single unit, and thereby assesses the impact of the entire program rather than each of its separate parts. NRDC challenged the programmatic statement on the grounds that the scope of the grazing program warranted a more specific assessment. Robert Nelson has asserted that NRDC also "hoped to use the NEPA requirement to force a better balance between livestock grazing and other uses. In some areas NRDC believed that, if an analysis were objectively done, livestock grazing would probably be eliminated altogether."[40]

In its ruling the court listed three specific failures of the programmatic impact statement. First, although the programmatic statement contained specific criteria for environmental evaluation, there was no guarantee that the district staff would implement those criteria in the issuance of a grazing permit. Second, the programmatic statement did not provide "detailed analysis of local geographic conditions necessary for the decision-maker to determine what course of action is appropriate under the circumstances." Third, the programmatic "EIS does not allow those who are not part of the decision-making process to adequately evaluate and balance the factors on their own."

As a result of these findings, the BLM was directed to begin preparing 144 individual environmental impact statements on 170 million acres of grazing land. These statements were scheduled to be completed in 1988, but by 1978 the general trend had been identified: "In nine areas for which EIS's were completed in 1978, for example, downward adjustments for authorized livestock were required of 44 percent of the allotments while 14 percent were allowed increases and 42 percent remained essentially unchanged. Subsequent EIS's are likely to follow this trend."[41]

Following on the heels of the NRDC case, the stockgrowers confronted implementation of the wilderness review mandated by FLPMA. As discussed above, two provisions of Section 603 offered apparently contradictory directives regarding the wilderness review process. The non-impairment clause directed the secretary to manage potential wilderness areas to prevent degradation of their wilderness qualities. The grandfather clause protected uses authorized prior to the passage of FLPMA, even if those uses might otherwise be excluded from wilderness areas. Grazing was identified as one of the grandfathered uses.

In its "Interim Management Policy Guidelines for Lands Under Wilderness Review," BLM offered the following resolution between these clauses: "The grandfather clause does not freeze grandfathered uses at the same level as existed on October 21, 1976. The mandate, in section 603(c), to prevent unnecessary or undue degradation of the lands explicitly applies to the grandfathered uses. Thus, the grandfather provision will not prevent implementation of reductions in authorized use adopted in allotment management plans."[42] Given the contradictory nature of these provisions, BLM's interpretation seemed to frame a workable compromise. The problem, however, was that the specific language from FLPMA required "continuation of existing mining and grazing uses and mineral leasing in the *manner and degree* in which the same was being conducted on the date of approval of this Act" (emphasis added). Stockgrowers understood this passage to mean that wilderness review was not a justification for grazing reductions.

Combined, the EIS process and the wilderness review fueled two related suspicions on the part of the stockgrowers. First, and most obvious, both suggested a trend of reduced grazing allotments, but more important, they also created doubts about the BLM's motives. The site-specific EISs may have been required by a court decision, yet the court justified its ruling, in part, with a BLM report on grazing in Nevada. The primary contention of this report, cited in the NRDC decision, was that: "Uncontrolled, unregulated or unplanned livestock use is occurring in approximately 85 percent of the state and damage to wildlife habitat can be expressed only as extreme destruction."[43] Moreover, the Department of Interior's decision not to appeal *NRDC v. Morton* added further uneasiness about BLM's intent. Pacific Legal Foundation summarized these apprehensions in a supplemental brief filed on behalf of the stockgrowers' attempt to appeal the decision: "Viewing the events that led up to the filing of the instant suit many permittees felt besieged on two fronts: On the one hand NRDC was actively engaged in trying to run them off the range; on the other, BLM, which is nominally charged with fostering their interests under the Taylor Grazing Act, was preparing to give in to NRDC's demands by voluntarily preparing EISs."[44] Thus it is not difficult to understand why stockgrowers viewed the Interim Guidelines as part of a larger pattern to restrict grazing on the public lands.

The grazing EIS process and wilderness review were not the only issues that worried the livestock industry during the 1970s. Grazing authorizations on the public lands are measured in terms of animal unit months (AUMs). Because grazing forage is a scarce resource, the allocation of AUMs is a zero-sum game in which providing for one group of animals means reducing forage for another group. Historically, the major nonlivestock use of the public range has been forage for game animals. The BLM estimated that 1.8 million AUMs were required for support of big game animals in 1975. In addition, BLM estimated that some 627,925 AUMs were required to support wild horses and burros under the mandate of the Wild and Free-Roaming Horses and Burros Act. (In 1975, the wild horse and burro population was estimated at 60,100 head by 1978 the population had grown to 63,190 head.) Finally, the Endangered Species Act introduced yet more restrictive management practices to provide both forage and critical habitat.

One measure of the overall impact of these various demands on public range management is that authorized livestock AUMs decreased by 36 percent from 1959 to 1978. This total reduction has not been distributed equally among the Western states, but all the states except Montana experienced a decline (see Table 3.2).

From the stockgrowers' perspective, then, the issue was that despite a clear pattern of reduced grazing on the public lands, critics continued their attacks. For example, a 1977 GAO report suggested: "The Nation's public rangelands have been deteriorating for years and, for the most part, are not improving. . . . Livestock have been permitted to graze on public rangelands year after year without adequate regard to the detrimental effect on range vegetation."[45] It seemed conceivable, therefore, that the ultimate goal of these attacks might be the elimination of public land livestock grazing.

There is another criterion for assessing grazing on the public lands.

TABLE 3.2. Change in AUMs (in thousands)

State	1959	1978	% Change
Arizona	.611	.516	−16
California	.385	.234	−39
Colorado	.781	.441	−44
Idaho	1.398	1.105	−21
Montana	.896	.927	+3
Nevada	3.139	1.846	−41
New Mexico	2.152	1.412	−34
Oregon	1.124	.886	−21
Utah	2.333	.831	−64
Wyoming	1.925	1.182	−39

Source: U.S. Department of Interior, Bureau of Land Management, *Public Land Statistics* (Washington, D.C.: Government Printing Office, 1959–1979).

Although grazing is a traditional use of the public lands, it has never been a significant component of the livestock industry. Table 3.3 displays total cattle population estimates in the United States, the western states, and on BLM lands from 1935 to 1980.

These figures lead to several interesting observations. First, the number of cattle grazing on BLM lands has always been a small portion of both the total U.S. population and the western population. Second, the number of cattle on the public range has remained relatively constant over this 45-year period. Third, the total U.S. cattle population increased by 83 percent, and the western population by 170 percent, over the same period. In short, it is not at all clear that the growth in environmental regulations adversely affected the western livestock industry.

If stockgrowers had been the only commodity interest in the Sagebrush Rebellion, then it would be possible to conclude that the controversy represented nothing more than an unwillingness on the part of

TABLE 3.3. Total Cattle Population (in millions)

	United States	West	BLM
1935	60.67	6.91	1.58
1946	81.05	8.71	2.14
1960	101.52	17.04	2.46
1980	110.96	18.69	1.61

Source: Compiled from U.S. Department of Interior, Bureau of Land Management, *Public Land Statistics* (Washington, D.C.: Government Printing Office, 1936–1980) and U.S. Department of Commerce, Bureau of Census, *Census of Agriculture* (Washington, D.C.: Government Printing Office, 1936–1980).

grazing interests to accept the changing character of public land management. But they were not alone in their concerns about public land policy throughout the 1970s. Mining interests raised virtually identical complaints about declining access to public land resources.

MINING

Mineral development is the single most problematic commodity use of the public lands. The basic dilemma is that minerals are as vital to the well-being of an industrial society as their production is disruptive to the natural environment. Thus, mining interests are better situated than other public land users to articulate their demands in terms of an overriding national interest, yet the environmental dislocations produced by mineral activity frequently provoke complaints not only from preservation interests but from other commodity users as well.

Nevertheless, the train of events throughout the 1960s and 1970s created a condition summarized in a 1979 GAO report: "At one time, 90 percent of all Federal lands were available for mineral exploration and development. However, beginning with the passage of the Wilderness Act of 1964, which created 9.1 million acres of federally protected wilderness areas, successively more and more public land throughout the United States has been declared off-limits to mining."[46] At one level, then, the general pattern in the mining area mirrored that in the grazing area: the ascendancy of the environmental movement led to increasing restrictions on commodity use. However, two factors made the mining situation especially problematic. First, the trend of restricting mining activity occurred against a backdrop of relatively explicit statements of government policy to encourage domestic mineral production. Second, two crises in the mid 1970s provided further evidence of the need for increased domestic mineral production.

Before we examine the role that mining issues played in the Sagebrush Rebellion, there are a few background issues that we should consider. For our purposes, two categories of minerals are important: fuel minerals (primarily fossil fuel sources) and nonfuel minerals (primarily precious and strategic metals). The basic process for nonfuel mineral development was established by the General Mining Law of 1872, which allowed individuals to enter the public domain at will, stake out mineral claims, and secure title to lands containing mineral deposits. Fuel mineral development, on the other hand, is regulated by the Mineral Leasing Act of 1920 (MLA). In essence, the MLA established a leasing system administered by the Secretary of Interior. It also required royalty payments on mineral development, and importantly, it stipulated that the federal government would retain title to lands under development.

Another background feature is a shift in the source of supply for minerals that occurred after World War II. A variety of forces in the postwar years, not the least of which was lower production costs, created an attractive incentive for importation of foreign mineral supplies. A 1962 study by Resources for the Future, for example, found that imports accounted for about 20 percent of total U.S. consumption of oil, a level controlled by government policy, not market forces. The trend for nonfuel minerals was even more pronounced: "Until fairly recently, the growth in U.S. demands for metals was primarily met by increased domestic output. . . . Since the end of World War II, however, there has been a rapidly increasing reliance on imports, so that today the United States has become a net importer of the basic metals and their ores."[47] As long as foreign supplies remained available and lucrative, mining on the federal estate did not seem to pose a major problem.

However, 1962 was also the year that the Outdoor Recreation Resources Review Commission (ORRRC) published the results of its study. Among the components of the ORRRC report was an investigation by the Wildlands Research Center (WRC) of the potential mineral resources in areas being considered for the wilderness system proposed in what would become the Wilderness Act of 1964. The WRC's report contained troublesome implications in this regard.

> The Bureau of Mines in reviewing mineral potential of 30 National Forest wilderness and primitive areas, indicates that discovery potential for metalliferous minerals is high in 18 areas, and medium to low in the other 12. Potential for nonmetalliferous minerals discovery is listed as high in 9 areas, medium or low in the other 21; while mineral fuel discovery potential is high for one area and mostly low for all other areas.[48]

Moreover, the WRC admitted that the data used for these estimates were far from conclusive. In six of the areas, for example, there was simply no available information on the potential for fuel minerals. The problem, then, was that banning mining from wilderness ran the risk of locking up both known and unknown mineral deposits. Yet the WRC remained optimistic: "Legislation restricting development and access to legitimate deposits and mining activities appears to be the most effective, practical and fair solution to this problem."[49]

The WRC's recommendation, in turn, provided a plausible framework for constructing a compromise in the proposed Wilderness Act. The basic premise of the compromise was that wilderness mineral deposits would be treated as "bank accounts" to be used only as a last resort during times of pressing national needs. Implementation of this compromise presented some problems, however. The first problem was how to extend the bank account approach to both categories of minerals. Fuel minerals were less troublesome, in that wilderness leases could be denied unless situations arose creating an overriding national need. Although this approach placed considerable power in the hands of the secretary of Interior it was generally consistent with the terms of the MLA. Exercising similar control over nonfuel minerals, however, required repeal or amendment of the General Mining Law. And while environmental interests were more than willing to entertain modifications to that act, the mining industry was not.

A related problem centered on the issue of information. To work effectively, the bank account approach required an accurate inventory of mineral deposits within the wilderness system. Mineral exploration, though certainly less disruptive than extraction activity, is nonetheless an antagonistic intrusion on the primeval character of wilderness. Although wilderness advocates were convinced that mineral exploration, if successful, would create significant pressure for development, an accurate mineral inventory served their cause more than they cared to admit. An accurate mineral survey would determine the extent to which mineral deposits were, in fact, locked up by the proposed system. Equally important, it would also provide a concrete measure of accountability should the secretary of Interior attempt to authorize mineral development in wilderness.

Although still uncomfortable with the entire situation, wilderness advocates realized that the minerals question might lead to further delays in the enactment of the Wilderness Act. In consequence, they relented, and these implementation problems were resolved by two provisions contained in the final act. Section 4(d)[2] addressed the exploration issue: "Nothing in this Act shall prevent . . . any activity, including prospecting, for the purposes of gathering information about minerals or other resources, if such activity is carried on in a manner compatible with the preservation of the wilderness environment." It also called for mineral surveys on a "planned and recurring basis" to be conducted by the U.S. Geological Survey and the Bureau of Mines in order to "determine the mineral values, if any, that may be present." The results of these surveys were to be made available to the public.

The more problematic part of the compromise was spelled out in Section 4(d)[3]: "Notwithstanding any other provisions of this Act, until midnight December 31, 1984, the United States mining laws and all laws pertaining to mineral leasing shall, to the same extent as applicable prior to the effective date of this Act, extend to those national forest lands designated by this Act as "wilderness areas." Thus mining activity could be permitted within the wilderness system for twenty years, but after that time the system would be withdrawn from mineral activity. There were two qualifications to this general rule. The ban on mining activity after 1984 pertained only to new exploration; any claims and leases established before that date could be developed. As before, Paragraph 3 contained a proviso requiring stringent regulation of any authorized mineral activity, including "restoration as near as practicable of the surface of the lands disturbed . . . as soon as they have served their purpose."

In a sense, the argument over mineral development in wilderness was a "tempest in a teapot." Once again, the amount of land under consideration for wilderness in 1964 was a tiny fraction of the total federal estate, and the relatively stable supply of foreign minerals reduced demands for domestic sources. Nevertheless, the Wilderness Act established an important precedent—wilderness designation did not exclude mineral activity.[50]

By the late 1960s, however, concerns about the potential hazards of reliance on foreign sources for mineral supply began to emerge. During 1969 hearings, for example, Representative Ed Edmondson (D-Okla.) explained:

> We have gone out and invested literally hundreds of millions of American dollars in developing resources in Latin America, and in Africa and in the Middle East, and we have increased our own dependence upon those resources, and we have been discovering . . . that they are not dependable sources of supply for us . . . that they are subject to outright confiscation [and] interdiction.[51]

The topic of these hearings was the need to establish a national mining and minerals policy that encouraged greater attention to domestic production. This effort, in turn, paralleled the work of the PLLRC, which noted in its summary report:

> As our demands for minerals have grown, we have become more dependent on foreign sources of supply. Over one-third of our mineral supplies are imported. This reliance on foreign sources may well increase according to current indications. Experience in Peru, the Middle East, and elsewhere demonstrates that total reliance on foreign sources would be a hazardous economic and political policy. We strongly favor, therefore, an overriding national policy that encourages and supports the discovery and development of domestic sources of supply.[52]

One product of these endeavors was the Mining and Minerals Policy Act (MMPA), adopted in December 1970.

Although the only specific action required by this act was an annual statement by the secretary of Interior on the state of the domestic mining industry, MMPA contained an explicit statement of support for domestic mineral production.

It is the continuing policy of the Federal Government in the national interest to foster and encourage private enterprise in (1) the development of economically sound and stable domestic mining, minerals, metal, and mineral reclamation industries, (2) the orderly and economic development of domestic mineral resources, reserves, and reclamation of metals and minerals to help assure satisfaction of industrial, security and environmental needs.[53]

It could be argued, of course, that MMPA's lack of specific requirements, and its brevity (a mere three paragraphs) made it little more than a rhetorical device intended to placate the mining industry, but in form and specificity, MMPA was not substantially different from the National Environmental Policy Act (NEPA). Thus MMPA carried as much potential for increasing attention to domestic mineral production as NEPA did for increasing attention to environmental values.

Two events in the mid 1970s provided graphic evidence of the need for the policy commitment contained in MMPA. The key event was the oil embargo by the Organization of Petroleum Exporting Countries (OPEC). The second event, the resulting energy crisis, captured national attention with one of the most complicated policy debates the United States has ever experienced. The second event was a brief disruption in world nonfuel mineral supplies in 1974 created by several unfavorable market forces. While not directly related to the energy crisis, these shortages added further concerns about the nation's vulnerability to a nonfuels mineral crisis. Since the nation's dependence on foreign supplies represented a major component in both crises, a plausible strategy was greater utilization of domestic resources. Yet two studies released in 1976 raised serious questions about the efficacy of this strategy.

The Department of Interior (DOI) and the congressional Office of Technology Assessment (OTA) carried out independent assessments regarding the availability of federal lands for mineral development. The DOI estimated that mining activity was either formally excluded or highly restricted on 58.1 percent of the federal lands and mineral leasing was banned or highly restricted on 61.3 percent of the federal lands. The OTA's estimates were more conservative: mining was banned or restricted on 44 percent and mineral leasing on 48 percent.[54] To some extent, the totals in both reports were artificially inflated by the inclusion of Alaskan lands slated for eventual disposal under the auspices of the Alaska Native Claims Settlement Act. However, as the DOI Task Force on the Availability of Federally Owned Minerals noted: "Until the Alaskan land ownership issues are resolved, large portions of the State will remain closed to mineral development."[55]

Public hearings conducted by the task force offered some early glimpses of the complaints raised in the Sagebrush Rebellion. For example, Calvin Black, Chairman of the San Juan County Commission and former state legislator, complained that federal land use planning had locked up nearly two-thirds of the state of Utah. Land use plans "developed by bureaucracies authorized by congress . . . with the input and far more influence from people in the extreme environmental groups living outside" of Utah. Black went on to suggest:

> I believe that most of [the federal lands] ought to be transferred to the State of Utah and the other states in which they belong so that we in the states can determine what these lands are used for. I know that a congressional act would be required, and I am told that it's unlikely that that will ever happen, but I think the odds of it happening are every bit as good as George Washington's odds were something over two hundred years ago, and I feel very strongly that that's a similar issue.[56]

It might be noted that San Juan County is located directly south of Grand County, the setting for the Moab incident.

U.S. Senate candidate Orrin Hatch echoed Black's sentiments:

> Although we are one of the most mineral rich states in the country, we have not been able to develop our minerals within the State of Utah, and I believe it is because of repressive actions on the part of the government and inactions on the part of the Department of Interior. . . . [O]ne of the biggest issues that Utahns have raised with me . . . has been that they feel like we are very, very poorly treated by the federal government with regard to the federal lands. They feel like you are stymieing the agriculture industry, livestock grazing, use of federal lands by Utahns, and the orderly development of minerals on our federal lands.[57]

Three months later Hatch won his first term in the Senate, and three years later he introduced a bill that provided a mechanism for the transfer of federal lands to the states.

At a general level, then, the configuration of the mineral development controversy pitted the perceived need for greater domestic production against a pattern of increasingly restrictive regulation on the federal estate. Two events that occurred in the mid 1970s provide a specific focal point for the dispute. One was the announcement of a major natural gas discovery in southern Utah within a complicated geological formation called the Overthrust Belt. This formation runs through the western United States from Alaska to Mexico, and since roughly 60 percent of the surface above the Overthrust Belt is federal land, the Utah discovery set off a flurry of demands for further exploration. The other event was the enactment of FLPMA. Although FLPMA contained several provisions regarding mineral development, two provisions were particularly important to the brewing frustration with public land management decisions. First, FLPMA called for the "implementation of the Mining and Minerals Policy Act,"[58] and second, Section 603 of FLPMA mandated a wilderness review of BLM lands.

As with grazing, the primary issue was how the BLM intended to harmonize the troublesome grandfather and nonimpairment clauses with mineral activity in potential wilderness areas. The BLM's response was the "surface-disturbing impact" rule. If a mining or mineral activity under question had a surface-disturbing impact prior to the enactment date of FLPMA (October 21, 1976), the activity would be allowed to continue, even though it might impair the wilderness character of the area. If the activity had not disturbed the surface, BLM required preparation of an environmental assessment (EA) or EIS to determine whether or not the proposed activity should be authorized.

Although this approach seemed more consistent with the intent of FLPMA than that used for grazing, other issues intervened. The surface disturbance rule clearly implied that the BLM had the authority to deny access where no disturbances had occurred. However, FLPMA linked the BLM's review to the Wilderness Act, which permitted exploratory activity as long as it was "carried on in a manner compatible with the preservation of the wilderness environment." Moreover, MMPA carried an explicit statement that federal policy should encourage the "orderly and economic development of domestic mineral resources" in an environmentally responsible manner. Thus, though the requirement for an EA or EIS was compatible with both the Wilderness Act and MMPA, a question remained as to whether or not BLM actually had authority to deny access.

Another aspect of Section 603 raised yet more questions. In defining the wilderness review process, Section 603 required that "prior to any recommendation for the designation of an area as wilderness the Secretary shall cause mineral surveys to be conducted by the Geological Survey and the Bureau of Mines to determine the mineral values, if any, that may be present in such areas."[59] On the one hand, this provision strengthened the BLM's position vis-à-vis the mining industry. Since mineral surveys by these agencies were required before an area could be designated wilderness, there was little reason for additional private exploration. On the other hand, the BLM's review process became dependent upon the ability of the Geological Survey and Bureau of Mines to carry out surveys in a timely manner.

The question of timeliness was, in turn, the subject of a 1978 General Accounting Office (GAO) report. Based on its review, GAO concluded that at the existing funding and staffing levels it would take the U.S. Geological Survey fifty years to complete required mineral assessments. Doubling the survey's budget would cut the assessment time to twenty years. However, even that time frame presented problems, as GAO explained: "BLM officials stated that they have other priorities and commitments arising under legislation that required updated land use plans in a shorter time, and BLM cannot delay its plans to accommodate the Survey schedule."[60] In fact, GAO found at least one instance of BLM officials using "obsolete geologic maps prepared in the 1880s and 1890s because, in many instances, this was the only information available."[61] A possible consequence of this situation, GAO argued, would be the need to revise land use plans as future mineral surveys were completed. Even this avenue suggested adverse repercussions: "BLM and the Forest Service could have difficulty reversing land use decisions, even if the Survey programs were later to identify high mineral resource areas that were previously designated for nonmineral use, because lawsuits from environmental groups and others could result."[62]

Further complications emerged in 1978 when the Rocky Mountain Oil and Gas Association (RMOGA) filed suit in the Federal District Court of Wyoming challenging the BLM's surface-disturbing impact rule. At dispute was the BLM's decision to deny access for mineral exploration within wilderness study areas overlying a portion of the Overthrust Belt in southern Wyoming. RMOGA argued that in denying access, BLM's interpretation of Section 603 violated the intent of both FLPMA and the Wilderness Act. In 1980, the court ruled in RMOGA's favor, basing its decision on the fact that the congressional intent of the Wilderness Act was "to keep lands already designated as wilderness areas open to oil and gas leasing until at least December 31, 1983."[63] In consequence, denying mineral activity in study areas represented an unlawful imposition of more stringent requirements on potential wilderness than designated wilderness. At the time, this ruling raised unsettling implications for the BLM wilderness effort. As then BLM Director Frank Gregg explained when the final wilderness study inventory was released: "Many areas will have high conflicts between energy and wilderness characteristics."[64] The Wyoming ruling was subsequently overturned in part by a 1982 appeals court decision.

While the conflict over wilderness preservation and mineral development is only one among many controversies surrounding mineral activity on the federal estate, it provides the most insight into the sources of the attitude that gave rise to the Sagebrush Rebellion. In this regard, a charge raised by the House Subcommittee on Mines and Mining, chaired by James Santini (D-Nev.), is instructive: "Land managers have utilized administrative planning policies or misinterpretations of statute to administer the lands on an ad hoc decision basis, prohibiting mineral exploration and development or inhibiting such use through time consuming and costly regulations."[65] The wilderness controversy seems to buttress this view. Confronted with inconsistent, even contradictory, mandates, federal managers did appear to choose wilderness over mineral development.

It could be argued, of course, that federal policy placed the BLM in a "no-win" situation. Had the agency emphasized mineral development, the environmental community probably would have been equally critical. And yet, understanding the BLM to be caught between the proverbial "rock and hard place" actually supports the Sagebrush Rebels' reading of the political landscape. The BLM's apparent bias in favor of wilderness preservation offered a tacit recognition of the environmental community's growing influence within the policy arena.

RECREATION

Growing public demand for outdoor recreation during the post–World War II era provided a considerable boost for the cause of preservation. Many recreation activities (camping, hiking, hunting, fishing) require management policies that emphasize the preservation of environmental values, and increasing public demand also afforded preservation interests the mass support they needed to expand their influence within the policy arena. In short, outdoor recreation proved to be a useful means for advancing preservation goals.

Nevertheless, the relationship between preservation and recreation has also had its stormy episodes. An ongoing source of conflict over the national parks, for instance, centers on the question of whether or not roads and concessions (hotels, restaurants) within the park system diminish the nature experience it was intended to provide. Ski resorts in the national forests have periodically invoked similar criticism. More recently, swelling use of the wilderness areas has been viewed as a threat to the system's environmental integrity and "outstanding opportunities for solitude." But amid the various points of contention between recreation and preservation interests, one of the more heated controversies is the use of off-road vehicles (ORVs).

Generally speaking, ORVs include motorcycles, fourwheel drive vehicles, dune buggies, half-tracks, minibikes, snowmobiles, and air boats. Though a relatively recent phenomenon, ORV use is a prominent feature in public land recreation. In 1978, for instance, BLM estimated that about 2.95 million visitor days were used by ORVs on the public lands, and ORV use has been blamed for widespread environmental damage.

> ORVs have damaged every kind of ecosystem found in the United States: sand dunes covered with American beach grass on Cape Cod; pine and cyprus woodlands in Florida; hardwood forests in Indiana; prairie grasslands in Montana; chaparral and sagebrush hills in Arizona; alpine meadows in Colorado; conifer forests in Washington; arctic tundra in Alaska. In some cases, the wounds will heal naturally; in others they will not, at least for millennia. Remnant wild and semiwild areas near urban environments in the West have been particularly hit by ORVs.[66]

The first attempt to limit ORV use occurred in the context of the Wilderness Act, with its expressed concerns about the consequences of "growing mechanization." In practical terms, this reference meant that motorized vehicles were essentially banned from the wilderness system. Although some opposition emerged to this aspect of the Wilderness Act, it was largely futile. The strongest argument centered on the practical difficulties this ban might pose for required mineral surveys. The only serious recreational complaint came from users of the Boundary Waters Canoe Area (one of the "instant wilderness" areas created by the Act), who would be denied the use of motor boats.

Although it contained no specific discussion of ORV use, the PLLRC report expressed a position on the issue through two photograph captions in the recreation chapter. One caption reads, "Off-road vehicle use is becoming a threat to the physical environment in many public land areas," and the other, "Motorcycle racing can grind a desert range to pulp."[67] Moreover, both photographs appeared in the section of the discussion entitled "Regulation of Recreation Use."

In 1971 a special task force was created within the Department of Interior to formulate recommendations for ORV use regulation. And though the task force concluded that ORV use should be primarily a state regulatory matter, President Nixon moved in a different direction. On February 8, 1972, Nixon issued Executive Order 11644, which directed federal land agencies "to provide for administrative designation of the specific areas and trails on the public lands on which the use of off-road vehicles may be permitted, and areas in which the use of off-road vehicles may not be permitted." Pursuant to the executive order, the BLM published draft ORV regulations on April 15, 1974. The BLM's regulations, in turn, became the subject of a suit filed by the National Wildlife Federation (NWF).[68]

At issue in the suit was whether or not the BLM regulations complied with the terms of the executive order. The BLM regulations stated, in effect, that any area not specifically denied access was open to ORV use pending further study. BLM defended this approach on the grounds that it simply codified the status quo while providing the time necessary to make a final determination regarding suitable and unsuitable areas. The NWF and subsequently the U.S. District Court of the District of Columbia adopted a different view.

The court faulted the BLM's regulations on several counts, including failure to observe the criteria contained in the executive order, failure to elicit adequate public participation, and a procedural violation of the terms of NEPA. One passage in the court's ruling is especially noteworthy. The court ruled that the structure of the regulations would require BLM officials to "employ the criteria in determining whether a specific area or trail's existing 'open' status should be *changed* to 'closed' or 'restricted.' This distinction creates a subtle, but nevertheless real, inertial presumption in favor of ORV use"[69] (emphasis in the original). The court also ruled, however, that the approach suggested by NWF—closing BLM lands to ORV use until a thorough study could be completed—was unacceptable.

Two years later, President Carter amended Nixon's order by directing federal land agencies to "immediately close" all areas of the public lands where ORV use "will cause or is causing considerable adverse effects on the soil, vegetation, wildlife, wildlife habitat or cultural or historic resources." The reaction to Carter's policy is best summarized in the following excerpt from a Department of Interior news release: "Some 80,000 concerned citizens have written to the White House and the Interior Department this spring expressing concern that the new Executive Order would result in a general ban against off-road vehicle use on Federal lands."[70] Thus, in the span of five years ORV use was transformed from a virtually unregulated activity into one that presumably would be allowed very limited access.

In constructing an interpretation for this controversy, as with the grazing and mining controversies, we can move in two directions. There seems little doubt that ORV use produces potentially serious environmental degradation. Regulating the activity and thereby minimizing damage is a reasonable and prudent management goal. Indeed, ORV proponents' charge that federal managers sought to ban their access to the public lands can be seen as simply an attempt to avoid regulation.

But if we are interested in understanding the roots of the Sagebrush Rebellion, then we must suspend judgments and confront the attitude this controversy helped create among some public land users. As one disgruntled advocate of snowmobiling and motorcycling explained to a national Sagebrush Rebellion conference: "I doubt if any bureaucrat or extreme environmentalist gives a hoot about our situation. That's fine with me, because as it stands right now, I don't give a hoot for them or their goals. I intend to fight for my rights to use public land and wrest its control from their obsessive and greedy paws."[71] Whether or not the facts of the situation justify this extremist stand is less important than the fact that increasing numbers of public land users shared similar sentiments and were willing to take action in the form of the Sagebrush Rebellion.

URBAN AND SUBURBAN GROWTH

The last conflict area to be considered here is, in some respects, as old as the nation. From the time the first Europeans set foot on the Atlantic seaboard, the drive to populate and settle the entire continent has characterized the American experience. Although frequently portrayed in terms of mission and character, as in John L. O'Sullivan's "manifest destiny" and Frederick Jackson Turner's "frontier thesis," this expansionist tendency received important encouragement from public land policy. Indeed, from the 1780s to the 1880s (the "Disposal Era"), roughly two-thirds of the public domain was transferred to states, individuals, and corporate entities.

Even when federal land policy shifted to retention, the drive for settlement remained alive. Perhaps the best example is the enactment of the 1902 Reclamation Act, which authorized construction of federal water projects as a stimulus for western development. Moreover, recognizing that federal ownership of large areas created problems for western states, Congress earmarked significant portions of revenues generated from the national forests, mineral leasing, and grazing districts for return to those states.

Despite these and other concessions by the federal government, the perception of federal landholdings as a potential impediment to western growth has been a recurring issue in policy discussions. The Multiple Use and Classification Act of 1964 identified community expansion and economic development as potential justifications for the sale of public lands. The PLLRC reinforced this point with its call for a legislative framework that would make "large units of land . . . available for the expansion of existing communities or the development of new cities." In what seemed the culmination of this effort, Section 203 of FLPMA authorized disposal of small tracts of BLM land for "expansion of communities and economic development, which can not be achieved prudently or feasibly on land other than public land."

While the legislative evolution of the community expansion issue seems clear enough, other factors have made its implementation a point of contention. Primary among these factors, as Frank Popper suggests, was the environmental movement.

> Some of the activists in the environmental movement had a more specific concern: land-use reform. Prior to the 1970s, the role of government in land use consisted largely of local planning and zoning. Local governments appeared weak or indifferent to the nation's land-use and environmental difficulties. . . . Those in the land-use reform movement therefore called for more regulation at higher levels of government—an objective that I shall call "centralized regulation."[72]

Popper's term was indeed accurate.

In 1970, for example, Senator Henry Jackson introduced the National Land Use Policy Act. This act required states to prepare statewide land use plans, covering both public and private lands, based on guidelines established by the federal Land and Water Resources Council (LWRC). Moreover, the LWRC was given authority to approve state plans, and states that failed to secure such approval faced termination of federal funding. Neither Jackson's bill nor more moderate proposals introduced by Aspinall and the Nixon administration were able to gain enough support for adoption. Nevertheless, planning became an integral component of the federal agenda throughout the 1970s.

Since urban sprawl was a primary focus of the land use reform movement, the West, with its wide open spaces and low population density, might seem an unlikely arena for conflict. The rural image of the West is deceptive, however. In 1970, the Census Bureau classified about 73 percent of the population in the Rocky Mountain states as urban; by 1980, this figure had grown to 76 percent. In addition, the overall population in these states increased by 37 percent during the 1970s. Thus the West experienced urbanization problems similar to those in other regions, but because of the large federal landholdings, the West also experienced a unique problem: communities surrounded, or landlocked, by federal land. This issue, in turn, figured prominently in the complaints raised by Sagebrush Rebels.

Dean Rhoads described the circumstances confronted by one such landlocked community:

Hawthorne is a small town in western Nevada and is exactly 1 square mile of nonfederal land completely surrounded by Federal land. When the ammunition depot that has been there for decades began to cut back employment, the town began to look for replacement industry but there was no place to put it. It took a special act of Congress to allow the sale of some 3,000 acres of public land to allow Hawthorne to expand. That law took 3 years to pass.[73]

James Santini echoed similar concerns when he asked a national television audience during a 1980 edition of *The McNeil/Lehrer Report*: "Why should the town of Alamo, Nevada, that wanted to get a little league baseball park, have to go through the federal agency locally and in the district and Washington, D.C. to get the baseball diamond transferred to the local entities?[74] The federal agency here, as might be expected, was the BLM.

Another area of contention between Nevada and the BLM was public land located in the Reno–Las Vegas areas. Alberta Sbragia offered the following comments regarding this situation. "BLM is seen as owning large amounts of land both in the Reno and Las Vegas areas. Some of this land would be suitable for development, and land speculators have continually asked political leaders to try to force BLM to sell it or transfer it to the state who would then re-sell it to individuals."[75] It should be noted that Nevada interests did not raise a unified voice on these matters. As Sbragia suggests, BLM was often "simultaneously criticized for 'landlocking communities' and for 'adding to urban sprawl.'"

Although the landlocked community phenomenon is an especially sensitive issue in Nevada, where over 80 percent of the land is federal property, the problem is not limited to that state. All the western states contain areas in which the federal government dominates land ownership patterns. Equally important, the landlocked community issue was, in many important respects, part of a broader complaint about the extent to which federal planning efforts violated the autonomy of local communities in the West.

The drafters of FLPMA were not oblivious to this predicament. Section 201, which directed the Secretary of Interior to "develop, maintain, and when appropriate, revise land use plans" for the public lands, also stated: "Land use plans of the Secretary under this section shall be consistent with State and local plans to the maximum extent he finds consistent with Federal law and the purposes of this Act." At first glance, these provisions seem attentive to the issue of local autonomy. As long as BLM plans are consistent with state and local plans, it would be difficult to sustain an image of heavy-handed federal managers imposing their will on local interests. The fly in the ointment here, however, is that FLPMA made the secretary of Interior the final arbitrator on the question of whether or not BLM plans are consistent with state and local plans, a situation that, as Sally Fairfax observed, "caused many to look with dismay on the 'consistency' requirements."[76] But dismay over the consistency language paled in comparison to reactions spawned by the ruling in *Ventura County v. Gulf Oil Corporation.*[77]

In 1974, the BLM issued a lease for oil exploration in the Los Padres National Forest to Gulf Oil Corporation. Though in the national forest, the area leased by Gulf Oil was also zoned as Open Space (O-S) under the auspices of Ventura County's land use plan. According to the county zoning ordinances oil exploration and extraction were prohibited in O-S areas unless the county planning commission had issued a use permit. In 1976 Gulf Oil secured a drilling permit from the U.S. Geological Survey and began exploratory activity without securing an O-S use permit. Ventura County sought injunctive relief in federal district court, lost, and appealed to the Ninth Circuit Court of Appeals. On August 3, 1979, the appeals court upheld the district court's ruling.

Although the language of the Ventura ruling clearly indicated that it addressed a "particular case," events of the day made broader interpretations inevitable. In an amicus curiae brief filed in support of Ventura County's appeal to the U.S. Supreme Court, the Western Governors' Policy Office (WESTPO) argued: "The decision . . . radically curtails traditional state power to secure the public interest, just at a time when burgeoning private development of public land resources is giving new urgency to that long established state and local role."[78] The WESTPO brief went on to recognize the relationship between the Sagebrush Rebellion and the Ventura ruling: "Nevada, which is not a WESTPO state, seeing the constitutional basis of its sovereignty over eighty-six percent of its territory exploded by the rationale endorsed by this Court . . . has launched a widely publicized 'Sagebrush Rebellion,' . . . as a means to restore the traditional legislative power that has been lost."[79] Even former Colorado Governor Richard Lamm, an outspoken critic of the Sagebrush Rebellion, acknowledged that

> for the West, the implications are frightening. The courts, in effect, have denied *any* local government the right to apply its laws, zoning ordinances, and environmental and land-use regulations to lessees of the public lands. If Ventura stands, western communities will have lost one of their oldest and most precious rights to the federal government—the right to control activities on federal lands on or

near the communities, the power to extend legislative sovereignty over the land on which they live.[80]

In 1980 the U.S. Supreme Court upheld the lower court's decision.

It is arguable, of course, whether or not the intensity of western reaction to the Ventura case and federal land use planning efforts in general was warranted. After all, the autonomy of western communities, landlocked or not, has always been linked to federal policy. The earlier land disposal policies encouraged the creation of western communities, and federal reclamation policies made the existence and growth of those communities possible. Moreover, in a predominantly arid region, planning is an essential mechanism in dealing with the inevitable conflict produced by water scarcity.

But here, as with the issues considered above, our concern is simply to reveal yet another facet of the attitude that gave rise to the Sagebrush Rebellion. Indeed, in the words of the press release with which we began this chapter, the recurring theme among critics of federal land use policies was a belief "that federal policies affecting the West . . . are made in ignorance of conditions and concerns in the West, that those policies are made for a so-called national constituency without regard for western problems, and that this 'colonial' treatment is going to get worse."

CONCLUSIONS

Richard McArdle who, as Chief Forester, helped shepherd the Multiple Use–Sustained Yield Act (MUSY) through Congress, once said: "Let me make it perfectly clear that I think being in the middle is exactly where we ought to be. I believe that our inability to satisfy completely each and every group of national forest users is a definite sign of success in doing the job assigned to us. When each group is somewhat dissatisfied, it is a sign that no group is getting more than its fair share."[81] McArdle's comment provides a useful approach for interpreting the disputes considered in this chapter. Each area discussed certainly offered examples of dissatisfied public land users, and the structure of federal policy, most notably FLPMA, did place federal managers in the middle of the conflict. Moreover, since none of the dissatisfied users discussed here were actually excluded from either the public lands or the decision process, their complaints could simply be viewed as an attempt to get more than their fair share.

Yet the fact that these disgruntled users embarked on the Sagebrush Rebellion suggests a turn of events unaccounted for by the logic of McArdle's argument. Indeed, conflict serves as a sign of success in multiple use discussions only to the extent that competing user groups continue to support the decision process, whether or not they agree with the actual decisions produced. What we have discovered in sorting through these various conflicts, however, is a recurring complaint that federal managers and environmentalists had conspired to willfully violate the *true* intent of public land policy mandates. Conspiracies are far easier to imagine than to substantiate, of course, but in this case it is important to understand that charges of conspiracy indicate a lack of support for the decision process.

From this perspective we can begin to construct an explanation for the attitude underlying the Sagebrush Rebellion. Though there were a variety of specific problems, the root problem from the Sagebrush Rebels' perspective was that the policy arena was distinctly biased in favor of environmental values. Although troublesome in its own right, this situation was complicated by two other factors.

First, Sagebrush Rebels and environmentalists simply disagreed on the meaning of the public lands. As Samuel Hays has noted: "At the root of these controversies was not just 'interest' in the conventional sense of an economic stake but values. The economic interest of producers undergirded their opposition. But at a deeper level of human response was the degree to which producers' values were offended. They could not accept the notion that what environmentalists thought was useful and valuable was, in fact, so."[82] One example of this value clash is the battle over wilderness. While part of the opposition to wilderness is motivated by economics—the image of wilderness as an all-purpose tool for stopping economic activity—another part is simply an inability to understand how saving portions of the federal estate in an unaltered condition serves a valuable purpose. Herein lies a connection between the public land controversies of the 1970s and the redefinition of conservation in the 1960s. Under the auspices of traditional conservation, the production of food, fiber, timber, minerals, and materials was understood to be the primary value of the federal estate. In consequence, resource development and national purpose were largely synonymous. With the advent of new conservation came a reassessment of the value of federal lands. Although they did not deny the need for commodity production, preservationists succeeded in politicizing the notion that commodity production represented the primary national purpose served by the public lands. Thus the disputes of the 1970s were as much about national purpose as they were about vested self-interest.

A second and related factor was whether or not the environmentalists' view of the public lands should dominate management decisions. Despite growing public support for environmentalism, the nation's demand for public land resources had not decreased, and in the case of minerals, it had actually increased. Moreover, mandates enacted by Congress, such as MMPA and FLPMA, seemed to contain clear assurances that resource development remained an important component of public land policy. A case could be made, therefore, that while environmental protection was necessary, it should not eclipse development activity. Nevertheless, the regulations promulgated across a diverse array of public land use categories appeared to the Sagebrush Rebels to form a common pattern: protection of environmental values had become the principal goal of public land management.

We are now in a position to answer the question posed at the end of Chapter 2—why did the Sagebrush Rebellion not erupt earlier in the 1970s? Although there were clear indications of a realignment within the public land policy arena at the beginning of the environmental decade, the full consequences of that change did not become manifest until the late 1970s. Equally important, disgruntled public land users, though quite vocal, discovered that their protests had little impact on the direction of management decisions throughout the 1970s. In consequence, they confronted two basic options: they could submit to increasingly restrictive regulations, or they could, in the words of James Santini, resort to "more dramatic and emphatic statements." The Sagebrush Rebellion provides graphic evidence of the option they chose.

Frustration with the perceived environmental bias in public land policy is part of the explanation for the Sagebrush Rebellion, but a question remains. Why did the Sagebrush Rebels believe that their action might affect a change in the policy arena? After all, if the environmental community's claims were accurate—if the shift in public land management did reflect broad-based public sentiment—then there would be little reason to believe that the Sagebrush Rebels could mobilize much support for their cause. However, there was widespread dissatisfaction with the scope of federal regulations in the late 1970s, which led President Jimmy Carter to suggest that the nation confronted a "crisis of confidence" in government. At the same time, regional tensions pitted the western states against the East. Taken together, these factors suggested that the Sagebrush Rebel's complaints might be part of a broader anger developing in the West.

CHAPTER FOUR

Western Anger and the Sagebrush Rebellion

It is a complex of sections and parties—this West—and only under stress does it find a community of policy.

—*Frederick Jackson Turner, 1932*[1]

This is our West.
And it is dying.

—*Richard D. Lamm and Michael McCarthy, 1982*[2]

As part of an annual public opinion survey, the Advisory Commission on Intergovernmental Relations (ACIR) asks a sample of national respondents: "From which level of government do you feel you get the most for your money?" In 1978, 35 percent of the total sample and 32 percent of the western sample picked the federal government. A year later, however, only 29 percent of the total sample and 18 percent of the western sample picked the federal government.[3]

In a nationally televised speech on July 15, 1979, roughly two months after the ACIR poll, President Jimmy Carter observed: "It's clear that the true problems of our Nation are much deeper—deeper than gasoline lines or energy shortages, deeper even than inflation or recession. It is a crisis of confidence. It is a crisis that strikes at the very heart and soul and spirit of our national will."[4] Part of this crisis, Carter argued, came from general apprehension about the future: "A majority of our people believe that the next 5 years will be worse than the past 5 years."[5] But another part came from the government itself: "Looking for a way out of this crisis, our people have turned to the Federal Government and found it isolated from the mainstream of our Nation's life. . . . The gap between our citizens and our Government has never been so wide."[6] And as the ACIR poll indicated, this crisis of confidence in the federal government was especially acute in the West.

Indeed, the cover of the September 17, 1979, issue of *Newsweek* carried a photograph of a cowboy on horseback below the title: "The Angry West: 'Get Off Our Backs, Uncle Sam.'" The accompanying story noted:

Suddenly the Old West has become the Angry West, a region racked by an increasingly bitter sense of isolation and political alienation.

. . . One measure of the anger now firing up the West is the way it has united an otherwise maverick group of states and rugged individualists with a sense of common cause—and a conviction that the rest of the country doesn't share, understand or sympathize with the region's most vital concerns.[7]

In short, public land users were not the only ones who expressed frustration with the federal government during the late 1970s.

It is not surprising then, that the Sagebrush Rebels believed their complaints might have currency with an audience larger than disgruntled public land users. As Nevada state Senator Richard Blakemore, one of the sponsors of the Nevada Sagebrush bill, explained: "While the particular issues on which the Sagebrush Rebellion is based are more common to the west, the principles behind the movement are national in scope. It is a question of the extent to which the destiny of the country is controlled by federal agencies and bureaucrats. States, local governments, and the people should make more of these determinations and the federal government less."[8] The intent of this chapter, then, is to complete our examination of the attitude underlying the Sagebrush Rebellion by exploring the connection between the Sagebrush Rebellion and these broader tensions.

REBELLIONS PAST AND PRESENT

There have been at least two controversies similar to the Sagebrush Rebellion during this century. The first occurred in the 1920s after the U.S. Forest Service announced plans to increase grazing fees for the national forests. In response, Senator R. M. Stanfield (R-Ore.) held hearings throughout the West that, in the words of Samuel Dana, "not only permitted but encouraged the malcontents to air their grievances, real and imaginary, against the Forest Service."[9]

Though unsuccessful in blocking the proposed increase, this controversy did force the Forest Service to replace its original plan with one designed in consultation with representatives of the national livestock associations. The hearings also focused national attention on the public lands, leading President Herbert Hoover to establish a Committee on the Conservation and Administration of the Public Domain in 1929. The primary recommendation offered by the Hoover committee was that states be given the remaining public domain on one condition: the federal government retained title to the mineral estate. The committee further proposed that any lands not accepted by the states be placed under active federal management.

The prevailing response in the West to this apparently generous offer was skepticism. Utah Governor George H. Dern explained:

The Western States appreciate the compliment of being assured that they are now man grown and that they can be trusted to administer the proposed new heritage more wisely than it can be done from offices in the Nation's Capital, but they can not help wondering why they should be deemed wise enough to administer the surface rights but not wise enough to administer the minerals contained in the public lands.[10]

Dern went on to ask if the national government had been unable to sell, lease, or even give the public lands away, "by what process of reasoning are they worth anything to the states?" Refusal by the states to pursue the title issue, in turn, set the stage for the next round of controversy.

Realizing that federal management of the public lands was inevitable, western stockgrowers redirected their energies to the task of designing a management scheme that simultaneously acquiesced to federal intrusion but retained as much of the status quo as possible. The result of this effort was the Taylor Grazing Act of 1934. The Taylor Act directed the secretary of Interior to create grazing districts and regulate their use through a permit/fee process, but it also required that "preference shall be given in the issuance of grazing permits to those within or near a district who are landowners engaged in the livestock business."

This conspicuous tilt in favor of western stockgrowers did not pacify all ranchers, however. In 1936 Nevada ranchers instigated a legal battle over the authority of the Grazing Service to assess a uniform grazing fee. After finding early success in the Nevada courts, the stockgrowers' cause was ultimately defeated by the U.S. Supreme Court. Undaunted by this setback, the stockgrowers mobilized a replay of the Stanfield gambit, directed this time by Senator Pat McCarran (D-Nev.).

From 1941 to 1946 McCarran conducted hearings throughout the West, assembling over six thousand pages of nearly uniform criticism directed at the Grazing Service. Out of this controversy emerged two legislative strategies. In 1946, Senator Edward V. Robertson (R-Wyo.) revived the disposal issue by introducing legislation calling for the conveyance to the states of virtually all federal lands. Although this proposal generated some interest, in the end a more complicated ploy by McCarran resolved the dispute.

Using what Foss described as a "triple play between a Senate committee which refused to allow increased fees, a House committee which cut appropriations because fees were not raised, and a powerful interest group which supported both committees," McCarran succeeded in cutting the Grazing Service's 1946 budget almost in half, reducing it to little more than a "paper organization."[11] The Grazing Service was then merged with the General Land Office to create the Bureau of Land Management. And to add insult to injury, for a brief period during this time the salaries of many BLM field personnel were actually paid by the stockgrowers from the portion of federal grazing fees returned to the states.

When viewed against this background, it is not surprising that many critics dismissed the Sagebrush Rebellion as merely the latest in a long series of attempts by exploiters to "rip off" public property. Indeed, the basic form of the Sagebrush Rebellion—a noisy protest against federal management policies—does fit the general pattern established by these earlier episodes. But this similarity in form masks important contextual differences.

For example, the ultimate outcome of the Stanfield controversy—the Taylor Grazing Act—may seem a "rip off" in contemporary context, but at the time grazing appeared to represent the most suitable use of the public domain remnants. The outcome of the McCarran controversy carries similar implications. Although the hearings and budget maneuvers were clearly intended to demonstrate the political muscle of the stockgrowers, their ability to exercise sustained influence was a direct product of the structure of the policy arena. Describing that structure as a "mono-political culture," Foss argued that BLM administrators found themselves

> in substantially the same position as the consumer who is confronted with a monopoly producer. He has no real alternatives. His public is narrow and restricted. . . . The administrator and his staff are alone—except for the stockmen who are with them always. As time goes by, they are likely to identify themselves closely with the stockmen. When they make decisions of a regulatory nature they are forced to consider essentially the same factors as do their clientele, so, over time, such decisions will tend to come close together.[12]

Indeed, the Taylor Grazing Act, which defined grazing as the dominant use for the public lands, created this monopoly situation. But equally important was the fact that range management was defined in terms of traditional conservation.

A popular 1949 college textbook on conservation defined range management as the "art of restoring and maintaining the range lands so that they will provide feed continuously for maximum numbers of livestock without impairment of their productivity."[13] Such a "conservation policy," the authors argued, "is essential for the continued prosperity of the livestock industry."[14] It seems plausible, therefore, that the training

TABLE 4.1. NABC Composition

Interests	1940	1949	1967	1975
Cattle	10	10	10 ⎱	10[a]
Sheep	10	10	10 ⎰	
Wildlife	—	3	10	6
Other[b]	—	—	12	20
Total	20	23	42	36

Source: U.S. Department of Interior, Bureau of Land Management.
[a]In 1975 the category "Livestock" replaced "Cattle" and "Sheep."
[b]Alaska, Washington, mining, forestry, leasable minerals, outdoor recreation, urban/suburban development, soil/water conservation, county government, state government, environmental quality, public utilities, and public information.

of BLM managers was as responsible for the monopolitical culture as the political clout of the livestock industry. Stated differently, the points of disagreement between managers and stockgrowers centered on the amount of permitted grazing and the fees charged for grazing, not on the premise that grazing represented the appropriate use of the public lands.

In contrast, the Sagebrush Rebellion emerged in an arena reflecting at least three important structural changes brought about by the events of the 1960s and 1970s. First, the transformation of the BLM into a multiple use agency converted the earlier monopolitical culture into a more competitive marketplace. Symbolic of this change was the evolving composition of the National Advisory Board Council (NABC), which was the primary vehicle used by the livestock industry to "capture" the BLM. Table 4.1 displays the changing configuration of the NABC from 1940 to 1975, suggesting that stockgrower dominance was reduced both by decreasing livestock interest representation and by increasing representation from other public land user interests.

Second, legislative mandates and the redefinition of conservation served to provide land managers with real alternatives in making public land regulatory decisions. The train of events beginning with the Multiple Use Classification Act of 1964 and culminating in the Federal Land Policy and Management Act of 1976 offered conclusive evidence that grazing was no longer the dominant use of the public lands, even though the Taylor Grazing Act was never repealed. Moreover, the discussion in Chapter 3 demonstrates how new conservation, with its emphasis on preservation and restoration of environmental values, affected public land management decisions.

Third, the Sagebrush Rebels, unlike their predecessors, had to confront the opposition of a national environmental movement. Although certainly not a monolithic force, environmentalists did maintain a relatively unified front in federal land policy discussions. And perhaps more important, environmentalists could buttress their claims by pointing to an apparent groundswell of public support for environmental concerns.

Thus, the political milieu that had previously underpinned commodity users' dominance in public land policy no longer existed in the late 1970s. Moreover, the experiences of the 1970s suggested that little would be accomplished as long as the discussion was confined to the public land policy arena. Indeed, the kind of intervention contemplated by the Sagebrush Rebels required demonstrating that their frustration involved more fundamental issues than the relative balance between preservation and development in public land policy.

As it turns out, the political climate of the late 1970s provided ample opportunity for the Sagebrush Rebels to recast their complaints. After a decade of political scandals, escalating inflation, rising unemployment, and energy crises, the mood of the American public had taken a decidedly cynical turn. Moreover, reactions to these national problems varied from region to region. In consequence, regional quarrels among the states intensified. In such a political climate, then, complaints about heavy-handed federal bureaucrats and diminished states' rights had currency with a wider audience than disgruntled public land users.

"SECOND WAR BETWEEN THE STATES"

In his 1978 keynote address to the first annual meeting of the Western Governors' Policy Office (WESTPO), Colorado Governor Richard Lamm warned: "We meet at a time when feelings of sectionalism and regionalism are the most intense of any time since the Civil War. . . . Unlike the last war between the states—which pitted the North against the South and only tangentially involved the West—in the 'Second War between the states,' the West is very much involved. In fact, the West appears to be the chief area under attack."[15] The primary situation prompting this caution was the pronounced population shift from the northeastern and northcentral (the frostbelt) regions of the country to the South and West (the sunbelt) that developed in the first half of the 1970s. But as might be suspected, more was at stake than the relocation of people. Like the Civil War, the frostbelt-sunbelt controversy emerged from growing regional economic disparities.

A major recession in the opening years of the 1970s triggered this confrontation, but its roots can be traced to trends developing throughout the post–World War II era. Hoping that the lure of lower capital and labor costs, as well as lower taxes and cost of living, would be attractive to industry, the sunbelt states launched largely successful campaigns to entice industry into the region. Reflecting this trend, from 1950 to the mid 1970s, manufacturing employment grew by 76 percent in the Southeast and by 141 percent in the Southwest. Similarly, new capital investments in manufacturing grew by 21 percent and 19 percent in the Southeast and Southwest, respectively.[16] Although industrial expansion proceeded at a much slower rate in the frostbelt, the historical economic advantage of that region combined with overall growth in the economy held promise that all regions could benefit.

The recession in the early 1970s, generally viewed as the worst since the Great Depression, exposed a different trend. Declining demand led to plant closures, and the older, less efficient frostbelt facilities were generally the first closed. Confronted with rising unemployment and decreasing tax revenues, frostbelt states were forced to increase taxes and reduce services. These actions served, in turn, to intensify the problem by creating incentives for additional out-migration of businesses and people. In short, the frostbelt states found themselves gripped by an apparently self-sustaining downward economic spiral that offered little prospect for a quick recovery.

Troublesome as these conditions were, the frustrations of the frostbelt states were further aggravated by an economic boom in the sunbelt, where industrial in-migrations had created new markets and employment opportunities. The energy crisis and consequent attention to domestic production generated even more growth, because the lion's share of domestic energy resources are located in the South and West. The influx of population and firms also allowed the sunbelt states to maintain low tax rates while increasing services. Taken together, these factors enhanced the image of the sunbelt as an avenue of escape from the economic hard times in the frostbelt.

It took little imagination to see economic events of the 1970s as a zero sum game in which the sunbelt's growth came at the expense of the frostbelt, but politicizing this issue presented certain problems. First, it was difficult to sustain a charge that the sunbelt had consciously organized these trends, and second, there was virtually no way the frostbelt states could prevent out-migration. Unable to address these problems directly, frostbelt states found ways to vent their frustration indirectly. One such avenue was an apparent regional disparity in federal taxing and spending policies.

The initial ammunition for this attack came from a 1976 *National Journal* article. Using per capita federal spending and per capita federal tax burden by state and region in the nation for 1975, the authors of this article created a ratio that measured the amount of money returned to the states and regions per tax dollar raised. Their results seemed to provide graphic evidence supporting the frostbelt's claims. For example, for every dollar they generated in federal tax revenue, the Northeast got 86 cents back in federal spending, while the Midwest got only 76 cents. In contrast, the West received $1.20 and the South $1.14. In aggregate terms, the Northeast and Midwest sent over $30 million more to the federal government than they received from it, while the South and West received over $22 million more from the federal government than they sent to it.[17]

Although these revenue disparities are minor in budget discussions about billions and trillions of dollars, they nevertheless provided frostbelt states with a convenient political issue. Regardless of the amounts involved, the disparities offered evidence of a reverse Robin Hood syndrome in federal revenue policies—taking from the "have-nots" and giving to the "haves." And unlike out-migration, federal policies were an area in which the frostbelt states could take action. Consequently, the mid 1970s witnessed concerted efforts by the frostbelt states to develop regional coalitions, especially among their congressional delegations.

As the battle over federal funding took shape, regional tensions emerged in the energy arena as well. In 1970 Congress adopted the Clean Air Act, which gave coal-burning facilities two options for reducing smokestack emissions: installation of scrubber technology, or increased use of low-sulfur (hence "compliance") coal. The cost of scrubber technology, as well as questions about its durability, made compliance coal the preferred option. Since about 85 percent of the nation's stripable, low-sulfur coal is located in the West, the Clean Air Act stimulated a flurry of western coal production. With the advent of the energy crisis, western coal production became a full-fledged boom. In 1970, for example, midwestern mines produced 138 million tons of coal, while mining operations in Montana and Wyoming produced a mere 10 million tons. By 1980, midwestern production had increased about 22 percent to 173 million tons; however, production in Montana and Wyoming had grown over one thousand percent to 124 million tons.[18]

Although the boom in western coal production carried obvious economic benefits, it also carried costs. Surface mining may be a cost-effective production technique, but as the coal fields of Appalachia have demonstrated, it leaves serious, long-term environmental disruption in its wake. Westerners recognized a certain irony associated with massive disruption of their environment in order to preserve the nation's air quality. The coal boom also created other costs for the human environment, most notably a surge in the population of small, rural towns located close to federal coal fields. The rapid influx of people disrupted lifestyles, and more important, overburdened the towns' infrastructures (schools, hospitals, police and fire protection, water and sewer systems). Westerners also understood that the energy boom was temporary. Eventually the energy resources would be depleted, leading to an economic bust of about the same magnitude as the boom.

It remained to be seen, then, whether the benefits from western energy development would outweigh the costs. However, it was clear that a passive stance would not bring attention to western concerns. In consequence, western states began to mobilize around a theme summarized by New Mexico Governor Jerry Apodaca: "Let there be no mistake—the West will not become an energy colony for the rest of the nation. We will not sacrifice our greatest assets—our blue skies and clear streams, our unblemished plains and mountains—to an endless national thirst for energy."[19] The point for Apodaca and other western governors was not to stop energy development, but to insure that the development proceeded in an orderly, controlled manner.

One avenue pursued by the western governors was the establishment of the Western Governors' Regional Energy Policy Office (WGREPO) in 1975. Designed to provide a collective western voice in federal energy policy decisions, WGREPO identified as high priorities the enactment of federal strip mining legislation, a federal assistance program for communities experiencing rapid growth from energy development projects, and guarantees against federal preemption of state laws.[20] From a western perspective, these demands were necessary steps to insure that the costs created by national policies were distributed nationally.

Other regions, and to some extent federal officials, viewed the situation from a different perspective. Portraying westerners as "blue-eyed Arabs," opponents charged that the West was simply attempting to secure the benefits of energy production while exporting the costs to the rest of the nation—a charge that fit the rhetoric of the broader frostbelt-sunbelt controversy.

Nevertheless, western efforts proved largely successful. In 1977 Congress adopted the Surface Mining Control and Reclamation Act (SMCRA), which did concede the important point that western coal development would proceed under stringent environmental regulation. Western states also gained additional federal funds, though the goal of a federal assistance program for impacted communities was not realized. The Payment in Lieu of Taxes Act of 1976 provided federal payments to counties based on the amount of federal land within their boundaries. And FLPMA justified increasing the states' share of federal mineral lease royalties from 37.5 percent to 50 percent, on the grounds that the additional 12.5 percent be earmarked for impact mitigation.

The issue of the preemption of state laws proved more problematic, however. In 1975 the Montana legislature enacted a coal severance tax, and in so doing, set the stage for a major confrontation over the authority of state law. Severance taxes are predicated on the argument that nonrenewable resources (primarily minerals) represent a source of wealth that is lost when the resource is extracted. In an attempt to reclaim potentially lost wealth, then, states assess a charge, usually a percentage of the resource's market value, at the time it is extracted. An additional justification for severance taxes is that they provide a way to pass production costs on to the resource consumer. Since thirty-three states use some form of severance taxation, Montana's act was not inherently problematic, but the rate charged by Montana—20 or 30 percent of the contracted sale price, depending upon the heating value of the coal—made it the highest in the nation. Wyoming was second with a 17-percent coal tax.

While a 30 percent tax rate may seem high, several factors must be considered before drawing a final conclusion. First, the price of Montana coal is well below the national average. In 1979, for example, the average price for a ton of Montana coal (including severance tax) was $9.76, the national average was $23.75 per ton.[21] Second, the single largest cost factor in the delivered price of Montana coal comes from transportation. In some cases, the rates charged by railroads can double the coal's delivered price, and importantly, transportation costs are added after the severance tax. Finally, even though Montana's severance tax rate was the highest in the nation, it generated substantially less revenue than lower rates charged by other states. In 1979 Montana's tax produced $54 million, while Texas raised over $1 billion with its 12.5 percent tax on oil and gas production.[22] Despite these factors, Montana and Wyoming found themselves the target of attacks typified by Texas Congressman J. J. Pickle's assertion that "a number of states, including Texas, are being skinned alive by unreasonable severance taxes on coal coming out of Montana and Wyoming."[23]

These rhetorical attacks became a legal challenge in 1978, when eleven utility companies from the Midwest and Texas, as well as four coal companies, filed suit in Montana state court. The primary legal text charged that the Montana severance tax violated the supremacy and commerce clauses of the U.S. Constitution. The political subtext came from the frostbelt-sunbelt controversy, however. Montana's tax represented a strategy by which the state could export its tax burden to utility companies and their consumers. The Montana state supreme court found neither the legal nor political arguments persuasive in its 1980 ruling upholding the constitutionality of the severance tax. Undaunted by this setback, the litigants filed an appeal with the U.S. Supreme Court.

This move heightened western apprehensions, and for good cause. The 1979 ruling in the Ventura County case (discussed in Chapter three) suggested that the Supreme Court might be less than sympathetic to states' rights in energy-related issues. In addition, opponents of Montana's tax had launched a second prong of attack in the form of congressional bills to establish a national limit on the amount states could charge in severance taxes. If Congress became the arena for the severance tax controversy, Montana would confront an uphill battle. Texas and Illinois had fifty-two votes in Congress compared to Montana's four votes. In fact, Texas and Illinois had more votes than the combined congressional delegations of the Rocky Mountain states and Alaska. Overall, then, the political and legal climates in 1980 did not bode well for Montana's cause.

Although the Supreme Court eventually ruled in Montana's favor, the attack on the Montana tax in combination with the other regional battles during the 1970s reflected a pervasive attitude that many western political leaders found both dangerous and frustrating. Actions they viewed as attempts to protect the West's political integrity in the face of external intrusions were consistently interpreted as efforts to "impose their will on the rest of the country." Time and again, the western leaders found their struggles to manage growth either vilified or thwarted by decisions over which they had little control.

The dispute over Montana's severance tax also pointed to another facet of the controversy. While never particularly cordial, the relationship between the West and the federal government became increasingly antagonistic during the 1970s, especially after Jimmy Carter moved to the White House. It is to this set of controversies that we now turn.

THE WEST AGAINST THE FEDS

Historically, confrontations between the federal government and western states over land use decisions have followed a fairly predictable script. They usually begin with an aggressive assertion of national prerogative by the federal government that precipitates an equally aggressive assertion of states' rights. The political climate in the 1970s, then, made confrontation virtually inevitable. The rise of the environmental movement, in combination with the energy crisis, led to an expression of national prerogative that rivaled the activism of the early conservationists. At the same time, pressures from growth and emerging regional tensions made western leaders especially defensive about decisions affecting their states. Thus, it was just a matter of time until these countervailing forces exploded in open conflict.

During the first half of the decade, western complaints centered on the disjointed and often contradictory character of federal policy initiatives. In the energy arena alone, over a dozen federal agencies pursued seemingly independent paths with virtually no effort to coordinate their activities. Indeed, the formation of WGREPO was in large measure an effort by the western governors to bring a semblance of order to an otherwise chaotic situation. It was not surprising, therefore, that Jimmy Carter's victory in 1976 raised optimism among western leaders.

Although Carter was not persuasive with the western electorate (Carter carried none of the western states), several aspects of his campaign platform offered hope for a more constructive dialogue between the West and the federal government. Promises to gain control of the federal bureaucracy through reorganization, to balance energy development with environmental protection, and to create a new national energy plan coincided with the basic goals of western governors. Furthermore, as a former southern governor, Carter was likely to be an important ally for the West in the sunbelt-frostbelt controversies. What western leaders did not anticipate, though, was that a balanced federal budget would be Carter's first priority, or that federal water projects would be the instrument for demonstrating his commitment to this goal.

On February 21, 1977, about one month after his inauguration, Carter announced: "I have identified 19 (water) projects which now appear insupportable on economic, environmental, and/or safety grounds. . . . I am recommending at this time that no funds be provided for these projects in FY78."[24] Only eight of the projects on this so-called hit list were located in the West, but this fact did not seem to matter to westerners. Immediate reaction throughout the West portrayed Carter's move as a direct attack on the region. A political cartoon portrayed Carter showing two maps to the western congressional delegation: one depicting the location of the water projects on the hit list, and the other showing the states that did not vote for Carter in the 1976 election. The maps were identical: the western third of the nation.

The timing of Carter's announcement had virtually guaranteed a hostile reaction in the West. Serious drought had developed in 1976, and low snowfalls during the winter of 1977 promised no relief in the immediate future. Indeed, Carter's announcement came as western governors were meeting in Denver to discuss the drought. The projects on the hit list would do nothing to ease the immediate water shortages, of course, but that was beside the point. The fact that a president would even contemplate the elimination of water projects during a drought seemed to provide prima facie evidence that he was either ignorant of, or openly hostile to, western conditions.

Even if drought had not existed, the influx of people into the West and accelerating energy development assured increasing competition over scarce western water resources. This point was clearly recognized by the Ford Foundation in its ambitious study, *A Time to Choose*:

In the semi-arid western states where coal and oil shale is being extracted, water is a critical factor. Water in abundance will be required for reclamation of strip mined lands, generation of electric power from coal, and production of synthetic fuels. It is highly questionable whether adequate water exists to support massive development of federally controlled fossil fuel resources in the west, without the extensive reordering of regional water use priorities. It might even require federal funding for huge and costly interbasin water diversion projects.[25]

This report was especially pertinent because it provided the blueprint for Carter's national energy program.

Despite western protests, the hit list was neither surprising nor inconsistent with Carter's energy development plans. Carter's opposition to federal projects had emerged during his tenure as governor and continued into the presidential campaign with his promise to eliminate unnecessary projects.[26] Rather than an attack on the West, then, the hit list represented an attack on projects Carter believed should not have been authorized in the first place. Carter was also aware of the critical role water played in western energy development. In a major address on the environment delivered one month after the hit list, Carter explained: "Because extensive use of coal requires huge amounts of water, I am directing the Secretary of Interior to prepare a nationwide evaluation of the water supply needs and availability for development of various energy resources."[27] This evaluation, in turn, dovetailed with his call for a "comprehensive reform of water policy" later in the message.

Although the hit list was the focal point of the dispute, western leaders were equally troubled by Carter's decision style. The list had been composed without consultation with the affected states, and the environmental message did not identify a direct role for states. Thus Carter seemed intent on disrupting the water policy arena by minimizing, if not eliminating, state participation. A move such as the hit list would have created a confrontation at any time, but in the existing atmosphere of regional antagonisms it amounted to a declaration of war. It did not help reduce tensions when frostbelt states gave nearly unanimous support to the hit list as it moved through congressional deliberations.

Had the announcement of the hit list been an isolated event, western animosity might have been dismissed as arising more from parochial self-interest than states' rights issues. As it turned out, however, the hit list was only a prelude to the more dramatic moves by the Carter administration in the battle over Alaskan lands. The Statehood Act of 1958 had granted Alaska the right to claim over 110 million acres from the unreserved federal estate within its boundaries. This grant, justified by the fact that roughly 99 percent of Alaska was federal property at the time it joined the Union, became mired in a complex set of controversies that lasted over twenty years.

Initially, the selection process served as a focal point for racial tensions between Alaska's native and white populations. Another layer of conflict emerged with a major oil discovery on the North Slope in 1968, and the ascendancy of the environmental movement turned the disposition of Alaskan lands into a major confrontation between development and preservation forces. As is frequently the case, Congress's attempt to resolve these conflicts precipitated yet more controversy. The Alaska Native Claims Settlement Act of 1971 (ANCSA) allowed Congress to take up to 80 million acres for inclusion in the federal land system. Because these federal lands would be excluded from both state and native claims, this provision also made settlement of the matter dependent on congressional action. ANCSA originally gave Congress five years to act, but Congress subsequently extended the deadline to 1978.

When Carter assumed office, then, Congress had less than two years to meet the deadline. In January 1977, Interior Committee Chairman Morris Udall (D-Ariz.) introduced an Alaska lands bill weighted heavily in favor of land preservation. The intensity of opposition to Udall's bill did not bode well for a final settlement before the deadline. Congress could, of course, extend the deadline as it had in the past, but in his environmental address Carter clearly indicated that he wanted action, not another delay. "The Congress now has an opportunity of historic dimensions to conserve large sections of the American wilderness in Alaska. . . . We can double the size of the Wildlife Refuge and the Park Systems, as well as add to the Forest and Wild and Scenic River Systems, at no acquisition cost. . . . But if Congress fails to act by December 1978, the opportunity will be automatically lost."[28] The language of this statement also clarified which side of the preservation/development debate Carter's administration would support.

In September 1977 the administration submitted its proposal. Though more moderate than Udall's bill, it still reflected a heavy preservationist influence, as demonstrated by the call for ten new national parks, nine new wildlife refuges, and thirty-three wild and scenic river designations. By May 1978, a compromise between Udall's bill and the administration's proposal had been hammered out and adopted on a 277 to 31 vote in the House. The prognosis for Senate action was not good, however. Senator Mike Gravel (D-Alaska), already noted for his unorthodox tactics in the Pentagon Papers affair, launched a campaign to block passage of the bill. Gravel's efforts, in combination with deliberations on Carter's energy bill, succeeded in stalling progress on the Alaska lands matter throughout the summer. Finally, on October 9, with only five days remaining in the legislative session, the Senate Energy Committee reached agreement on the bill. Despite an eleventh hour frenzy of activity, no compromise could be reached on a final version and the bill died at the close of the session.

The first warning of Carter's unwillingness to accept congressional inaction came with the October 25 release of an environmental impact statement (EIS) assessing various administrative actions for preserving Alaskan lands. Although the public comment deadline for the EIS was November 22, Interior Secretary Andrus invoked Section 204(e) of FLPMA on November 16 as authority to withdraw 110 million acres in Alaska from state selection and mineral entry. Section 204(e) authorizes the secretary of Interior, House Interior Committee, and/or Senate Energy Committee to declare an "emergency situation" and thereby withdraw areas of the federal lands from all development activity for a period of up to three years. Prior to this incident, Section 204(e) had been used only once before in an effort to protect drinking water from possible contamination by uranium mining in Ventura County, California.

Senator Ted Stevens (R-Alaska) immediately labeled Andrus's action a classic example of arbitrary and capricious bureaucratic behavior. Such was not the case, however. The day before his announcement, Andrus received a letter from Udall urging the secretary to take "extraordinary measures" to resolve the "emergency situation" over the Alaskan lands.[29] Moreover, Section 204(e) was originally intended as a stopgap measure to allow Congress time to take action. Thus, the effect of Andrus's action was simply to extend the congressional deadline administratively, not to resolve the issue administratively. Nonetheless, Stevens and other opponents viewed the administrative withdrawal of the Alaska land as a first step in broader actions planned by Carter. And their apprehensions were quickly confirmed.

On December 1, 1978, Carter invoked the Antiquities Act of 1906 to set aside 56 million acres as seventeen new national monuments in Alaska. This classification barred all development activity on the land unless Congress subsequently removed it from national monument status. While Theodore Roosevelt had used the Antiquities Act in similar fashion during the early 1900s, the scale of Carter's action was unprecedented. In one set of proclamations, Carter doubled the area of the national park system by adding a land mass roughly the size of Minnesota.

Not surprisingly, Alaskans were less than receptive. As one disgruntled Alaskan exclaimed: "Environmentalists have infiltrated the government too far. And now those park planner parasites are locking up Alaska as wilderness and excluding mankind. They want food for the soul. *We* need food for the body. The federal government has always acted like a foreign power up here."[30] And in an action foreshadowing the activity in Moab, Utah, two years later, the city council of Eagle vowed to "disobey any new park regulations and threatened mass trespassing on federal property."[31] In contrast, the environmental community's reaction was perhaps best summarized by Edgar Wayburn's assertion: "The President's quick and decisive actions place him in history as the greatest conservation president of our time."[32]

The environmental community's assessment of Carter soon changed, however. Writing in the September 1979 edition of *Audubon*, Robert Cahn observed:

> The long honeymoon of the environmental movement with Jimmy Carter is over. In the space of a few days last July, the President turned, in the eyes of environmental leaders, from staunch friend to potential enemy. The cause: Carter's new energy production proposals—the $88 billion Energy Security Corporation and an Energy Mobilization Board. If carried out . . . they threaten to undo the hard-won environmental gains of the past fifteen years while bypassing many of the laws and rights now protecting all citizens.[33]

The event that led to this reassessment was Carter's "crisis of confidence" speech.

The topic of the speech was the national energy crisis. Although the gasoline lines and other manifestations of energy shortages had disappeared, the energy crisis was still a major concern. Escalating crude oil prices fueled rampant inflation and created a balance of payments problem that drove down the value of the dollar in international money markets. In many respects, these economic implications were more troublesome than the shortages themselves, because they lacked a focal point for mobilizing public attention. And though Carter's attempt to link the energy crisis with broader public alienation was an accurate reading of the times, his solutions were fraught with ambiguity.

On the one hand, Carter seemed to side with the environmental community in its ongoing insistence that reducing energy consumption (conservation) was the most appropriate response to the energy crisis. Calling on Americans to reduce their use of automobiles and to lower their thermostats, Carter explained: "Every act of energy conservation like this is more than just common sense—I tell you it is an act of patriotism." A commitment to conservation, Carter argued, would also help resolve the crisis of confidence by rekindling "our sense of unity, our confidence in the future, and give us a new sense of purpose."[34] But on the other hand, increased domestic production remained a major component of the overall national energy plan. Carter called for the creation of an "energy security corporation" to implement an $88 billion plan for converting coal, oil shale, and tar sands into synthetic fuel sources (syn-fuels), which could be substituted for oil and natural gas. Indeed, Carter argued that this proposal could "replace 2½ million barrels of imported oil per day by 1990."[35]

Synfuels production also offered several other advantages. First, synfuels were not subject to political or economic manipulation by for-eign powers. Second, they could help reduce the growing balance of payments problem by lessening the outflow of American dollars to oil-producing nations. Third, major synfuel production would increase oil supplies and thereby drive down international oil prices. Finally, the availability of primary technologies for synfuel production made it an immediate solution. In fact, Congress had already begun deliberations on proposals similar to Carter's.

Despite these advantages, synfuel development presented poten-tially serious environmental consequences. Synfuel production creates a rather nasty mix of carcinogenic compounds, toxic substances, and trace metals, which means that both the production process and disposal of its by-products pose dangerous health threats. In addition, the Council on Environmental Quality (CEQ) estimated that synfuel production at lev-els proposed by Carter would require strip mining five hundred square miles of western lands for coal and mining another one hundred to two hundred square miles for oil shale. Water presented yet another prob-lem. CEQ noted that mining, reclamation, and production of synfuels would consume enough water to "irrigate roughly 100,000 acres of agri-cultural land per year."[36] To this list can be added a host of secondary im-pacts created by the population influx needed for expanded mining op-erations, as well as the construction and operation of the synfuel plants.

Support for synfuel production, therefore, did not seem consistent with the description of Carter as the "greatest conservation president of our time." But troublesome as the synfuels proposal was to the environ-mental community, another part of Carter's plan was even more so—the Energy Mobilization Board (EMB). Modeled after the War Production Board from World War II, Carter explained that the EMB would have the "responsibility and authority to cut through the red tape, the delays, and the endless road blocks to completing key energy projects." Carter then went on to say: "We will protect our environment. But when this Nation critically needs a refinery or pipeline, we will build it."[37] The message seemed clear enough—environmental regulations would not impede de-velopment of energy resources.

If Carter had intended to rekindle confidence in the federal govern-ment, his speech produced exactly the opposite effect in the West. Por-traying Carter's initiatives as tantamount to declaring large portions of the West "national sacrifice areas," a broad coalition of western political leaders, environmentalists and indigenous western commodity interests (primarily stockgrowers) quickly mobilized opposition. But even as battle lines were being drawn over the administration's energy proposals, Carter launched yet another salvo.

In September 1979 Carter formally approved an air force proposal to develop a multiple protective shelter (MPS) basing mode for MX missiles. The roots of this proposal dated back to early 1970s and growing concerns about the vulnerability of land-based nuclear missiles in the United States. In 1973 authorization was given for the development of a new generation of intercontinental ballistic missiles: the "missile experimental," or MX. The advantage of the MX is that it carries ten warheads, each with a theoretically high targeting accuracy. Thus the MX is a useful first strike weapon, capable of neutralizing Soviet missiles before they leave their silos.

The missiles, however, were only part of the system. In order to be effective, the MXs must be based so that they were not vulnerable to a first strike by the Soviets. Although various basing modes had been considered by the air force, the preferred system at the time of Carter's approval seemed to be the "race track" MPS located in the Great Basin area of western Utah and eastern Nevada. The basic design of this system required the construction of two hundred tunnels (race tracks) connecting 4,600 shelters. Missiles would then circulate through the race tracks to the shelters on a secret schedule. Since the Soviets would not be able to predict where the missiles were at any given time, they would be forced either to commit a huge component of their arsenal to the destruction of the system (one estimate suggested 9,200 Soviet missiles would be needed), or view the cost as too high and therefore be deterred from launching a first strike. Defense planners speculated, of course, that the Soviets would choose the second option. However, even if the Soviets went with the first option, the MX system would draw their fire, giving the United States time to activate its other defense systems.

Despite historically strong support for national defense in the West, the prospect of being made the potential target for 9,200 Soviet missiles was unsettling. As Senator Paul Laxalt (R-Nev.) asked rhetorically: "Wouldn't Nevada, as home of the nation's top defense apparatus, be subject to a mighty nuclear attack if war comes?"[38] The possibility of nuclear holocaust was less troublesome, though, than the more immediate environmental and social impacts associated with the construction of the MX system. Although estimates varied, some representative statistics help establish the scale of the proposal. The deployment area ranged from 8,200 to 40,000 square miles of land. A workforce of around 10,000 people was required for construction of the system, and construction would consume 140,000 tons of cement per year, 150,000 tons of steel, 27,000,000 tons of sand, 9,000 acre feet of water, and 180 megawatts of electricity.[39] In short, the MX represented the largest construction project ever undertaken in the history of the United States.

More important, the MX race track proposal, like Carter's energy initiatives, had a galvanizing effect in the West. Paul Culhane, for example, noted: "In my research, I discovered only one standard public land constituency that favored MX. The Air Force planned to locate its main MX operating base at Coyote Springs Junction (Nevada), . . . [and the] chamber of commerce, recognizing the base's potential contribution to the local economy, supported the MPS deployment."[40] Stockgrowers and mining interests opposed the system because it would restrict access to large areas of the public lands far more effectively than wilderness designation. Environmentalists objected to the long-term, perhaps permanent, destruction of the desert's fragile ecosystems. State and local officials recited the familiar litany of socioeconomic impacts associated with the boom conditions the system would bring. And everyone wanted to know where the air force intended to get the water needed both for construction and operation of the system.

Though certainly not the only points of disagreement between the West and the federal government, these issues provide a clear picture of the frustrations that produced the Angry West. They also demonstrate how confusing the political landscape had become. Environmentalists who had showered Carter with praise during the hit list and Alaska lands controversies were transformed into ardent opponents by the energy and MX initiatives. Disgruntled public land users, who viewed the hit list and Alaska lands controversies as further evidence of the federal government's antidevelopment posture, recoiled at the scale and nature of the development promised by aggressive energy production and the MX installation. And western political leaders viewed all of the issues as further evidence of the extent to which, in the words of Richard Lamm and Michael McCarthy, "the West has become legally emasculated, that it is treated with arrogance and indifference, and that it still is living with the old, archaic federal-eastern assumption that the federal government is better equipped to rule the West than the West is to rule itself."[41]

CONCLUSIONS

Sorting through the myriad issues and controversies discussed in this chapter and Chapter 3, we can now isolate several themes that help establish a context for the Sagebrush Rebellion.

We have witnessed the development of a pattern of growing dissatisfaction in a diverse assembly of public land interests. Within that pattern are three key themes. First, the interests expressing dissatisfaction advocated uses that are environmentally disruptive. Second, the source of their discontent was a belief that public land management decisions during the 1970s exhibited a distinct bias in favor of environmental preservation. Third, they shared a belief that the environmental bias represented an overt violation of the actual intent of policy initiatives adopted during the 1970s. Taken together, then, these themes point to an interpretation of the Sagebrush Rebellion as principally a protest against the growing political influence of environmentalists and the consequent realignment within the public land policy arena. This interpretation, in turn, is embellished by several additional themes.

Though western commodity users had successfully employed a strategy similar to the Sagebrush Rebellion in earlier public land conflicts, the policy arena of the 1970s presented a fundamentally different political landscape. The combination of the legal mandate for multiple use management (FLPMA), a redefined meaning of conservation, and the rising influence of the environmental movement clearly indicated that the structural advantages commodity users once possessed were no longer in place. Thus, confronted with a changed political arena that produced objectionable policies, public land users needed a way to expand the scope of their complaints.

Indeed, as E. E. Schattschneider argued, the "most important strategy of politics is concerned with the scope of conflict [because a] change of scope makes possible a new pattern of competition, a new balance of forces, and a new result."[42] Herein lies the importance of the tensions and antagonisms that produced the Angry West. Although the details of these controversies were only tangentially related to the public land disputes, the language in which they were articulated proved extremely useful to disgruntled public land users. Recurring themes of ignorance about western concerns, heavy-handed federal bureaucrats, and violation of states' rights were well suited for the complaints raised by public land users.

More specifically, public land users could portray their complaints as a facet of the general frustration throughout the West, rather than as expressions of economic self-interest. The connection was not spurious—the presence of the federal estate in the West was a key source of the regional and intergovernmental tensions. Phrasing their complaints in the language of the time afforded public land users an opportunity to expand the scope of the conflict and thereby renew the hope of securing a "new balance of forces" within the public land policy arena.

And yet, within this discussion are other themes that disrupt the otherwise straightforward story line of the Sagebrush Rebellion. First, and perhaps most important, the realignment within the policy arena and consequent shift in management direction did appear to reflect broad-based public sentiment. Second, the Sagebrush Rebels' reading of policy intent was far more problematic than they maintained. As we have seen, FLPMA and other policy initiatives were open to a variety of interpretations. In short, the justification for the disgruntlement of the public land users was not as self-evident as they assumed.

Moreover, public land users were not necessarily assured of western unity behind their efforts. Commodity users and environmentalists might find grounds for an alliance in blocking proposals like synfuels development, the EMB, and the MX race track, but that did not mean their historical animosities over public land management had been resolved. In addition, despite their pointed attacks against the Carter administration's pattern of "policy through mandate," western governors seemed unwilling to participate in an open confrontation over the ownership of the public lands. Instead, western governors pursued an institutional response by transforming WGREPO into the Western Governors' Policy Office (WESTPO) in 1978. Though WESTPO had a broader mission than its predecessor, it nevertheless underscored the governors' continuing commitment to a path of bargaining and negotiation with the federal government.

CHAPTER FIVE

The Sagebrush Rebellion: Issues and Tactics

The success of it would require not merely a factious majority in the legislature, but the concurrence of the courts of justice and the body of the people.
—*Alexander Hamilton, 1787*[1]

In the courts, we need to speak with one voice in support of our case, even if it be from more than one state. In the state legislatures, we need to enact a uniform series of bills that will ensure that the states have demonstrated that they are willing and ready to accept their rightful stewardship of the public domain. In the Congress, we need to pursue the passage of legislation, . . . by which the states can elect to accept the public domain if they agree to meet certain conditions.
—*Senator Orrin G. Hatch, 1980*[2]

In November 1980, over five hundred people gathered at the Little America convention center in Salt Lake City to attend a national conference on federal land policy sponsored by the League for the Advancement of States' Equal Rights (LASER). According to its promotional literature, LASER was a nonprofit foundation organized "to create a broad base of support in favor of divesting the federal government of the public domain." Calvin Black, who had consistently raised complaints about federal land policy since deliberations over the Federal Land Policy and Management Act (FLPMA) in the early 1970s, served as chairman of LASER's board of directors. Other members of the board included Senators Barry Goldwater (R-Ariz.), Orrin Hatch (R-Utah), and Ted Stevens (R-Alaska).

The conference program read like an inventory of the issues and interests that characterized the Sagebrush Rebellion. One set of panel discussions served as a forum for grazing, mineral, timber, recreation, and other public land user interests to voice complaints about federal management policies. Another set offered legal, political, and economic arguments in support of state ownership of the federal public lands. In his keynote address, Hatch told the participants that they were involved in an event of "great historical significance," an event, he argued, that "will constitute the major factor in the political and economic future of the West."[3] But after the LASER conference, history seemed to be repeating itself. Reminiscent of the tactics used by both Stanfield and McCarran during earlier conflicts, hearings of the House Subcommittee on Mines and Mining were scheduled by James Santini to begin in Salt Lake City immediately following the close of the LASER conference.

A mood of excitement permeated these meetings, and for good cause. It had been a little over a year since Nevada launched the Sagebrush Rebellion, and much had happened in that time. As Dean Rhoads explained to the subcommittee: "Some months ago, in January 1979, I never realized that when I walked down the hall and put the first bill on the chief clerk's desk in the Nevada Legislature that it would ever grow into the movement that it is today. It has grown from a handful of legislators and supporters in Nevada to broad-based Western support that now has seven Western States that have passed some type of sagebrush rebellion legislation."[4] The Sagebrush Rebellion, it seemed, had become more successful than anyone dared imagine a few months earlier.

Important as these efforts were, the outcome of the 1980 elections clearly overshadowed them. President-elect Ronald Reagan sent a telegram to the conference that read in part: "I renew my pledge to work toward a Sagebrush solution."[5] Equally important, Republicans gained control of the U.S. Senate, which meant that western senators sympathetic to the Sagebrush Rebellion would move into key leadership positions. Combined, these events indicated that a major policy realignment loomed on the horizon. Indeed, earlier doubts about the efficacy of the national policy apparatus faded in the face of speculations about what could be accomplished with the new administration.

Sagebrush Rebel leaders understood that the battle was far from over. The movement's apparent success resulted as much from the absence of organized opposition as from support for it—a situation destined to change now that the Sagebrush Rebellion had become an established feature on the political landscape. Furthermore, the Sagebrush Rebellion had fallen prey to a problem plaguing all political movements: its success in mobilizing support also gave rise to related but potentially divisive issues. The task before the Sagebrush Rebels, then, was to galvanize support behind a common strategy. As Hatch explained: "Only with a unified effort can we expect to meet the challenge before us."[6]

In the end, the LASER participants adopted a package of resolutions anticipating that future battles would center in the nation's capital. For example, recognizing that "the people of the United States have chosen to elect a new national Administration and a Congress substantially altered in philosophic composition," one resolution encouraged

all organizations in sympathy with the goals and objectives of this conference to work immediately to establish strong liaison and effective means of communication with the new Administration and Congress so as to assure the maximum possibility of immediate and meaningful effort on behalf of the federal government to alleviate the causes of grievance and distress associated with the past administration of the public lands.[7]

What the participants did not anticipate, however, was that some members of the new administration would use the Sagebrush Rebellion to advance their own political agenda.

This chapter divides the evolution of the Sagebrush Rebellion into two parts. We begin with an examination of the original intent of the movement—to effect the transfer of public land ownership from the federal government to the western states. We then turn to a consideration of the events after the 1980 elections.

STATE OWNERSHIP

Whether or not the Sagebrush Rebels' view of events during the 1970s represented an accurate assessment, they believed it did. Summarizing that view, Nevada State Senator Richard Blakemore argued:

> For many years, the public domain was open to ranching, mining, and outdoor recreation. But a number of federal acts, passed to protect and conserve the environment, have closed great parts of the public domain to traditional uses. Westerners see these restrictions in the use of the public lands as a portent of things to come—that eventually most of today's public lands will be locked up in wilderness or other restrictive uses.[8]

The question, then, was how to articulate these complaints within the political landscape of the late 1970s.

It seemed clear that the existing pluralist bargaining arena did not provide an acceptable avenue. Environmentalists had been largely successful in portraying environmentally disruptive activities as at best a necessary evil associated with the concept of multiple use, and at worst a violation of the national interest connected with the public lands. The Carter administration, in turn, had expressed little sympathy with either the Sagebrush Rebels' complaints or the broader concerns of the western governors. In consequence, there appeared to be little recourse for them but to provoke a showdown in the hope that such a disruption would create the possibility for restructuring the dialogue.

Invocation of the traditional call for state control of the public lands offered an appropriate text. On the one hand, it created a bridge between the Sagebrush Rebels' demands and the frustration expressed by western governors. On the other hand, if articulated correctly, it could also undermine environmentalists' influence without violating the basic principle of multiple use management. The initial strategic move entailed securing passage by the state legislature of AB 413, asserting Nevada's moral and legal claim to BLM lands. This maneuver accomplished several purposes. First, it guaranteed attention from the national news media and therefore a national platform from which the Sagebrush Rebels could voice their complaints. Second, it accentuated the intergovernmental character of the issue, thus subordinating the preservation/development debate. Indeed, AB 413 specifically excluded "congressionally authorized national parks, monuments, national forests, [and] wildlife refuges," as well as lands controlled by the Department of Defense, Department of Energy, Bureau of Reclamation, and Indian reservations. In addition, AB 413 required the conveyed federal lands to be managed "in such a manner as to conserve and preserve natural resources, wildlife habitat, wilderness areas, historical sites and artifacts, and to permit the development of compatible public uses for recreation, agriculture, ranching, mining and timber production . . . under principles of multiple use which provide the greatest benefit to the people of Nevada." Interestingly, this management mandate was virtually identical to that contained in FLPMA. Change in ownership of the public lands, therefore, did not imply a change in management philosophy.

But the most sophisticated aspect of the Nevada strategy was that it formulated a confrontational situation based on threat rather than action. Asserting a claim to the public lands, even through state law, represented nothing more than a statement of philosophy unless it was coupled to an attempt to actually take control of the public lands. Hence, the federal government and other opponents were more or less without options for action until Nevada officials decided to make good on their threat. But the Sagebrush Rebels were in no hurry to take the next step.

The Sagebrush Rebels intended to escalate the controversy by seeking passage of bills similar to AB 413 in other states as a prelude to initiating an original jurisdiction case in the U.S. Supreme Court. Recognizing that the legal precedents were not encouraging, the rebels hoped these legislative efforts, if successful, would strengthen their position by demonstrating broad-based support for their cause. Such support, in turn, might help sway the court.

Moreover, politicizing the issue also offered the possibility of engendering a conciliatory attitude among federal land managers, which had certainly been the case during earlier controversies. Equally important, the process of working bills through the state legislatures would delay the need to take further action until after the 1980 elections. And while it was too early to make predictions, a major controversy like the Sage-brush Rebellion might well catch the attention of campaigning politicians. In short, far from a spontaneous outburst of frustration, the Nevada strategy was a skillfully designed ploy that allowed the Sagebrush Rebels to mobilize public opinion before initiating legal action.

However clever the Nevada strategy might have been, its success ultimately depended upon the degree to which the issues raised could generate broad-based support in the West and elsewhere. As Schattschneider reminds us: "The outcome of the game of politics depends on which of a multitude of possible conflicts gains the dominant position."[9] The battle lines drawn in Nevada focused attention on two issues: First, whether or not federal land ownership violated the states' equal footing in the Union; and second, whether or not the states could carry out a multiple use management mandate. We now turn to an analysis of these issues.

The Equal Footing Doctrine

As was the case with most of the states carved out of the public domain, Nevada was required, as a condition for admission to the Union, to "forever disclaim all right and title to the unappropriated public land" within its boundaries (hence, the "disclaimer clause"). In asserting a claim to the BLM lands, then, Nevada established a basis for challenging the constitutionality of the disclaimer clause. Although Nevada linked this challenge to specific conditions regarding its admission, the broader issue—one pertaining to all western states—centered on the argument that federal land ownership violated the states' equal footing. Assessing Nevada's claim, and therefore the utility of the issue for the Sagebrush Rebels' cause, requires a brief review of history.

Almost immediately after adopting the Declaration of Independence the Continental Congress began deliberations on the Articles of Confederation. While several disagreements animated these discussions, none was more troublesome than the disposition of the western territories. The basic question was whether the future of the western territories should be a matter of state or national prerogative. The ensuing argument stalled ratification of the Articles but was eventually resolved by making the territories the property of the national government.

In 1784 Congress adopted the Northwest Ordinance, which defined the procedures for creating states out of the western territories. For our purposes, however, the importance of the 1784 ordinance is that it contained the origins of both the equal footing doctrine and the disclaimer clause. The 1784 ordinance declared that new states "shall be admitted . . . on an equal footing with the said original states."[10] It also established the principle of congressional preeminence over the federal estate by prohibiting states from imposing taxes on "the property of the United States" or interfering with the "primary disposal of the soil by the United States in Congress assembled, nor with any regulations which Congress may find necessary." Congressional preeminence, in turn, is the legal basis for the disclaimer clause.

In 1787 Congress revised the 1784 ordinance, but the new version contained the equal footing and congressional preeminence clauses. Interestingly, the same month Congress adopted the 1787 ordinance, the Constitutional Convention delegates resolved their disputes over the same issues. Although they rejected the equal footing language, the delegates agreed (with only one dissenting vote) to congressional preeminence. In consequence, the second clause in Article IV, Section 3 of the Constitution states: "The Congress shall have power to dispose of and make all needful rules and regulations respecting the territory or other property belonging to the United States." As it turned out, the rejection of the equal footing doctrine was only temporary. After ratification of the Constitution, Congress reenacted the 1787 ordinance, including the equal footing clause. With a few exceptions, then, all the states created under the auspices of the Constitution have been admitted on an equal footing basis and have been required to affirm congressional preeminence with a disclaimer clause.[11]

Although this brief background sketch tends to discount Nevada's claim of unequal treatment, there are other issues to consider. For example, since the original thirteen states were formed before the federal estate had been created, they contained no public domain lands. In consequence, it could be argued that the presence of federal lands within new states made them unequal with the original states. This issue was addressed by the U.S. Supreme Court in the case of *Stearns v. Minnesota*. At dispute in this case was the question of whether or not Minnesota could tax lands granted by Congress for the construction of railroads. Several issues were involved in this case, but part of the Court's ruling established an interpretation of the equal footing doctrine that has continued to serve as the dominant precedent. In essence, the Court ruled that the equal footing doctrine was not a guarantee of either social or economic equality to new states, but only an assurance of political equality. The Court further held that the existence of federal property did not create a political hardship for the state. Thus federal land could not be construed as a violation of the equal footing doctrine.

This ruling did not bode well for Nevada's effort, but a possible strategy was to convince the Court that Nevada's claim represented a substantially different situation than Minnesota's. If this argument could be substantiated, then Nevada would be in a position to challenge the applicability of the *Stearns* ruling, and thereby open the door for a reconsideration by the Court. One passage from the *Stearns* ruling was especially useful in this regard:

> It is true that Congress might act so as in effect to keep withdrawn a large area of the State from taxation. . . . It had the power to withdraw all the public lands in Minnesota from private entry or public grant, and, exercising that power, it might prevent the State of Minnesota from taxing a large area of its lands, *but no such possibility of wrong conduct on the part of Congress can enter into consideration of this question.* It is to be expected that [Congress] will deal with Minnesota, as with other States, and in *such a way as to subserve the best interests of the people of that State.*[12] (emphasis added)

Based on this language, Nevada could raise several credible arguments.

In the first place, at the time of the *Stearns* ruling in 1900, there were roughly five million acres of unappropriated federal land in Minnesota. In comparison, roughly sixty million acres (or about 86 percent) of Nevada was federal property in 1979, and forty-eight million acres of this total were BLM lands. This fact alone offered a significant difference between Nevada's complaint and that of Minnesota. Indeed, it could be argued that Congress had participated in precisely the kind of wrong conduct anticipated in the *Stearns* ruling.

Moreover, since the *Stearns* ruling came before the creation of federal land management agencies and related legislative management mandates, Nevada could establish further differences. A recurring theme throughout federal public land policy is that land management decisions are to serve national interest. As such, federal policies did not seem to fit the Court's expectations about serving the "best interests of the people of that State." Nevada could point to the Sagebrush Rebellion as evidence that the people of the state did not view federal policies as serving their interests.

Finally, because of the large federal land holdings and federal management policies, Nevada (as well as other western states) confronted rules and regulations that limited both state and private activities, not only on the federal lands, but also on state and private property. Viewed in this light, the earlier position that federal property did not inhibit the state's political equality seemed less supportable. On the face of it, then, Nevada was well situated to challenge the contemporary relevance of the *Stearns* precedent, especially if a significant number of western states joined in Nevada's complaint.

Another ruling that encouraged optimism on behalf of Nevada's cause was the case of *Coyle v. Oklahoma*.[13] The subject of this ruling was whether or not preadmission requirements could be enforced once the state had been admitted to the Union. The enabling legislation for Oklahoma required that the state capital remain in Guthrie for a specified number of years after admission. Once admitted, and before the specified time period had elapsed, Oklahoma's capital was moved to Oklahoma City.

Calling upon the equal footing doctrine, the Court held that all states have the right and power to move their capitals without federal concurrence. Since Oklahoma had been admitted on an equal basis, it too had the right to move its capital. Thus, although the preadmission requirement was both legal and constitutional, it became unenforceable following Oklahoma's admission. At the very least, then, the *Coyle* ruling introduced a question regarding the authority of the federal government to compel Nevada's compliance with the disclaimer clause.

However, even if the disclaimer clause were unenforceable, it would not necessarily follow that the federal lands would be transferred to the states. Nevada still needed a basis for challenging the constitutionality of federal land ownership. A brief prepared by Robert List, who had served as Nevada state attorney general before he became the governor who signed AB 413 into law, provided this basis. List cites two rulings, *Pollard's Lessee v. Hagan* (1845) and *Oregon v. Corvallis Sand and Gravel Co.* (1977), in which the Court upheld the principle that "under [the] equal footing doctrine new States, upon admission to the Union, acquire title to the lands underlying navigable waters within their boundaries." Building on this principle, List goes on to argue:

> Assuming *arguendo* that the scope of the equal footing doctrine is broad enough to treat the unappropriated public lands in identical fashion as the soils underlying navigable waters, there would be little doubt that a state seeking title to its public domain lands would prevail in its recovery efforts before the courts. Herein lies the rub because no court has extended the doctrine this far and equally important the issue has never been addressed by the United States Supreme Court. These circumstances are perhaps fortunate, however, because having never directly ruled on the issue the Court is not bound by prior precedent.[14]

Taken together, then, these factors appeared to provide a credible foundation for taking the issue to the U.S. Supreme Court.

But even if the Supreme Court agreed to hear the case, there was no guarantee that Nevada would win. Indeed, the fact that Nevada's complaint was filed in the shadow of the fuels and nonfuels mineral crises suggested that the Court's ruling in *The United States v. Texas*[15] would have direct bearing on the situation. At dispute in this case was the attempt by the federal government to assert control over the Outer Continental Shelf (OCS) lands in the 1950s.

Invoking language similar to that used by critics of the Sagebrush Rebellion, President Harry Truman summarized the federal government's position:

> The minerals that lie under the sea off the coast of this country belong to the federal government—that is, to all the people of this country. . . . if we back down on our determination to hold these rights for all the people, we will act to rob them of this great national asset. That is just what the oil lobby wants. They want us to turn the vast treasure over to a handful of states, where the powerful private oil interests hope to exploit it to suit themselves.[16]

In response, the state of Texas argued that since it had entered the Union as an independent republic, the federal government had no original claim to its land, including the OCS lands. Lacking such a claim, therefore, there was no legal basis for federal control of the Texas portion of the OCS.

Conceding that Texas raised a valid claim regarding its preadmission status, the Court ruled that Texas had nevertheless been admitted on an equal footing basis. Since none of the other coastal states possessed a claim to OCS lands, allowing Texas' claim to stand would make it unequal with the other states. Therefore, in order to preserve its equal standing, Texas had to relinquish claims to the OCS lands.

It should be noted, however, that the equal footing doctrine was a subsidiary issue. The primary ruling accepted the argument that the mineral wealth contained in the OCS lands constituted a matter of national security. National security, in turn, is the sole jurisdiction of the federal government. Given the level of national attention to domestic mineral supplies in the 1970s, it seemed unlikely that the Supreme Court would be willing to consider divesting federal control of the mineral estate. And if control of minerals remained with the federal government, there was little reason to believe that control of the land would be turned over to the states.

Nevada's legal case, then, was tenuous at best. Though there appeared to be salient arguments for reevaluating the relationship between federal land ownership and the equal footing doctrine, there did not seem to be any compelling justification for the Court to rule in Nevada's favor. More important, an adverse Supreme Court ruling would represent a serious, if not fatal, setback for the Sagebrush Rebels' cause. It is not surprising, therefore, that the Sagebrush Rebels were in no rush to instigate litigation. Their first, and perhaps most important step, was to mobilize public support. The legal arguments were more useful in this regard than in court.

There was another reason to postpone legal action: the Sagebrush Rebellion had begun attracting attention in Congress, and the Constitution vests Congress with the power to dispose of public lands. Thus, if Congress enacted legislation that authorized the transfer of federal lands to the states, then there would be no need to take the matter to the Supreme Court.

The Western Lands Act

Several bills addressing the transfer issue emerged during the ninety-sixth Congress. By the fall of 1979, they had been harmonized into the Western Lands Distribution and Regional Equalization Act (the Western Lands Act), introduced in the Senate as S. 1680 by Hatch (R-Utah), and in the House as H.R. 5436 by Santini (D-Nev.). The purpose of the Western Lands Act was to provide a mechanism for the conveyance of BLM and Forest Service lands, including mineral rights, to the states. However, it specifically excluded the transfer of national parks and monuments, military lands, Indian reservations, and national wildlife and bird sanctuaries created prior to January 1, 1979.

The governors were given five years from the enactment date to initiate the conveyance process by requesting that the president establish a Federal Land Transfer Board (FLTB) for their state. Each FLTB was to have seven members: a chairman appointed by the president; three members appointed by the secretaries of Interior, Agriculture, and Defense; and three members appointed by the president from recommendations submitted by the governor. Once created, the FLTBs had complete authority to transfer title of the federal lands to the states and to resolve all disputes that might arise during the conveyance process. However, all FLTB decisions were subject to review by the Federal Court of Appeals for the circuit in which the federal lands were located. Finally, after the federal lands had been transferred, the FLTBs were to be abolished.

The actual conveyance process required the state to submit an application to the FLTB, but the amount of land claimed in the application was left a matter of state discretion. Thus adoption of the Western Lands Act did not necessarily imply a wholesale transfer of federal land to the states. Moreover, the conveyance of land was contingent upon the state establishing a land commission empowered to carry out specific functions defined by the act. The most important of these functions was to manage the conveyed lands:

in conformity with the established concepts of multiple use and in such a manner which will maximize the conservation and preservation of natural resources, wildlife habitat, wilderness values, historical values, artifacts, and antiquities, and in such a manner which will permit development of compatible public uses for recreation, agriculture, grazing, mineral and timber production, and development, production and transmission of energy and other public utility services.[17]

In addition, the commission was charged with preventing any disposals of the transferred lands without specific statutory authority enacted after the legal conveyance.

Recognizing that these commissions would require financial resources, the Western Lands Act authorized a low interest loan program for the states. The program was to be administered by the secretaries of Interior and Agriculture, and the amount of the loans was limited to the "anticipated mineral, timber, and grazing revenues to be received by such State from such transferred lands for any prospective ten-year period." Loans were to be repaid from the actual revenues generated by those activities.

On the face of it, then, the Western Lands Act seemed to define a carefully constructed process that allowed states to claim federal lands while preserving both the public character of those lands and the principles of multiple use management. What made this bill especially attractive to Sagebrush Rebels, and troublesome to their opponents, was that it avoided the awkward legal arguments for state ownership. Indeed, if the Western Lands Act was adopted, there would be little, if anything, opponents could do to block the transfer.

It remained to be seen whether or not the Western Lands Act could successfully traverse the legislative process. Even if it voted in a unified block, the western states' congressional delegation was too small to secure the act's passage. Moreover, the Congress being asked to consider divestiture of the federal estate was essentially the same body that had enacted the policies that Sagebrush Rebels found objectionable. However, the general elections were approaching, and even though divestiture of the federal estate was a radical idea, the Western Lands Act provided a convenient vehicle for mobilizing public complaints about the federal government. Equally important was the question of whether or not the western states were willing and/or able to carry out a multiple use management program. It is to this question that we now turn.

State Management

The Sagebrush Rebels' assurances that state ownership would not alter the fundamental character of public land management created something of a quandary for their opponents. If the states embarked on a full-fledged multiple use management program, then conveyance represented far less of a threat than critics charged. Indeed, guarantees of protection for wilderness and other environmental values contained in both the Western Lands Act and bills under consideration by the state legislatures seemed to affirm the Sagebrush Rebels' sincerity. The major change brought about by conveyance appeared to be simply the relocation of the conflict from the nation's capital to the various state capitals. But opponents realized this move carried other implications.

The Sagebrush Rebellion, as Public Lands Institute president Charles Callison explained, was a known entity:

> Observing the [Sagebrush Rebellion] and listening to the arguments give conservationists over the age of 60 a sense of *deja vu.* . . . [The Western Lands Act] eerily echoes a bill introduced by Senator Edward V. Robertson of Wyoming in 1946. It is so nearly like the Robertson bill that I suspect some officer of the Cattleman's Association who is as old as I am extracted the earlier measure from among his keepsakes and gave it to the Utah Senator. Some member of the Hatch staff must have updated the bill, written in some language about the environment, and, plop, we have S. 1680.[18]

Callison's message was clear—the Sagebrush Rebellion represented nothing more than the most recent chapter in the ongoing land heist saga initiated during the Stanfield era and continued in the McCarran era. In that case, the language of the Sagebrush legislation was less important than the intent behind it. The real strategy, Callison argued, involved transfer of federal lands to the state as a prelude to converting public lands into private property. Stated differently, for Callison and other Sagebrush Rebellion opponents, the promise that transferred lands would be managed under a multiple use mandate was a smokescreen that masked the movement's true goal. In consequence, I have dubbed this position the smokescreen theory.

Although aspects of the Sagebrush Rebellion were clearly reminiscent of the Stanfield/McCarran eras, the parallels were not complete. In neither of the earlier episodes had the state legislatures been directly involved, nor had the states pledged to manage transferred lands under a multiple use mandate. Thus, questioning the sincerity of the Sagebrush Rebels came dangerously close to maligning the integrity of the state legislatures. Environmentalists, having consistently complained about the power of commodity interests in western state legislatures, were not bothered by this implication. Their complaints had historical and contemporary foundations.

Given the importance of resource extraction activity in the econo-
mies of western states, commodity users have always played an important role in state politics. Using data compiled by the League of Conservation Voters, Samuel Hays notes that throughout the 1970s the Rocky
Mountain states had one of the poorest voting records in Congress on
environmental matters, and that "[e]nvironmental voting strength increased in all regions except the Mountain states" during that time.[19] Finally, in analyzing legislative voting patterns on state Sagebrush bills, for
example, John Francis noted that the western legislatures had a higher
proportion of representatives identifying themselves with ranching and
agricultural occupations than the general populations of the states.[20]
Since ranchers occupied a prominent role in the Sagebrush Rebellion, as
well as earlier episodes, the smokescreen theory advanced by Callison
and others seemed credible.

But other factors added complexity to the situation. The wave of environmentalism that swept the country in the 1970s did not miss the
West. Western states joined the national trends by taking steps to develop state institutional capacities for environmental regulation. Three
states (Nevada, Oregon, and Wyoming) even created agencies modeled
after the Environmental Protection Agency.[21] Average western state expenditures for environmental programs in 1979, expressed as a percentage of total expenditures, were consistent with the national average: .6
percent for the West and .7 percent for the Nation.[22] Although categoriz-
ing the western states as bastions of environmentalism would be unwarranted, it would also be unfair to portray them as lacking commitment to
environmental goals.

Indeed, the siege mentality that gripped the West during the 1970s
fostered a political climate that made the smokescreen theory even more
implausible. Controversies over federal initiatives in combination with
regional confrontations accentuated the need for greater state control of
growth and development in order to preserve the region's environmental
quality. More important, these tensions frequently precipitated cohesion
among otherwise diverse western interests. The possibility of massive
reallocation of western water resources from agriculture to energy, for instance, created a common threat for both ranchers and environmentalists. It seemed unlikely, therefore, that the states would be either willing
or able to divest their control over conveyed lands. In addition, the dialogue surrounding proposals like the Energy Mobilization Board and
limitations on state severance taxes offered reason to suspect that state
policies might actually restrict development activity more than federal
policies.

There is a sense, then, in which the motives of the western states as
envisioned by opponents to conveyance did not fit the practical circum-

stances in the West. Nevertheless, opponents were also willing to talk about practical matters. In a *Wall Street Journal* editorial, Interior Secretary Andrus pointed out: "There are institutional barriers to balanced management of public lands by the states. In Idaho, for example, the state constitution says state lands must be managed for the highest return to school endowment fund. If they followed that to the letter, as the State Land Board must do, it would mean a lot of those lands would be sold, or leased for single-purpose harvest—either timber or mineral."[23] Andrus's contention was subsequently reinforced by a study commissioned by the Public Lands Institute.

> Most of the western states have mandates of one type or another specifying the uses to which their trust endowments may be put. Three, Colorado, Idaho, and Wyoming, have constitutional provisions stipulating that their trust lands must be utilized to secure the maximum possible revenue therefrom. Montana statutes contain a like provision. The other states have adopted corresponding policies. It can therefore be stated that without exception, the principal goal—the overriding purpose—of the trust land administrative agencies is to secure the highest monetary revenues.[24]

In short, it seemed that the existing legal mandates would leave the states little recourse but to manage conveyed federal lands for revenue maximization. Under such a mandate, moreover, uses that did not generate revenue (such as wilderness) would have to be ignored.

Yet there were other issues to be considered. First, and most important, the state lands in question originated from grants made by Congress. These grants, in turn, stipulated the purposes for which the lands could be used. In the General Land Ordinance of 1785, for example, Congress granted one section per township to the states for the support of education. In 1850 Congress increased the school land grants to two sections per township, and Utah, New Mexico, and Arizona received four sections per township. The original and continuing intent of Congress, then, was to provide the states with a revenue source specifically earmarked for education (hence, "trust" lands). Thus, in selling or leasing these lands for the highest monetary return, the states were fulfilling a congressional mandate.

Second, the assumption that the conveyed lands would automatically fall prey to revenue maximization was simply not true. State school lands were one of several categories established by Congress under the general classification of internal improvement grants. Like the school lands, these internal improvement grants were designated for specific purposes (roads, canals, railroads, public buildings, colleges and univer-

sities). Strictly speaking, then, grants made under the Western Lands
Act constituted a new category of state lands, not an addition to preexisting categories. This interpretation is reinforced by a provision in the
Western Lands Act that obligated the states to create a state land commission empowered to carry out multiple use management on the conveyed
lands prior to their transfer.

Finally, a provision in the Western Lands Act, apparently overlooked
by critics, required state land commissions to "provide for the conduct,
in conjunction with the respective boards of county commissioners and
county planning commissions, of an inventory and study of the public
lands of the State with a view to determining the best methods of utilization and management of such lands in order to meet the needs and interests of the people of the State." The key phrase here is "public lands of
the State." Elsewhere in the act, references to the lands subject to conveyance are specifically identified as such ("lands acquired by the State
pursuant to this Act," and "lands conveyed to the State pursuant to this
Act"). This passage, then, is clearly intended to address preexisting state
lands.

A plausible interpretation of this provision is that drafters of the
Western Lands Act, understanding that the management mandate for
the conveyed lands was not consistent with the mandate(s) for preexisting state lands, created an opportunity for states to consider incorporating existing state lands within the multiple use framework of the conveyed lands. Following from this, a likely outcome of the Western Lands
Act might have been just the inverse of that predicted by opponents.
Rather than conveyed lands being managed for maximum revenue, all
state public lands (conveyed and preexisting) would be managed according to the principles of multiple use.

It seems apparent, then, that the Western Lands Act anticipated
much of its opposition. But if the smokescreen theory was correct, then
the language of the Western Lands Act amounted to nothing more than a
set of platitudes intended to divert attention from the Sagebrush Rebels'
actual goal. In short, the promises contained in the Western Lands Act
required a level of trust that critics of the Sagebrush Rebellion were obviously reluctant to accept.

Another objection raised by opponents proved more troublesome
for the Sagebrush Rebels—the cost of managing public lands. Assuming
the states were willing to mount a full-fledged multiple use program,
critics asked, would they also be willing to appropriate the funds necessary for the program? This was an appropriate question to ask in light of
the traditional fiscal conservatism of western legislatures and the developing national tax revolt, exemplified by California voters' approval of
Proposition 13 in 1979.[25]

One response to this question came from a study conducted by the American Farm Bureau Federation (AFBF).[26] In summary, the study identified a "profit" of $439,807,265 earned by BLM from its management activities in the eleven western states. This figure was calculated by subtracting BLM's 1978 management expenditures ($181,270,339) from the revenues generated in the same year by grazing, mineral, and timber activities ($621,078,339). The immediate conclusion, and the one advanced by AFBF, is that after conveyance this profit would accrue to the states. Thus, the states would have the revenues to carry out multiple use management without the need for additional appropriations. A closer examination of the situation suggests that some qualifications are in order.

First, the AFBF study indicated that BLM's profit was not equally distributed among the western states, with BLM experiencing a net loss in the management of Arizona and Idaho public lands. Second, a significant portion of BLM revenues are returned to the states and counties in which the public lands are located. In 1978, over 40 percent of BLM's revenues ($280 million) were returned to the states; of that total about $278 million went to the western states (excluding Alaska).[27] Deducting this amount from BLM's total revenue figure (since it already goes to the states), the potential new revenue accruing to the states after conveyance is about $443 million. A corresponding adjustment to BLM's profit margin would reduce it to $161 million.

Though this adjustment does not negate the basic point—that conveyance would provide additional funds for state management programs—there are additional adjustments to be considered. For example, $159 million of the BLM's 1978 revenues were deposited in the Reclamation Fund. This fund was originally created in 1902 to provide money for the construction and maintenance of western water projects, but the cost of western water development quickly outstripped the revenues it produced. As a result, western water projects have been financed through a mix of revenue sources, including congressional appropriations. Considering the implications of Carter's Hit List, however, it seemed plausible that western states would, at the very least, have to contribute a larger share in financing water development. This factor alone could devour the $161 million profit gained by the states from conveyance.

In addition, states receive federal funds based on the presence of federal lands in their jurisdiction but derived from sources other than those generated on the public lands. Two such programs are the Land and Water Conservation Fund (LWCF) and the Payment in Lieu of Taxes (PILT) program. The primary funding source for the LWCF is mineral lease money from the Outer Continental Shelf. Its purpose is to provide funds for the acquisition and development of outdoor recreation opportunities by state and local governments. Forty percent of the LWCF is dis-

TABLE 5.1. BLM Management Revenues and Expenditures

State	Adjusted Revenues	Expenditures
Arizona	$1,405,088	$8,269,825
California	3,639,311	23,484,000
Colorado	2,464,426	17,399,000
Idaho	2,001,507	14,389,000
Montana	3,741,058	16,469,000
Nevada	3,552,979	10,922,200
New Mexico	6,733,949	15,292,600
Utah	3,944,444	12,389,515
Wyoming	22,684,200	18,208,000

Source: Compiled from U.S. Department of Interior, Bureau of Land Management, *Public Land Statistics* (Washington, D.C.: Government Printing Office, 1978); and Leonard H. Johnson, "Comparison of BLM Management Costs and State Land Management Agency Costs," a study prepared for the American Farm Bureau Federation, 1979.

tributed equally among the fifty states, and 60 percent is allocated on the basis of need. One of the factors considered in need assessment, in turn, is the amount of federal land within the state. In 1978 the western states received about $60.8 million, a portion of which would be jeopardized by conveyance.[28]

The PILT program, on the other hand, is completely dependent on federal lands. Created in 1976 but originating in a PLLRC recommendation, PILT provides general appropriation revenues to local governments through two formulas, both based on the amount of federal land within the government's jurisdiction. In 1978 the western states received about $77.2 million in PILT payments. Conveyance, therefore, could jeopardize all of the PILT payments.[29]

Another qualification emerges when the relative weight of the various revenue sources in the BLM's total revenue figure is examined. The lion's share of the BLM's revenues come from mineral development: about 62 percent of the BLM's 1978 total revenues were generated by mineral activity. There is a sense, then, in which mineral activity can be understood as subsidizing BLM's management mission. For example, Table 5.1 compares the amount of revenue generated in the western states by sources other than mineral development (Adjusted Revenues) with the BLM management expenditures. Again, this chart is based on 1978 figures. The immediate conclusion, of course, is that BLM experienced a net loss in all the states except Wyoming.

Herein lurked a particularly troublesome dilemma for the Sagebrush Rebels. On the one hand, the importance of mineral revenues in the overall financial picture made the viability of the transfer proposal heavily dependent upon the conveyance of the mineral estate. On the other hand, the fuels and nonfuels mineral crises, as noted above, created a persuasive argument, based on national security, for retaining the mineral estate in federal ownership.

If the BLM revenue picture was problematic, the Forest Service situation seemed worse—transfer of the Forest Service lands carried a significant cost. Estimates prepared in Utah and Wyoming, for instance, indicated that 1978 Forest Service expenditures outstripped revenues by a substantial margin: $30 million and $20 million respectively.[30] These assessments were subsequently reinforced by the 1980 *Report of the Forest Service*, which listed total receipts from national forest lands as $1.3 billion and total expenditures as $1.7 billion.[31] Thus, the Forest Service experienced a $400 million shortfall.

The analysis here, like that done by AFBF, is predicated on two basic assumptions: first, that all federal lands would be conveyed to the states; and second, that existing revenue patterns would remain unchanged. Both assumptions, however, are open to discussion. For example, the Western Lands Act, unlike state bills, did not require a complete divestiture of the federal estate. Therefore, the states might not have needed to assume the full management cost. Moreover, after conveyance the states might have contemplated other revenue enhancement measures.

State grazing fees, as BLM critics have consistently pointed out, are generally higher than federal fees. It is plausible, therefore, that fees on the conveyed lands might be increased to the level of existing state charges. Additionally, Montana and Wyoming demonstrated the efficacy of severance tax as a revenue generating mechanism. Yet another possibility, one articulated by the opponents, was that the states might sell portions of the public lands to help finance management of the remaining portion. While these actions might improve the overall revenue picture, they most certainly would not be welcomed by many of the commodity interests within the Sagebrush Rebellion.

Despite questions and uncertainties surrounding both the legal and management issues, Sagebrush Rebels pursued the conveyance strategy throughout 1979 and 1980, chalking up an impressive track record along the way. Arizona, New Mexico, and Utah enacted bills similar to AB 413, with the Arizona legislature overriding Governor Bruce Babbit's veto. Wyoming also adopted a Sagebrush bill, which claimed both BLM and Forest Service lands. Colorado, Idaho, and Alaska passed legislation calling for feasibility studies of land transfers, and the Hawaii legislature adopted a resolution endorsing the Sagebrush Rebellion without actually joining the movement. Actions in California and Washington added further twists.

The California legislature adopted a Sagebrush bill during its 1979 session without a dissenting vote. Governor Jerry Brown vetoed this bill, but rather than challenging the veto, the legislature adopted a compromise bill calling for a feasibility study. The 1980 Washington legislature adopted both a Sagebrush bill and a constitutional amendment that would eliminate that state's disclaimer clause. The fate of the Sagebrush bill was tied to the outcome of the constitutional amendment in the 1980 elections. Indeed, the only states that did not take some form of action were Oregon and Montana; neither state's legislature met during this time.

Although these actions exposed an undertow of opposition to conveyance in the West, they were nevertheless sufficiently successful to capture national news attention and put the Sagebrush Rebellion on the political map. The Sagebrush Rebels understood that events in the national political scene had direct bearing on their efforts. Reagan's support for the movement, for example, led to the following statement in *Coalition Comments*, a newsletter published by the Nevada Legislative Counsel Bureau:

> The results of the 1980 elections will give Sagebrush Rebellion supporters a better idea of popular support for the movement as well as future strategy and direction. If Ronald Reagan is elected President, there will be a new opportunity to seek more responsible and responsive public land management by the Federal Government. Selection of the Secretary of Interior under a Reagan administration will be extremely important.[32]

It might be noted parenthetically that the story preceding this comment foreshadowed events to come. It praised the "excellent job" being done by the Mountain States Legal Foundation (MSLF), the firm headed by James Watt. And though Watt was not mentioned, an excerpt reprinted from MSLF's Annual Report summarized part of the argument Watt would subsequently use during his confirmation hearings. The root problem, according to the report, was that

> greater concentration on the identification and preservation of wilderness areas has resulted in the halting of mineral development, timbering, oil and gas exploration, and recreation on vast portions of the public lands. Not only has access to the lands for these purposes been denied by the Government, but those who lease the lands for agricultural purposes have found the Bureau of Land Management is no longer a 'good neighbor,' but rather a demanding and arbitrary landlord lacking in understanding of the economics of ranching and farming.[33]

These comments bring us back to the LASER Conference and the 1980 elections.

DEFUSING THE REBELLION

Testifying before an interim committee of the Colorado legislature in August 1980, Dean Rhoads explained that court action on the Sagebrush Rebellion would be initiated sometime after the general elections. During a subsequent telephone interview in October 1980, one of Rhoads's staff members indicated that court action was planned for April 1981. However, in an interview at the LASER Conference, Rhoads suggested that although the Supreme Court would eventually have to rule on the issue, litigation might not be instigated for "ten years." He went on to identify two factors accounting for this change in strategy: an assessment predicting that the Sagebrush Rebels would lose on a five to four decision if the existing Court heard the case; and the outcome of the 1980 elections, which opened new and unanticipated possibilities. The likely future of the Sagebrush Rebellion, Rhoads concluded, lay in the direction of "piece-meal legislation, administrative actions, executive orders, and revamping of regulations," all geared to addressing the grievances underlying the movement.[34] Conveyance, either through court or congressional action, no longer seemed to be the dominant goal of the Sagebrush Rebellion.

Herein lies a definite parallel between the Sagebrush Rebellion and the controversy of the 1940s. As William Voigt observed, the resolution of the McCarran era carried disturbing consequences:

> It would be nice to say that the victory against the land grab had lasting values, but it would be untrue. That turned out to be little more than a holding action followed by a more subtle threat. Somewhere along the way the livestock leadership came to the conclusion that outright ownership was not necessary if other measures could assure the perpetuation of its privileged status on the public lands. Why own if you could have all or nearly all the prerogatives of ownership without the cost and bother?[35]

Although Reagan's election did not suggest that Sagebrush Rebels would necessarily gain the "prerogatives of ownership," it did mean that the Sagebrush Rebellion was suddenly transformed into a profound threat.

Reagan's open support for the movement combined with his equally open criticism of environmental regulation in general created a potentially devastating blow to opponents of the Sagebrush Rebellion. If Reagan fulfilled his campaign promises, the argument that federal management would be more sympathetic to environmental concerns than state management no longer carried the certainty it had before the election. Moreover, Reagan's election in spite of his blunt attack on environmental regulations challenged the environmentalists' insistence that the public supported their cause. As one *Wall Street Journal* editorial suggested: "Environmentalism is a worthwhile cause, but the voters have grown tired of environmental excesses."[36]

The situation was further aggravated by the Republican senatorial victory. Although environmentalists had made a concerted effort to maintain bipartisan support throughout the 1970s, it was clear that the new Senate would present a formidable problem. Writing in the February 1979 edition of *Atlantic Monthly* Sanford Ungar identified a group of Senators he dubbed the "New Conservatives." Among the more influential members of this coalition were Jake Garn and Orrin Hatch of Utah, Paul Laxault of Nevada, Malcolm Wallop of Wyoming, Harrison Schmidt of New Mexico, James McClure of Idaho, and Jesse Helms of North Carolina. This group, Ungar argued,

> managed to filibuster and kill the Carter Administration's labor reform bill; they effectively prevented legislation for public financing of congressional elections from reaching the floor; they supported the sale of sophisticated fighter planes to Arab countries of the Middle East as well as to Israel; they opposed the original version of the Humphrey-Hawkins full employment bill; and they came close to denying ratification of the Panama Canal Treaty.[37]

A key to their success, Ungar continued, was their ability to "construct ad hoc coalitions around particular issues and to use what [is called] 'the inside-outside punch'—producing pressure from back home on senators who are wavering on a given matter, and thereby winning votes without having to make any rash trade-offs within the Senate."

After the 1980 elections, this coalition not only remained intact, but moved into various leadership positions within a Republican controlled Senate. For example, James McClure became chairman of the Energy and Natural Resources Committee, and Jesse Helms became chairman of the Agriculture, Nutrition, and Forestry Committee. Both of these committees had oversight power on federal land policy matters, and both new chairmen had publicly supported the Sagebrush Rebellion.

Thus it is clear why the Sagebrush Rebels were willing to set aside conveyance in favor of less dramatic policy adjustments. Indeed, the root complaint raised by public land users during the 1970s was that federal land managers consistently *interpreted* federal management policies as a call for environmental protection. Thus, a sympathetic secretary of Interior could accomplish a great deal by simply altering the interpretation of existing policies. And on December 22, 1980, this possibility became a reality when Reagan announced that James Watt was his choice for secretary of the Interior.

Environmentalists lost little time in mounting opposition to Watt's appointment. Concentrating on his involvement with Mountain States Legal Foundation and his support for the Sagebrush Rebellion, environmentalists portrayed Watt's nomination as a blatant conflict of interest. "As far as we can tell," suggested one spokesperson for Friends of the Earth, "[Watt] has spent the last few years ardently representing the anti-environmental point of view; and he would become the guardian of our national environmental heritage."[38] Sierra Club Executive Director Brock Evans echoed the sentiment: "For ten years we've been saying the secretary of interior is the No. 1 environmental position in the country. . . . We would hope that the secretary would at least have environmental values. Watt appears to have no environmental values whatsoever."[39] The environmental community's message was clear. They viewed Watt as an overt threat, and therefore he should not expect the grace period traditionally extended to new political appointees. Watt, as it turned out, had no illusions about what lay ahead.

In an interview with the *Rocky Mountain News*,[40] published the day after his nomination, Watt acknowledged that he expected to "receive criticism from some of the extreme environmentalist groups." Although he viewed this criticism as "part of the game," Watt conceded that such attacks had potentially debilitating consequences: "We've seen in recent history what the severe, brutal attack has done to other candidates for the secretary of Interior and it has affected their ability to manage" (an obvious reference to Hickle; see Chapter 2). Nevertheless, Watt indicated that he was "prepared emotionally, spiritually and intellectually to withstand that onslaught." Watt remained confident, moreover, that the "established environmental groups will look at [my] record, . . . and they will not oppose me." Further delineating the distinction between extreme and established environmental groups, Watt added: "I will be able to work with those who have not damaged my hearing." The battle lines he sought to establish, then, were not between development and preservation, but between obstructionist and conciliatory political behavior on the part of the environmental community.

Rather than the flagrant antienvironmentalist stance ascribed to him by environmentalists, Watt's views throughout the interview appeared well within the traditional expectations for a secretary of Interior. For example, he argued that the primary threat to environmental concerns

came from an unwillingness to recognize the nation's need for energy resources. "If we continue to block development of energy resources on
the public lands," he insisted, "the pressures will build," pressures like
those behind the "Energy Mobilization Board, which would have had
the authority to override state environmental laws." The appropriate response, therefore, was a "reasonable, environmentally sound development program to meet the energy and resource needs of America."
Through such a program, Watt contended, "we [can] define the terms
and move in an orderly fashion."

Watt's comments on the Sagebrush Rebellion followed a similar pattern. Affirming that he was "part of the Sagebrush Rebellion," Watt
maintained that the conveyance effort was a "waste of money." The
cause of the controversy, he argued, was a Department of Interior that
had "become almost hostile to many interests of the West." Watt admitted, "BLM has a right to dictate how leased federal lands should be
used, but BLM goes beyond that, dictating to the land user how he must
use the state-leased lands, and private land he owns or leases." The goal
of his administration, then, would be to "manage [the public] lands as a
good neighbor . . . and let the sagebrush rebellion die because of
friendly relations."

It appears, then, that environmentalist opposition to Watt was motivated by something other than his expressed positions. Indeed, Watt's
assessment of the EMB and opposition to the conveyance proposal were
consistent with the environmental community's positions. Moreover,
rather than openly challenging the legitimacy of environmental concerns, Watt seemed to agree with the environmental community's belief
that environmental protection should be a key component of future energy development plans. The question was why environmentalists
refused to accept the sincerity of Watt's expressed positions.

One insight about the underlying threat posed by Watt emerged
during his confirmation hearings. Brock Evans argued, for instance, that
Watt's initiatives simply fell outside a well-defined consensus:

> For at least the *past fifteen to twenty years*, not only the Congress, but
> every Administration, Republican or Democrat, and indeed the
> whole American people, have all advanced together to give *new
> meaning to the terms of "environmental protection" and "conservation"*
> first pioneered by President Theodore Roosevelt and those who
> came before him in the last century. And for all of this time, each
> Secretary of the Interior, again whether Republican or Democrat,
> has subscribed to these principles and this value system.
>
> The present nominee for Secretary of the Department of Inte-
> rior, however, seems to have called into question much of this tradi-

tion of reverence and care for the land, so carefully nurtured and built up over the past two centuries, and given a special force and life over the *past two decades*.[41] (emphasis added)

Despite Evans's attempt to link the environmentalists' position with the roots of the conservation movement, the highlighted passages offer clear indication that the tradition supposedly being called into question by Watt was new conservation. Indeed, when situated in an historical context, Watt's antienvironmentalism looks very much like a revitalized traditional conservation.

For example, when Watt explained that "we can have reasonable development of our energy resources, and preserve our natural environment, if we are given an opportunity to phase in, with proper safeguards, the expansion being demanded by the Nation. . . . [b]ut this can be done only if there is a common sense approach to the balanced use of our natural resource base";[42] there was an unmistakable echo of Wayne Aspinall's definition of conservation: "Accepting all the material resources that nature is capable of providing, taking those natural resources where they are, and as they are, and developing them for the best use of the people as a whole. Conservation means that we do not waste; however, it does not mean that we save merely for the sake of saving."[43] Both of these statements reverberated with Gifford Pinchot's insistence: "The first great fact about conservation is that it stands for development. . . . Conservation does mean provision for the future, but it means also and first of all the recognition of the right of the present generation to the fullest necessary use of all the resources with which this country is so abundantly blessed."[44]

In short, the argument between Watt and the environmental community looked very much like a replay of the 1960s. Watt's insistence that the conservation tradition embraced both resource development and preservation was virtually identical to Aspinall's posture in the 1960s. Moreover, the environmental community's insistence that Watt was not sincerely committed to environmental preservation sounded curiously similar to the charge raised by stockgrowers against Udall in the 1960s. Indeed, with one modification, Watt might have borrowed Udall's lament: "Words which my associates and I use seem to get twisted and we are pictured as relegating grazing to an inferior place."[45] The modification, of course, is substituting environmental protection for grazing.

Environmentalists, like the stockgrowers before them, understood the full force of Watt's challenge. Their policy gains throughout the 1970s rested on the efficacy of the basic premise underlying new conservation—environmental preservation should serve as the primary criterion for determining reasonable levels of commodity use. The assumption underlying the *NRDC v. Morton* ruling, for example, was that grazing allotments should be based on the ecological carrying capacity of the range. Similarly, BLM's resolution of the grandfather clause for both mining and grazing in wilderness study areas was based on the presumption that preservation should be given greater priority than commodity use. The regulation of ORV use also fit this pattern. But most important of all, implementation of Section 4 of the Wilderness Act, permitting mineral exploration and extraction in the wilderness system, had been avoided because of continued adherence to the new conservation principles. All of these issues, then, would be open to further negotiation if Watt succeeded in reestablishing classic conservation.

Unsettling as these possibilities were, the more frustrating issue was Watt's unwillingness to accept two decades of adherence to new conservation as prima facie evidence of its validity. Without denying past precedence, Watt simply pointed to recent events as providing clear indication of the need for a new direction in public land policy. And once again, Watt might have borrowed text from Udall who, in 1962, suggested: "[Conservation] is a concept that grows. Each generation has to redefine it because it has new meaning."

Despite the concerted effort to block Watt's confirmation, there was little doubt about its outcome. Reagan's campaign position had been consistent with Watt's stance, and Watt laid to rest any doubts in this regard by recounting a conversation with the President-elect:

> We talked about the "Sagebrush Rebellion," and the frustrations, . . . we talked about the need to insure public access to the lands managed by the Federal Government: access for recreation; access for exploration; access for true multiple-use; . . . we talked about the vital urgency of developing a strategic minerals policy, so that this Nation would not suffer for military or national security reasons, so that our quality of life might be assured and enhanced.[46]

There was also little doubt about a Republican-controlled Senate confirming Reagan's nominee.

Once confirmed, Watt approached his new task with the enthusiasm of a general leading an invasion. He initiated budget and personnel changes directed at increasing the department's development emphasis and decreasing its environmental planning efforts. He also proposed changes in policies and regulations for virtually every area under the department's administration.[47] Among the more controversial of these changes were plans to begin processing mineral lease applications for areas within the wilderness system; accelerate leasing of OCS lands and federal coal reserves; reduce public participation in the BLM land planning process; reduce the likelihood of future grazing cuts; redirect Land and Water Conservation Fund revenues from land acquisition to park maintenance efforts; and dismantle both surface mining and ORV regulations. Although the environmentalists stepped up their attacks, it seemed that Watt represented a more formidable adversary than they had anticipated.

The Sierra Club, for example, launched a "Dump Watt" campaign that succeeded in collecting over a million signatures on petitions calling for Watt's resignation or firing. Although it captured media attention, the campaign was largely ignored by the Reagan administration. Indeed, writing in the *New York Times*, Philip Shabecoff suggested that the attacks against Watt had actually increased his popularity in some quarters: "Unrelenting criticism by environmentalists, members of Congress and the news media has transmogrified Mr. Watt into a martyr of the Republican right. . . . Mr. Watt is now the second most successful fund-raiser in the Republican party after President Reagan himself."[48] Shabecoff went on to point out that the reciprocal was also true. Environmental groups, he argued, "discovered that their fight with James Watt was an excellent base on which to build membership and fund-raising drives."

At the very least, then, the controversy surrounding Watt revitalized environmental politics to levels not seen since the heady days at the beginning of the environmental decade. But there were other, more subtle, forces at work. The game of politics is largely a struggle for control of the initiative. As Schattschneider maintained: "He who determines what politics is about runs the country, because the definition of the alternatives is the choice of conflicts, and the choice of conflicts allocates power."[49] Environmentalists demonstrated the practical application of this proposition throughout the 1970s by consistently portraying the destruction of the earth as the inevitable alternative to preservation policies. The growing frustration among groups allied in the Sagebrush Rebellion provided testimony to the tactic's effectiveness. In Watt, then, environmentalists confronted an opponent equally skilled in the battle for initiative.

Though frequently criticized as injudicious or misguided, Watt's aggressive, confrontational style represented a conscious strategy. As noted earlier, Hickel's experience convinced Watt that a traditional compromise and consensus approach merely played into the hands of the environmental community. His success, therefore, depended upon his ability to disrupt the established arena. As Watt explained in a 1981 interview: "I had to come in and yell commands that would be heard and obeyed. So I yelled, and the change came faster than I thought it would."[50] The change here was not implementation of the new agenda, but capturing control of the initiative. "[Environmentalists] were quite surprised and upset," Watt continued, "when we did not consult them on decisions. But we didn't need to. We knew exactly what we wanted to do." And the alternatives Watt pursued were those raised by the Sagebrush Rebellion.

It is not surprising, therefore, that the Sagebrush Rebels sensed victory close at hand. Through Watt, their claims had come to dominate the policy agenda, and the environmental community, though still a force to be contended with, could no longer find a sympathetic ear in the administration. Thus the Sagebrush Rebels had cause for guarded optimism. As an appraisal in the January 1982 edition of *Coalition Comments* suggested, "many of the goals of the Sagebrush Rebellion have been accomplished since James Watt became Secretary of Interior. The main future thrust . . . must now be to institutionalize and make permanent the changes that have been made through administrative decisions and changed attitudes of the new administration."[51] But once initiated, political controversies frequently develop in unexpected ways.

In June 1982 the Nevada Select Committee on Public Lands adopted a resolution that reaffirmed "its total dedication to the original 'Sagebrush Rebellion' concept."[52] The event that triggered this change in attitude was a proposal in Reagan's budget message of February 8, 1982. Explaining that the federal government owned 775 million acres of land and 405,000 buildings, he went on to suggest: "Some of this real property is not in use and would be of greater value to society if transferred to the private sector. During the next 3 years we will save $9 billion by shedding these unnecessary properties while fully protecting and preserving our national parks, forests, wilderness and scenic areas."[53] Subsequently, Reagan established a Property Review Board to direct the inventory and prepare recommendations for properties that should be sold.

While this so-called privatization initiative seemed to confirm the smokescreen theory advanced by opponents of the Sagebrush Rebellion, reactions to it suggested a different interpretation. In addition to reaffirming support for the original Sagebrush Rebellion, for example, the Nevada Select Committee adopted another resolution opposing the privatization effort. This resolution is particularly interesting because it was endorsed by a wide array of interests, including the Nevada Cattleman's Association, the Nevada Miners and Prospectors Association, the Nevada Wildlife Federation, and the Nevada chapter of the Sierra Club. Moreover, the privatization issue did not sit well with some of the congressional rebels. James Santini, for instance, pulled no punches when he exclaimed: "I would like to put this Administration on notice once and for all that I will not stand idly by and see Nevada or the West put on the auction block." He went on to suggest: "Quite frankly, this is hardly the behavior I would expect from a 'Good Neighbor.' "[54]

Santini's reference to Watt's efforts raised yet another issue. During his confirmation hearings, Watt had insisted that disposal of the federal estate would be unnecessary if he was successful in implementing his good neighbor policy. Indeed, one of the more lucid statements of this premise came in an exchange with Senator Gary Hart (D-Colo.):

> Senator Hart: If called upon to testify as Secretary of the Interior on the legislation which would provide for the systematic transfer of ownership of federally owned lands to States or private entities, what would be your present inclination?
>
> Mr. Watt: My present inclination would be that that would be a premature piece of legislation that would be a divisive force in Congress, unlikely of being passed at this stage and not advancing the good neighbor policies that we need to advance at this time.
>
> If I failed in my mission, pressures would be so great on you Senators to do that, that you would have no other alternative.[55]

Little had occurred between the time of Watt's confirmation hearings and the emergence of the privatization issue to suggest that Watt's good neighbor policy had failed. In fact, Watt's initiatives proved more successful than even he had anticipated. Unless Watt had changed his mind, there was no reason to believe that privatization and the good neighbor policy were compatible initiatives. And as we will see in the next chapter, despite allegations to the contrary, Watt did not support the privatization initiative.

CONCLUSIONS

One of the recurring analytical problems encountered in this study is the fact that the Sagebrush Rebellion had no formal organization or leadership and in consequence, no formal membership roster. In fact, the process by which someone became a Sagebrush Rebel was apparently no more complicated than declaring support for the movement. For example, when presidential candidate Ronald Reagan declared "count me in as a [sagebrush] rebel," he became, for all intents and purposes, a Sagebrush Rebel. The problem, then, was that no authoritative source or spokesperson could be consulted to determine the official position of the Sagebrush Rebels. Nevertheless, the continuity and similarities in various public statements made by people purporting to be Sagebrush Rebels provided a sense of the issues and motives that animated the movement.

However, the lack of an official voice for the Sagebrush Rebellion makes the task of constructing an interpretation for the events considered in this chapter somewhat troublesome. Two points are relatively clear. First, the Sagebrush Rebellion grew from a seemingly minor symbolic act of the Nevada legislature to the focal point of a national controversy in an amazingly short time. Second, the path followed by the Sagebrush Rebellion encompassed a diversity of tactics and issues. It remains unclear whether these various issues represented a conscious strategy employed by the Sagebrush Rebels, or a difference of opinion among factions within the movement. Lacking a definitive answer to the question, we will take a practical approach and outline the contours of both interpretations.

The two interpretations share a common starting point. Initially, the Sagebrush Rebels faced a difficult situation. Environmentalists, buttressed by apparently widespread public support, had made significant gains in influencing the direction of public land management. Moreover, the character of congressional mandates and the implementation process carried out by federal managers throughout the 1970s offered every indication that environmentalist influence was rapidly becoming institutionalized. Thus, from the Sagebrush Rebels' perspective, some form of dramatic action was needed—an action like calling for the divestiture of the federal estate.

One reading of the ensuing events, then, is that the true goal of the Sagebrush Rebellion was to mount a counteroffensive against the environmental movement as a way to gain greater concessions in public land management decisions. From this perspective, effecting the transfer of the federal estate to the states was less important than demonstrating that it was a viable alternative. Stated differently, the Sagebrush Rebellion was an attempt to create something of a Hobson's choice in public land policy. Either the public lands could remain in federal ownership but with more attention to development activities, or they could become state property and be managed with greater attention to development activities. In either case, the complaints of disgruntled public land users would be placated.

Several aspects of the events discussed in this chapter argue in favor of this interpretation. First, surprisingly little substantive action occurred prior to the 1980 elections. Nevada and other western states enacted Sagebrush Rebellion bills, but as noted above, these bills in and of themselves amounted to little more than a statement of philosophy. Moreover, even though they outlined the basis for a legal challenge to federal land ownership, the Sagebrush Rebels were in no hurry to bring the matter before the Supreme Court. Finally, though Sagebrush bills were introduced in Congress during 1979, no hearings were held until the LA-

SER Conference, and those hearings were not specifically devoted to the Hatch-Santini bills.

Taken together, then, these activities do not paint a portrait of a movement actively pursuing the conveyance of federal lands to the states. Instead, they suggest an effort to mobilize support and thereby increase the credibility of the threat posed by the conveyance proposal— an effort that makes a certain amount of sense given the approaching elections.

The Carter administration had clearly not been sympathetic to the complaints raised by Sagebrush Rebels. The Carter administration's implementation of FLPMA fueled the public land conflicts and the Rebels' frustration, and the administration's positions on the hit list, Alaska lands, EMB, and MX controversies exhibited a consistent lack of commitment to states' rights. Thus there was no reason to suspect that if Carter was reelected, his second term would follow a significantly different path. In consequence, the Sagebrush Rebels' mobilization effort could be viewed as laying the groundwork for battles to be fought after the elections.

At the same time, Reagan's expressed support for the Sagebrush Rebellion and states' rights, as well as his attacks against the scope of federal regulations, raised another possibility. If Reagan won the election, then the Sagebrush Rebels would be dealing with a sympathetic administration. In that case, the support mobilized by the Rebels would provide a mandate for more development-attentive management of the public lands. In short, the initial moves by the Sagebrush Rebels created a useful posture regardless of the election outcome.

There is another interpretation for these events, however. Given the apparent lack of central organization and leadership, the Sagebrush Rebellion could be seen as a movement composed of people who shared a common perception of the problem, but disagreed over the appropriate response. Specifically, one group of Sagebrush Rebels may have viewed conveyance as a realistic solution, while another group pursued the strategy outlined above. In that case, the multiplicity of voices in the Sagebrush Rebellion prior to the 1980 elections represented expressions of the differing opinions within the movement.

Indeed, the LASER Conference discussed at the beginning of this chapter offers support for the diversity interpretation. It represented the first and only time supporters of the Sagebrush Rebellion gathered en masse. Moreover, Hatch set the tone for the conference by suggesting in his keynote address: "Only with a unified effort can we expect to meet the challenge before us." And though the conveyance proposal occupied center stage at the beginning of the conference, at the end the participants elected to "work immediately to establish strong liaison and effective means of communication with the new Administration and Congress" as a way to "alleviate the causes of grievance and distress associated with the past administration of the public lands." Thus, the LASER conference looked very much like a successful effort to unify an otherwise diverse movement.

At one level, then, it does not really matter which interpretation we follow. Whatever the original intent of the Sagebrush Rebellion might have been, the outcome of the 1980 elections and the LASER Conference made clear that conveyance of the public lands no longer represented the consensus of the Sagebrush Rebellion.

We now have a context useful in assessing the subsequent train of events. For example, while Watt's pledge to defuse the Sagebrush Rebellion appeared to contradict the thrust of the movement, it now seems obvious that his efforts were perfectly consistent with the movement's goals. His good neighbor policy promised a new era in public land management that would address the immediate complaints of the Sagebrush Rebels. But more important, Watt's openly confrontational approach raised hopes for an even more fundamental change. At base, Watt's challenge represented an attack on the very foundation of the environmental community's influence within the policy arena, an attack that, at least initially, seemed capable of withstanding the protests raised by the environmental community. Thus it seemed possible that a realignment within the policy arena had begun to take shape. If that were in fact the case, then the Sagebrush Rebellion might have been more successful than its original authors had imagined.

And yet the Sagebrush Rebels' victory celebration was cut short by Reagan's privatization proposal. As noted above, the privatization initiative seemed inconsistent with both the Sagebrush Rebellion and Watt's good neighbor policy. Therefore the question is, who did support privatization? In the next chapter, we attempt to answer this question by demonstrating that the roots of the privatization position can be traced to a curious combination of ideas derived from libertarian political ideology and environmentalism.

CHAPTER SIX

Privatization: A Flank Attack

Why does the (self-proclaimed) most conservative and loyal member of the president's cabinet oppose Mr. Reagan's land-sales program? This opposition arises because Mr. Watt, a celebrated "sagebrush rebel," believes in public land ownership—but at the state, rather than at the federal, level.

—*Steve Hanke, 1983*[1]

Some say I could have done more for the modern conservative cause if I had not spoken the truth so loudly so often. But the Liberal Establishment will never be shaken without confrontation. We must be willing to confront it if we want to restore America's greatness.

—*James Watt, 1985*[2]

On the face of it, the Reagan administration's Federal Real Property Initiative (the so-called privatization initiative) contained several obvious problems. First, although presented as a debt reduction strategy, the scale of the proposal simply did not make sense. In his budget message, Reagan proposed raising $9 billion over three years from the sale of surplus federal property. The Property Review Board, which Reagan created to oversee the sale process, increased the target amount to $17 billion over five years. However, estimates indicated that the federal deficit would exceed $100 billion in 1982, pushing the national debt to over $1 trillion. Thus the proposal would not make a significant dent in either the deficit or the debt.

The low revenue figures fed speculations that the initial proposal might be a prelude to a more ambitious sale planned by the administration. Increasing the scale of the proposal would help the revenue picture, of course, but it also raised other problems. The Federal Property and Administrative Services Act of 1949, which authorized the sale of surplus federal property, specifically excluded the bulk of the federal estate. Moreover, the lion's share of revenues generated from the sale of western federal lands was earmarked for western water projects and/or acquisition of park land and wildlife refuges. At the very least, then, using land sales to retire the national debt would require a significant revision of federal land law.

There was yet another problem with the scheme. It was not at all clear who might be interested in buying federal property. As Christopher Leman explained: "Western state and local governments went on record against the idea. Environmental, conservation, and recreation groups—including wilderness advocates, hunters, and off-road vehicle enthusiasts—achieved an unprecedented unity in opposition. Not a single major commodity sector supported privatization: livestock, mining, oil and gas, coal, or timber."[3] In short, the privatization initiative appeared to be an ill-conceived proposal, lacking any identifiable political support. It is not at all surprising, therefore, that the scheme produced more rhetoric than revenue, and consequently, was quickly abandoned by the administration.

Nevertheless, the argument advanced in this chapter is that the controversy precipitated by the privatization effort plays an important role in the Sagebrush Rebellion story. The fact that the proposal galvanized national attention, even if only briefly, demonstrated how thoroughly politicized the public land policy arena had become. It also served to convince Sagebrush Rebels, environmentalists, and the Reagan administration of the need to reevaluate their positions as a step toward staking out new claims in the policy arena. The intent of this chapter, then, is to trace the contours of the privatization controversy.

Contrary to the view prevailing at the time, privatization was neither a goal of the Sagebrush Rebellion nor part of Interior Secretary James Watt's agenda. Instead, privatization advocates were attempting to use the controversies surrounding the Sagebrush Rebellion to advance their own political agenda. As such, intervention by privatization advocates presented the kind of threat suggested by Schattschneider when he observed: "The greatest hazard to any faction is not a frontal attack by the opposition but a flank attack by bigger, collateral, inconsistent, and irrelevant competitors for the attention and loyalty of the public."[4]

PRIVATIZATION VERSUS ASSET MANAGEMENT

The August 23, 1982, cover of *Time* magazine carried a headline reading, "GOING, GOING . . . ! Land Sale of the Century." Beneath the headline was a portrait of James Watt superimposed over a three-dimensional representation of the United States. "With Watt leading the way," the cover story told readers, "the Reagan Administration is putting the Government back into the business of selling its real estate."[5]

There were several factors that cast doubts on this view, however. First, and perhaps most important, the privatization initiative did not emerge from the Interior Department. In October 1981 Senator Charles Percy (R-Ill.) introduced Senate Resolution 231, which proposed that the "liquidation of carefully selected Federal properties could contribute to restraining and ultimately reducing the national debt of the United States." Although Percy's resolution received little support in Congress, it caught the administration's attention. More specifically, Steve Hanke, a staff member of the Council of Economic Advisors and as we will see later, an early privatization advocate, used Percy's resolution as the basis for the Federal Real Property Initiative.

Second, Watt was not a member of the Property Review Board, which had been appointed by Reagan to oversee the inventory and sale process. In fact, the board was composed primarily of Reagan's top political advisors. Third, when Watt met with the Property Review Board, he reported that initial inventories had identified 4 million acres of BLM lands as potentially suitable for disposal, but that subsequent study would likely reduce the total to about 2.7 million acres. Taken together, these factors tend to discount the notion that Watt was leading the way in the privatization effort. Indeed, they portray Watt as an outsider and perhaps even a reluctant player in the land-sales program.

Moreover, the Interior Department's approach to privatization was not precisely consistent with the expressed intent of the effort. In testimony before the Senate Energy and Natural Resources Committee, for example, Interior Assistant Secretary Garrey Carruthers reported that the department had established the Asset Management Program in response to the president's initiative. A program, Carruthers explained

> that requires us to look at the lands we manage to determine how they can best be managed for the maximum public good. Sound management includes disposal of unneeded property. But the goals of the Asset Management Program are more than selling land or real property. It is a review of our land management practices to determine whether Federal Lands are being used to the best advantage, and if not, to correct that.[6]

During subsequent hearings, Carruthers insisted that the department was "enthusiastic" about the administration's program, and that "excess property will be sold with the proceeds being used to reduce the national debt." However, he also assured the committee: "Only a small portion of the [public] lands will be offered for sale. We do not foresee massive transfers of public lands, . . . [t]he Federal government will still have extensive landholdings."[7]

It appears, then, that the Asset Management Program represented an attempt to refocus the privatization effort from emphasis on land disposals to emphasis on improved management of the federal estate, a move that would have made privatization more consistent with Watt's good neighbor policy. But, given the fact that privatization had not been advanced by the Interior Department, the Asset Management Program also pointed to a possible disagreement about the administration's federal land policy.

One indication of such a disagreement emerged after Steve Hanke left the administration. Writing in the May 6, 1983, edition of the *New York Times*, Hanke noted:

> Scarcely a week passes in which the Interior Department's controversial Secretary, James Watt, is not castigated by environmentalists and others. . . . What is unfortunate is that Mr. Watt has become the issue. As much as he and the environmentalists might enjoy their cat-and-mouse game, we should recognize that he is largely irrelevant. . . . The real issue is: Do we want the Government to retain ownership of public lands and use political and bureaucratic processes to determine their uses, or do we want the Government to sell off some and let private owners and consumers determine their uses?[8]

Though Hanke clearly viewed Watt as an obstruction to the administration's program, it is unclear whether the problem was Watt's actions or his media presence. The answer to this question was provided by subsequent events.

In a July memo to western governors, Watt noted: "One of the areas that continues to draw criticism deals with the disposal of lands no longer needed by the Federal government. I am satisfied that the mistakes of 1982 are not being, and will not be, repeated."[9] Ten days later, the *New York Times* reported: "Interior Secretary James Watt has quietly pulled the public lands controlled by his department out of the Reagan Administration's program to sell off some property as a means of reducing the national debt."[10] The article went on to note: "An aide to Mr. Watt, who did not want to be quoted by name said, 'Watt has closed down the asset management effort because he regards it as a political liability to President Reagan. Selling off public lands to retire the national debt is not sound policy and never was endorsed by Watt,' the aide said."[11] Any doubts about the accuracy of this report were laid to rest by Hanke in a *Wall Street Journal* editorial on August 5.

Commenting on Watt's disengagement from the privatization effort, Hanke suggested: "Contrary to press reports and the wailings of critics of the administration's environmental policies, Secretary Watt has been opposed to the president's land-sales program from the beginning." He then went on to list specific actions taken by Watt designed to undermine the administration's program, including instructing "his staff not to use the words 'privatize' and 'privatization.'" But the full intensity of

Hanke's attack is suggested in the following passage. "Why does the (self-proclaimed) most conservative and loyal member of the president's cabinet oppose Mr. Reagan's land-sales program? This opposition arises because Mr. Watt, a celebrated 'sagebrush rebel,' believes in public land ownership—but at the state, rather than at the federal, level."[12] Hanke likened this position to the "one taken by socialists, who prefer decentralized, rather than centralized, state farms." Nevertheless, he also conceded that Watt's decision reduced the land-sales program to "only a shadow of its former self."

Though his accusations were certainly hyperbole, the tenor of Hanke's attack is instructive. It not only confirmed that the privatization initiative created tension within the administration, but also suggested that the roots of that tension had more to do with interpretations of conservative political ideology than federal land management. Furthermore, the intervention by privatization advocates presented a new and unexpected attack on Watt's efforts to effect a realignment within the public land policy arena. Thus the privatization controversy threatened to undermine the advances made by the Sagebrush Rebellion. However, before exploring this point more fully, we must establish the ideological backdrop against which the privatization controversy played out.

"WE'RE READY TO LEAD"

The modern conservative movement, as George Nash explains, first took shape in the 1950s:

> Where, just a few years earlier, only scattered voices of intelligent right-wing protest were audible, by the end of President Eisenhower's first term a chorus of articulate critics of the Left had emerged. . . . The Right consisted of three loosely related groups: traditionalists or new conservatives, appalled by the erosion of values and the emergence of a secular, rootless, mass society; libertarians, apprehensive about the threat of the State to private enterprise and individualism; and disillusioned ex-radicals and their allies, alarmed by international Communism.[13]

These factions may have shared aspects of a common vision, but there were important doctrinal differences among them as well. Particularly troublesome was an underlying disagreement between libertarians and new conservatives.

Libertarians insisted that releasing the economic system from government regulation would not only restore individual political freedom but also eliminate the need for the burgeoning bureaucratic apparatus characteristic of American government in the latter half of the twentieth century. The libertarian philosophy rested on two basic assumptions. First, since the give and take of free market economics forced individuals to make decisions among competing values, it represented an accurate measure of the "public interest."[14] Second, decisions by government officials were more frequently motivated by a desire to maintain the bureaucratic apparatus than by a desire to serve the public interest. Herein lay the disagreement.

Though equally alarmed at the growth of government and resulting decline in individual freedom, new conservatives remained skeptical about the extent to which individual decisions actually reflected the public interest. In their view, the primary duty of government was to establish and maintain core social values. These values, in turn, served to define the public interest, even if they appeared to be at variance with what individuals thought they wanted. The new conservative critique, therefore, centered less on the size of government than on the concern that government was no longer preserving core social values.

The underlying tension, then, was that "while libertarians tended to emphasize economic arguments against the State, . . . the new conservatives were little interested in economics—particularly what they regarded as an abstract and doctrinaire economics. Instead, they were fundamentally social and cultural critics, for whom conservatism meant the restoration of values, not the preservation of material gains."[15] If the Right had been only an intellectual movement, this tension would have been less problematic. However, the Right's "objective was not simply to understand the world but to change it, restore it, preserve it."[16] These internal disagreements continually frustrated the Right's efforts to secure the political power it wanted and needed.

Nevertheless, in the mid 1970s, a group of young conservatives undertook the task of forging the components of the Right into a new political movement. To emphasize their break with the past, these conservatives dubbed their movement the New Right. And as the founder of the Conservative Caucus, Howard Phillips, explained, the goal of the New Right was to establish conservatives "first as the opposition, then the alternative, finally the government."[17]

Initially, the New Right concentrated on building a grassroots constituency and winning seats in Congress. Indeed, the new conservative coalition in the U.S. Senate (discussed in Chapter 5) was one tangible manifestation of the New Right's success. Moreover, by 1980 the New Right had become a recognized feature on the political landscape, prompting Richard Viguerie, one of the New Right founders, to declare: "Liberalism is almost stone cold dead in American politics. And conservatism is ready willing and able to take its place, because the New Right has made a profound difference in conservative effectiveness and capacity these last few years."[18] Reagan's subsequent victory not only vindicated Viguerie's optimism but also gave the New Right its chance to lead.

In his first inaugural address, Reagan outlined the essential elements of the New Right agenda. "In this present crisis," Reagan insisted, "government is not the solution to our problem; government is the problem." To rectify this situation Reagan pledged: "It is my intention to curb the size and influence of the Federal establishment and to demand recognition of the distinction between the powers granted to the Federal government and those reserved to the States or to the people. All of us need to be reminded that the Federal Government did not create the States; the States created the Federal Government."[19] Reagan's goal, however, was not to eliminate government. "It is rather to make it work—work with us, not over us; to stand by our side, not ride on our backs. Government can and must provide opportunity, not smother it; foster productivity, not stifle it."[20] Relieving the burden created by government was a key step in nurturing the "healthy, vigorous, growing economy" needed to solve the nation's social ills.[21]

Thus, at the outset of Reagan's first term it seemed that the New Right had converted earlier tensions within the conservative movement into a unified front. But as the administration began to implement the New Right agenda, it became obvious that the tensions had not been resolved. One eruption of these tensions occurred in federal land policy.

THE NEW RIGHT AND FEDERAL LAND POLICY

Although the Sagebrush Rebellion emerged from growing frustration with federal land management decisions, there were also clear, albeit unacknowledged, connections between the Sagebrush Rebellion and the New Right. For example, among the people who helped forge the New Right coalition, Viguerie listed Orrin Hatch, James McClure, and Paul Laxalt. All three, as we have seen, were prominent spokesmen for the Sagebrush Rebellion. In addition, Viguerie identified financial support from Joseph Coors as an important ingredient in the New Right's success. Coors, as it turns out, was also a major sponsor for Mountain States Legal Foundation and influential in hiring Watt to head it.[22] Moreover, it was James McClure who first suggested Watt as a possibility for Reagan's Interior secretary, and Laxalt whose endorsement secured Watt's nomination.[23] Finally, the Sagebrush Rebels and the New Right faced a common enemy: the environmentalists. Though he offered no substantive discussion on environmental politics, Viguerie did catalog the Sierra Club and Wilderness Society among "some of the better known liberal single issue groups" opposed to the New Right.[24]

Viewed in this light, it is not at all surprising why the focus of the Sagebrush Rebellion shifted after the 1980 elections. The themes expounded by Reagan—reducing the federal establishment, increasing the states' role, and emphasizing economic production—went directly to the heart of the Sagebrush Rebellion. But nowhere was the internal consistency between the goals of the New Right and the Sagebrush Rebellion more apparent than in the guiding principles Watt sought to establish for the Department of Interior. Indeed, what critics frequently characterized as Watt's personal ideology was instead a skilful weaving of traditional conservation and Reagan's agenda into a cogent defense for prodevelopment policies.

In a January 1982 *Saturday Evening Post* article, for example, Watt argued: "What too many people fail to recognize is that being a good steward involves decisions on the *use* of resources as well as the *preservation* of resources." By failing to remain attentive to resource use, Watt insisted, "we unduly penalize and impoverish our people, weaken our nation and deny ourselves the economic base essential to good stewardship. Only economically strong nations can be good stewards. It is in the economically deprived countries that environmentally devastating practices abound."[25] Whether or not the similarity was intentional, these comments were nearly identical to arguments raised by Gifford Pinchot in the early days of the conservation movement. "There may be just as much waste," Pinchot maintained, "in neglecting the development and use of certain natural resources as there is in their destruction."[26] For Pinchot, as for Watt, a balanced stewardship program offered "the only form of insurance that will certainly protect us against disasters that lack of foresight has in the past repeatedly brought down on nations since passed away."[27]

The link between resource use and national stability also provided an opportunity to incorporate Reagan's antigovernment agenda. As Watt explained, government was the core problem. "It is true that in the past two decades the federal government has enacted a number of well-intentioned environmental protection laws—laws that I support and that I will enforce. But our government did not do a good job implementing the laws. . . . Instead of using resources to build a strong nation so we can be good stewards, we have deprived America of the raw materials it needs."[28] In short, Watt believed that misdirected implementation of environmental protection laws had smothered opportunity and stifled productivity. Part of the solution, then, was to make government work by restoring the balance between preservation and development; the other part was to curb the size of the federal establishment: "I have put a high priority on helping President Reagan cut government spending as part of his Economic Recovery Program. Most of our programs have been trimmed back, and some agencies have been consolidated as part of this effort. But the objective is to revitalize our national economy so that we Americans can be the kind of good stewards most of us want to be."[29]

In this article, as elsewhere, Watt simply confounded his critics. Air and water pollution, overgrazed rangeland, clear-cut forests, and gaping strip mines offered poignant reminders that, contrary to Watt's assertion, environmentally destructive practices could and did abound in economically strong countries. Moreover, Watt's belief that traditional conservation and the New Right's critique of centralized government were compatible seemed to contradict history. If anything, as Samuel Hays suggests, the conservation movement represented a persuasive defense for centralized government. "The broader significance of the conservation movement stemmed from the role it played in the transformation of a decentralized, nontechnical, loosely organized society, where waste and inefficiency ran rampant, into a highly organized, technical, and centrally planned and directed social organization which could meet a complex world with efficiency and purpose."[30] Despite these apparent inconsistencies, environmentalists discovered that mobilizing an effective attack against Watt presented a formidable challenge.

The Sierra Club, as noted earlier, launched a "Dump Watt" campaign that succeeded in securing over a million signatures on petitions calling for Watt's dismissal. However, not only did Reagan not fire Watt, he did not even bother to comment on the petitions, an indifference explained, at least in part, by the fact that Watt had become a top fund raiser for the Republican party and second only to Reagan in requests for public appearances. Some observers suggested, in fact, that attacks from environmentalists were largely responsible for Watt's growing popularity within the conservative camp.

But environmentalists were not Watt's only critics. In February 1982, one month after Watt's carefully crafted *Saturday Evening Post* article, Reagan delivered the budget message containing the privatization initiative. Watt's role as a leading spokesman for the administration led, logically, to the conclusion that he supported and had perhaps even authored the proposal. However, with hindsight it is clear that the privatization initiative posed a significant dilemma for Watt.

On the one hand, it seemed plausible that both environmentalists and Sagebrush Rebels would oppose the proposal. The initiative's authors admitted as much in their background memo to Reagan: "Altering present policies, either selling the lands or raising user fees, would likely generate considerable controversy." They went on to identify western ranchers, environmental groups, local communities, private landowners, and recreationists as groups that "would probably oppose major sales of public lands."[31] Pursuing the privatization initiative, therefore, might create a significant political threat for the administration.

On the other hand, Watt's efforts to redirect federal land policy were tied to the continuing vitality of the Reagan administration, and at the time it seemed that the administration's vigor resulted from the New Right coalition. The rub here was that the privatization initiative represented part of a broader push among libertarians to move the Reagan administration into a bolder free market posture. In consequence, by opposing the privatization initiative, Watt risked creating dissension within both the administration and the New Right coalition.

If nothing else, Watt's exchanges with environmentalists demonstrated his ability to finesse difficult political situations. The key in this case was to translate privatization into terms that seemed consistent with traditional public land policy. The Federal Land Policy and Management Act (FLPMA) provided precisely the text Watt needed.

The prevailing belief that FLPMA assured federal retention of the public lands in perpetuity, like other policy interpretations, was less clear than commonly assumed. The specific language from the act reads: "the public lands [will] be retained in Federal ownership, unless as a result of the land use planning procedures provided for in this Act, it is determined that disposal of a particular parcel will serve the national interest."[32] A subsequent provision identifies three conditions that could lead to divestiture of public lands:

(1) if the tract in question is "difficult and uneconomic to manage as part of the public lands"; (2) if the tract were acquired for a purpose no longer needed; and (3) if disposal of the tract "will serve important public objectives, including, but not limited to, expansion of communities and economic development, which cannot be achieved prudently or feasibly on land other than public land."[33]

These conditions, in turn, became the backbone of the Asset Management Program (AMP).

Despite its ultimate failure, the AMP initially appeared to be a brilliant political ploy. Portraying the AMP as an application of the privatization initiative to the special conditions associated with the public lands, Carruthers could explain that the AMP demonstrated the Interior Department's commitment to "fulfilling the objectives of the Administration's Federal Real Property Initiative." Moreover, the link with FLPMA provided a context for addressing the troublesome political problems raised by the privatization initiative.

First, it transformed an otherwise radical proposal into an extension of the existing public lands management mandate. In fact, the disposal provision of FLPMA granted the Secretary of Interior authority to unilaterally carry out land transactions on areas of the public lands less than 2,500 acres in size, demonstrating that privatization could be carried out without additional congressional action. Second, the limited scope of the AMP made the effort appear consistent with the good neighbor policy and thereby helped allay the fears of the Sagebrush Rebels. Third, since the proposal was based on FLPMA, environmentalists' protests could be dismissed as yet another example of their ongoing misinterpretation of public land policy.

Yet there was no escaping the fact that the AMP represented a clear deviation from the intent of the privatization initiative. The limited scale of the program would not produce significant revenues, so it failed to provide a meaningful solution for the national debt problem. More important, the AMP was firmly seated in the efficacy of public land ownership and therefore a violation of the libertarian agenda. Thus the AMP fit a broader pattern that added to growing dissatisfaction among libertarians. As Steve Hanke suggested: "What you have now in the White House is the Nixon-Ford Administration without Nixon or Ford. . . . The level of taxes and of government expenditures as a percentage of G.N.P. have gone up not down. They have done nothing substantive about deregulation. . . . There's a massive gap between rhetoric and reality."[34] The perceived failure of the Reagan administration to fulfill its promises to the free market cause led to a mass exodus of libertarians, a turn of events that brings us back to the clash between Watt and Hanke.

Although Hanke's attacks obviously reflected disagreement about public land policy, their character reveals that the true locus of the dispute centered on the meaning of New Right doctrine. The referent for Hanke's assertion that Watt was "largely irrelevant," for instance, was Watt's unwillingness to fully embrace the libertarian cause, a point Hanke made more forcefully in a *New York Times* letter. Responding to criticism from a Wilderness Society representative about Watt's national park policy "failures," Hanke declared: "When judged by authentic conservative standards, Secretary Watt has also been a failure. . . . It's time for the Secretary to stop talking and begin acting in an authentically conservative way."[35] For Hanke, authentic conservative actions included raising "park user fees by about 2,000 percent," and rolling "back the frontier of state ownership" by privatizing "some of the 73 million acres of Federal park land." It was two weeks later that Hanke accused Watt of socialist tendencies.

The point, then, is that Hanke's attacks had more to do with libertarian doctrine than public land policy. His ongoing challenge to Watt was to privatize public lands, not because it made sense as part of an overall management program, but to demonstrate his commitment to the conservative cause. Watt, on the other hand, remained unconvinced that large scale privatization made sense in the context of either public land management or the conservative political agenda. In the end Watt prevailed, and both the privatization initiative and the AMP quietly faded into oblivion. It is not without irony that Watt, who was commonly believed to be the author of privatization, would ultimately defeat the privatization initiative. Yet Watt's activities as spokesman for the New Right left little time for reconsideration of his role in the privatization battle.

Though always controversial, Watt's comments in 1983 exhibited a new and seemingly unexpected trajectory. He began the year by asserting: "If you want an example of the failure of socialism, don't go to Russia. Come to America, and go to the Indian reservations."[36] This observation was followed almost immediately by an equally controversial interview with *Business Week*. Speaking of his critics within the environmental community, Watt charged: "Their real thrust is not clean air, or clean water, or parks, or wildlife but the form of government under which America will live. The environment is a good vehicle to achieve their objectives. That is why you see the hard-line left drifting toward that interest."[37] Identifying his critics' real objective as "centralized planning and control of society," Watt proposed: "Look what happened to Germany in the 1930s. The dignity of man was subordinated to the powers of the Nazism. The dignity of man was subordinated in Russia. . . . Those are the forces that this thing can evolve into."[38] Not surprisingly, critics pointed to these remarks as evidence that Watt's baiting, confrontational style was simply out of control.

Further support for this interpretation emerged in April with allegations that Watt had replaced the Beach Boys with Wayne Newton as the entertainment for the annual Fourth of July celebration in Washington because he believed that the Beach Boys would encourage drug abuse and alcoholism, while Wayne Newton represented wholesomeness. However, the final straw was Watt's derogatory remark about the composition of a commission formed to investigate his coal-leasing policies,[39] a comment that led Senator Robert Dole (R-Kan.) to observe: "We just can't stand, every two or three months, Mr. Watt making some comment to offend another 20 or 30 or 40 million people."[40] Faced with significant opposition from all sides, Watt tendered his resignation on October 10, 1983.

It could be that his critics were correct. The endless barrage of attacks finally took their toll and Watt simply lost control. There is, however, an underlying consistency to his remarks. Although widely interpreted as an accusation that environmentalists were either Nazis or Communists, the actual point of his *Business Week* comments was that the environmental movement had become a tool of the "hard-line left." Similarly, the subtext to the Beach Boys controversy was a statement about the need to reclaim traditional social and familial values. Finally, his description of the coal commission members was intended as a criticism of the logic behind affirmative action. In short, each comment can be traced back to the litany of complaints that defines the new conservative branch of the New Right agenda.

Viewed in this light, Watt appears to have been responding to libertarian criticism—attempting to demonstrate that despite his opposition to the privatization initiative, he was an authentic conservative after all. In any event, by 1983, it was clear that the privatization controversy had deflected the momentum of the Sagebrush Rebellion. Although the Nevada Sagebrush Rebels attempted to rekindle support for the original conveyance proposal, they found little. Moreover, though Watt's departure resulted more from his bickering with libertarians than his stance on federal land policy, the environmental community quickly portrayed his resignation as vindication of their posture. Finally, given the approaching reelection campaign, it seemed plausible that the Reagan administration might moderate its posture in the hopes of mending fences with the environmental community. In short, the Reagan administration's promise of a new era in public land policy appeared to have collapsed.

However, there is one more aspect of the privatization controversy that warrants attention. Because conservative politics was central to the privatization initiative, it is not surprising that privatization advocates were frequently portrayed as a group of zealous economists who lacked an appreciation of the federal estate's heritage. Summarizing this view, Charles Callison observed:

> I am convinced that in their mind-set the [privatization advocates] cannot recognize or understand the public and national purposes for which public lands have been retained or taken into public ownership. Nor do they understand or recognize the historical currents in American culture—the development of certain values and customs held dear by the American people—that have led to the preservation of our National Parks and Wilderness Areas, the development of National Wildlife Refuges (the finest such system in the world), and the management under law of the bulk of our National Forests and BLM lands for multiple public uses.[41]

Preservation is certainly one of the historical currents that helped shape federal land policy. However, that history has also been shaped by calls for privatization of the federal estate.

Though merely a coincidence, it is interesting to note that the

Reagan administration's privatization initiative coincided with the two-hundredth anniversary of the founding of the public domain. Moreover, the original purpose of the public domain was to provide the national government with an independent revenue source for repaying Revolutionary War debts. Although that plan ultimately failed to raise significant revenues, it did establish the dominant federal land policy theme for the nineteenth century. Constantly "cash poor but land rich," the national government used land disposals to raise revenue, to promote internal improvements, and to encourage western settlement.

With the advent of the conservation movement, land policy increasingly favored retention and management, but the disposal impulse did not disappear. In 1872, for example, Congress signaled the beginning of the retention era by reserving Yellowstone National Park, yet it also continued earlier policy themes by adopting the General Mining Act. Intended to stimulate private mineral development on the federal estate, this act allowed individuals who discovered mineral deposits on the public domain to mine them without charge. In addition, individuals could claim title to land necessary for mining and milling activity. Another noteworthy example of the disposal impulse was the Reclamation Act of 1902, which originally financed the construction of western water projects with revenues generated from the sale of federal land.

Disposal has also been an ongoing component of the BLM's management mandate. Although the Taylor Grazing Act was generally viewed as the closing of the public domain, the congressional intent was to "promote the highest use of the public lands pending its final disposal." Furthermore, efforts to transform the BLM into a full-fledged multiple use agency during the 1960s were balanced by continued calls for disposal through the Multiple Use and Classification Act, the Public Land Sales Act, and the Public Land Law Review Commission. And as noted above, even FLPMA contained a disposal provision. In short, there has never been an unambiguous statement declaring an end to disposals of the public lands.

Indeed, the specific policy mechanism proposed by the Reagan administration was an adaptation of a plan developed by President Nixon. Growing demands for outdoor recreation during the 1960s provided an opportunity for environmentalists to expand their influence in federal land policy, and one way to increase recreation opportunities on the public lands was to restrict development activity. There were other possibilities, however.

In his 1970 address on the environment, President Nixon explained:

Acquiring needed recreation areas is a real estate transaction. One third of all the land in the United States—more than 750,000,000 acres—is owned by the Federal Government. . . . Until now, the uses to which Federally owned properties were put has largely been determined by who got them first. As a result, countless properties with enormous potential as recreation areas linger on in the hands of agencies that could just as well—or better—locate elsewhere.[42]

To remedy this situation, Nixon directed the "heads of all federal agencies and the Administrator of General Services to institute a review of Federally-owned real properties that should be considered for other uses." In addition, he established a Property Review Board to make recommendations on properties that could be either converted to recreation purposes or sold to finance acquisition of new recreation areas. The Reagan administration privatization proposal simply redirected this process from acquiring recreation areas to raising revenue.

Viewed against this background, the argument that Reagan's initiative violated the history of public land policy is difficult to sustain.[43] Nevertheless, critics were correct in suggesting that the contemporary privatization efforts were not simply an extension of earlier disposal policies. It seems useful, therefore, to briefly trace the origins of the modern privatization proposal.

OF COMMONS AND COERCION

In his 1962 work, *Capitalism and Freedom*, Milton Friedman argued:

Political freedom means the absence of coercion of a man by his fellow men. The fundamental threat to freedom is power to coerce, be it in the hands of a monarch, a dictator, an oligarchy, or a momentary majority. The preservation of freedom requires the elimination of such concentration of power to the fullest possible extent and the dispersal and distribution of whatever power cannot be eliminated—a system of checks and balances.[44]

At first glance this observation seems unrelated to issues of public land management, yet in a subsequent passage Friedman demonstrates a potential link. Speaking of Yellowstone National Park, Friedman asserts: "If the public wants this kind of an activity enough to pay for it, private enterprise will have every incentive to provide such parks. And, of course, there are many private enterprises of this nature now in existence. I cannot myself conjure up any neighborhood effects or important monopoly effects that would justify governmental activity in this area."[45] This comment, perhaps the first statement of the contemporary privatization position, does seem to fit the charge raised by Callison and others. Friedman's criticism of national parks is not situated in federal land history, but rather in libertarian economic theory. However, libertarian theory was only part of the intellectual watershed that produced the privatization initiative. The other, more important part was Garrett Hardin's 1968 essay, "The Tragedy of the Commons."

Like Friedman, Hardin's concern centered on the relationship between freedom and coercion. But unlike Friedman, Hardin viewed freedom as the problem, not the solution. "Freedom in a commons," Hardin asserted, "brings ruin to all."[46] This proposition followed from what Hardin identified as the "inherent logic of the commons," logic derived from examining the benefit/cost calculations confronting users of common resources. Individuals receive full benefit from their use of common resources but bear only a part of the cost, and any resource not used by one individual will be used by another. Combined, these factors create a strong incentive for users to claim an ever-increasing share of the commons' resources. However, benefit/cost calculations discourage efforts to improve the resource base. The costs of improvements are borne by the individual user, but because the resources are commonly owned, the benefits from improvements are shared by all users. Thus rational people pursuing their self-interest are locked into a system that makes the destruction of the commons inevitable. Yet Hardin remained convinced that tragedy could be averted.

"The tragedy of the commons as a foodbasket," Hardin suggested, "is averted by private property, or something formally like it."[47] Since private owners pay the full cost of their use and receive full benefit from improvement efforts, they have an incentive to balance desires for short-term gains against the need to sustain long-term productivity of the resource base. Thus, despite his disagreement with Friedman's initial premises, Hardin is nonetheless willing to concede the more important point regarding the efficacy of private market approaches, at least in some forms of the problem.

However, the issue that occasioned Hardin's essay was pollution, an issue that presents a different, though related problem, to that of the traditional commons.

> Here it is not a question of taking something out of the commons, but of putting something in—sewage, or chemical, radioactive, and heat wastes into water; noxious and dangerous fumes into the air; and distracting and unpleasant advertising signs into the line of sight. . . . The rational man finds that his share of the cost of the wastes he discharges into the commons is less than the cost of purifying his wastes before releasing them. Since this is true for every-

one, we are locked into a system of "fouling our own nest," so long as we behave only as independent, rational, free-enterprisers.[48]

Moreover, because the "air and waters surrounding us cannot be readily fenced," private property/market solutions were simply impractical. Instead, Hardin argued that averting pollution-induced tragedy required regulation of the commons following the principle of "mutual coercion, mutually agreed upon by a majority of people affected."[49]

As should be obvious, Hardin's essay provided a theoretical foundation for the kind of stringent regulatory programs advocated by environmentalists. It is not surprising, therefore, that in the dominant policy dialogue the "tragedy of the commons" quickly became a shorthand reference for government intervention. Nevertheless, a handful of writers insisted throughout the 1970s that useful, even if unconventional, solutions to natural resource problems could be discovered in libertarian economic theory. In 1973, for example, Steve Hanke coauthored a paper that advocated the use of market forces to augment wildlife management efforts in East Africa.[50] Though moderate in tone and free of New Right ideology, this article clearly foreshadowed his subsequent role in the privatization conflict.

Another 1973 article, written by Richard Stroup and John Baden, is more germane to the questions at hand. After surveying the myriad complaints lodged against national forest management practices, Stroup and Baden suggested:

> Proposed solutions to existing management problems range from small changes in criteria or practices to rather drastic changes in the form and function of management itself. In the latter category is a proposal, voiced by Milton Friedman and others, that government agencies should not manage these forests at all. Instead management would be left to private managers and the present value of *wealth* captured for public use by auctioning off rights (title) to the lands in question.[51]

Such a move, they argued, would create a "large revenue windfall to the government" without necessarily disrupting established use patterns. Traditional multiple use goals would be preserved, if not enhanced. "Just as we have restaurants of all kinds," Stroup and Baden argued, "in about the proportions people want and will pay for, we could expect an immense diversity in forest use and perhaps even the development of use patterns not yet attempted, as private owners tried to increase the usefulness (value) of their land."[52] Furthermore, "some wilderness areas could be expected to be more strongly protected than now as some entrepreneurs catered to those willing and able to pay for access to pristine wilderness."[53] If nothing else, these arguments suggest that, contrary to Callison's complaint, privatization advocates were quite cognizant of the public and national purposes served by the federal lands. Indeed, their challenge centered on the question of whether or not public ownership and government regulation were the only means for attaining those purposes.

It is important to understand that this article documents the origin of the privatization effort well in advance of both the Sagebrush Rebellion and the Reagan administration initiative. Moreover, these early expressions of privatization were clearly sympathetic to the cause of environmental quality, even if they disagreed with the mechanisms advocated by the environmental movement. As Hardin and Baden observed in their 1977 book, *Managing the Commons*: "In this crowded world of ours *unmanaged* commons are no longer tolerable: but how shall we manage them? What core norms of society need to be altered, and how? How can we best avoid the "tragedy of the commons" without provoking other evils?"[54] Summarizing the privatization response to these questions, Baden argued the problem inherent to government regulation was that it relied on "coercion rather than willing consent to coordinate behavior." In contrast, a market approach led "people voluntarily to participate [because] prices serve as effective and efficient coordinating, rationing, and incentive-generating devices."[55] The logic of Baden's argument is open to debate, but he was willing to pursue it.

Three years later, on the tenth anniversary of Earth Day, Baden published another collection of privatization essays under the title *Earth Day Reconsidered*. Though more critical in tone than his collaboration with Hardin, this volume expressed a similar commitment to the environmental cause. Acknowledging that environmental policies had "produced substantial benefits," Baden went on to suggest: "It is also obvious that they have generated costs, transferred wealth, and reduced efficiencies. . . . In brief, we have adopted extremely expensive mechanisms to buy increments in environmental quality. The relative contributions of altruism and self-interest have been misunderstood and hence incorrectly evaluated."[56] Through an accurate assessment of market incentives, Baden insisted, it becomes clear that "the Sierra Club member shares substantial ground with the classical liberal, the libertarian, and indeed with the fiscal conservative."[57]

These passages are particularly interesting interesting because they parallel comments Baden made in a slightly different context. Baden served as a keynote speaker, panel convener, and editor for the proceedings of the League for the Advancement of States' Equal Rights (LASER)

Conference on the Sagebrush Rebellion (discussed in Chapter 4). In the introduction to the conference proceedings, Baden explained:

> Activists during the environmental decade overwhelmingly favored increased governmental command. . . . Throughout this decade, however, a small number of academics ran a fundamentally different line. They believed that there is a natural coalition, still early in its gestation period, that could join together ecologically sensitive conservationists, fiscal conservatives, and individuals who place a high value on freedom. . . . The 1980 election suggests that this coalition has promise.[58]

He then sought to incorporate Sagebrush Rebels in this coalition: "A successful Sagebrush Rebellion can lead to the development of a responsible resource management system relatively free of distortions of political management. By designing and fostering a system of resource allocation based on monitoring the states' property rights and free exchange among consenting parties, we can systematically move resources to more highly valued uses."[59] It should be noted that "more highly valued uses" did not necessarily mean commodity production. The proposal advanced by Baden during his panel session was to "permit environmental interest groups, such as the Sierra Club, the Audubon Society, and the Wilderness Society, to patent and to obtain fee simple ownership of wilderness lands."[60]

This much is clear then: Privatization advocates represented a distinct faction within the natural resource policy arena. And though they appeared largely tangential to mainstream policy dialogue throughout the 1970s, they anticipated the themes that would dominate the nation's political agenda in the 1980s. It is not surprising, therefore, that privatization advocates would finally receive attention with the ascendancy of the New Right. Yet privatization advocates discovered, much to their chagrin, that recognition did not readily translate into policy success. Indeed, despite the intensity of their disagreements in other areas, neither environmentalists nor Sagebrush Rebels were ready to accept the radical changes implied by privatization.

CONCLUSIONS

In seeking to expand the scope of their movement, it seems that the Sagebrush Rebels encountered the kind of hazard described by Schattschneider at the beginning of this chapter. Initially, the Reagan administration offered promise of a new era in public land policy responsive to the complaints of the Sagebrush Rebellion. Moreover, Watt's melding of traditional conservation themes with Reagan's agenda created a powerful justification for the kind of prodevelopment management regime advocated by the Sagebrush Rebels. Equally important, Watt's stance appeared capable of withstanding the frontal attacks mounted by the environmental community.

Yet Sagebrush Rebels quickly discovered that the Reagan administration contained a more troublesome threat than their environmental adversaries. At one level, this threat took the form of privatization advocates who clearly fit the description of "inconsistent and irrelevant competitors for the attention and loyalty of the public." Whereas Sagebrush Rebels were attempting to rearrange power relationships within the public land policy arena, privatization advocates wanted to eliminate the arena altogether. Furthermore, privatization advocates consistently portrayed themselves as outside the traditional dialogue, a position clearly intended to divert public attention from both environmentalists and Sagebrush Rebels. And though they failed to mobilize an influential constituency, privatization advocates did succeed, at least for a brief time, in monopolizing public discussions.

Even though the privatization proposal was ill-conceived, the controversy it generated redefined the terms of the argument. Recognizing the common threat posed by privatization, environmentalists and Sagebrush Rebels set aside their other disagreements in order to oppose it. Furthermore, the growing split within the Reagan administration led Watt to emphasize his role as spokesman for the New Right over his role as spokesman for the Sagebrush Rebellion. Although these moves succeeded in defeating the privatization effort, they left most of the issues surrounding the Sagebrush Rebellion unresolved. Thus, when the Nevada Sagebrush Rebels adopted their resolution calling for a return to their original conveyance proposal, it was clear that they had lost most of their earlier momentum. At the same time, there was little evidence that the defeat of the privatization effort had strengthened the hand of the environmental community. In short, the privatization episode appeared to have defused the controversy surrounding the Sagebrush Rebellion far more effectively than Watt's good neighbor policy.

At first glance, then, it would seem that the Sagebrush Rebellion had ended. However, if the real goal of the Sagebrush Rebellion was to force a realignment within the public land policy arena, as I have argued throughout this book, then the apparent calm after the privatization conflict could be interpreted in another way. Having staked out new claims within the policy arena, the protagonists were engaged in the process of solidifying their relative positions. This is the primary issue we will explore in the next chapter.

CHAPTER SEVEN

The Aftermath

It is my view that my usefulness to you [Reagan] in this Administration has come to an end. A different type of leadership at the Department of Interior will best serve you and the nation.

I leave behind people and programs—a legacy that will aid America in the decades ahead. Our people and their dedication will keep America moving in the right direction.

—*James Watt, 1983*[1]

Moderate voices that try to achieve consensus on very, very difficult issues in the long haul are going to be more effective than kamikaze environmentalists. . . . Any of us can firebomb into an issue and perhaps stop the issue but, in the process, blow ourselves away. But that's not being effective, and that's not winning in the long haul.

—*Jay Hair, 1985*[2]

It is doubtful that the Sagebrush Rebels anticipated the kind of commotion their movement would create when they issued their initial call for conveyance. Nevertheless, the controversy surrounding the Sagebrush Rebellion produced a complicated argument centered around four competing demands for the future direction of public land management: a continuation of the 1970s new conservation agenda, conveyance of federal lands to the states, Watt's good neighbor policy, and privatization. None of these positions had sufficient support to dominate, and consequently the policy dialogue became stalemated.

By the fall of 1983 there were signs that the policy impasse might be lifting. The Sagebrush Rebellion had been defused; the Reagan administration had abandoned the privatization initiative; and Watt's resignation under fire raised uncertainties about the future of his good neighbor policy. Indeed, with Reagan's reelection bid looming on the horizon, it seemed that the administration might moderate its posture in order to placate the environmental community. There was a distinct possibility, therefore, that despite its success in disrupting the policy arena, the Sagebrush Rebellion would have no lasting influence on public land management.

But as we will see in this chapter, events after 1983 followed a different course. The Reagan administration remained committed to its prodevelopment policy stance forcing environmentalists into an openly oppositional role. Though environmentalists were successful in demonstrating public dissatisfaction with the administration's agenda, they couldn't convert that dissatisfaction into meaningful political power. More important, the environmental community's attempts to come to grips with the administration fueled latent tensions within the movement. In short, the disruption caused by the Sagebrush Rebellion proved to have more impact on the policy arena than was commonly recognized.

NO COMMON GROUND

On January 29, 1982, representatives from the National Audubon Society, National Wildlife Federation, and Sierra Club met with presidential counselor Edwin Meese to discuss differences between the administration and the environmental community. The outcome of this meeting was best summarized in the title of Russell Peterson's editorial report to Audubon Society members: "No Common Ground."[3] William Turnage of the Wilderness Society expressed a similar attitude about the Reagan administration. Noting that, throughout the 1970s the environmental movement had been a "collaborator with the administration and Congress," Turnage argued, "we're now in opposition to the administration. It's a profound change."[4]

During the 1980 campaign, Reagan made his opposition to the environmental movement quite explicit. The 1980 elections not only brought Reagan to the White House, but also gave the Republican party control of the Senate, thereby moving several western senators sympathetic to the Sagebrush Rebellion into key committee posts. Moreover, Reagan's choice of James Watt for secretary of Interior was tantamount to issuing a declaration of war on the environmental community. To further complicate matters, Reagan picked Anne Gorsuch Burford for the post of administrator of the Environmental Protection Agency (EPA). Frequently portrayed as Watt's protegé, Burford shared Watt's general political philosophy and his willingness to use a confrontational approach with the environmental community. Thus, with officials at the helms of two key environmental posts espousing an apparently antienvironmental philosophy, it is not difficult to imagine why the environmental community viewed itself as besieged.

Yet environmentalists quickly adapted to the new landscape. Most of the major environmental groups increased the size of their national staffs as well as funding levels for their lobbying efforts. Furthermore, environmentalists responded to the administration's attacks by taking their case to the public through a concerted media campaign. A spokesperson for the Interior Department attested to the success of this effort: "One thing that has amazed us here is the ease with which the environmental critics have penetrated the media."[5] In addition, the environmental community made a surprise move during the 1982 elections. Historically, the environmental movement had refrained from participating in electoral politics, but the threat posed by the Reagan administration called for new strategies. Thus, a coalition of environmental groups broke with tradition and endorsed a bipartisan slate of 48 congressional candidates. Although the role of environmental support in the elections was difficult to identify, 34 of the endorsed candidates won seats, a record that led one *Business Week* analysis to suggest that "the environmental movement has established a substantial beachhead in American electoral politics."[6]

By the end of 1982, then, it seemed that the environmental community's oppositional efforts had begun to pay off. Environmentalists could make credible claims that the policies of the administration did not have widespread support among the American public and that public opposition presented a potential electoral threat. These claims, in turn, were an important first step in moving the environmental community from a defensive to an offensive posture in the policy arena. As it turned out, events in 1983 gave environmentalists the opportunity to test their renewed political support.

The first event occurred on March 9, 1983, when Burford was forced to resign her position as EPA administrator. Although the story behind Burford's resignation is beyond the scope of this project, her connection with Watt gave the event symbolic importance by demonstrating the administration's potential vulnerability. When Reagan announced his choice of William Ruckelshaus to replace Burford, it seemed that the administration was attempting to placate the environmental community.

From 1970 to 1973, Ruckelshaus had served as the first EPA administrator, winning widespread praise from the environmental community for his aggressive commitment to environmental protection. In 1973 Ruckelshaus left EPA to become a deputy attorney general in the Justice Department, a position he lost for refusing to carry out Nixon's order to fire special prosecutor Archibald Cox during the Watergate scandal. Thus Ruckelshaus's environmental credentials, in combination with his demonstrated willingness to stand up to authority, suggested that he might not be another lockstep ideologue in the Reagan Administration. But there were other factors to be considered.

At the time of his nomination, Ruckelshaus was a senior vice president for Weyerhaeuser Company, a major lumber corporation. In that capacity, his public statements seemed sympathetic to the antiregulation

philosophy of the Reagan administration. It could be that these statements reflected his client's views, not his own. But as Sierra Club Director John McComb argued, it could be "that the Ruckelshaus EPA is simply the old Burford EPA with a new bow on its hat."[7] Indeed, of the five
environmental groups testifying at nomination hearings, only the National Wildlife Federation formally endorsed Ruckelshaus. The position
of the other groups was summarized by McComb. When asked whether
he was for or against Mr. Ruckelshaus McComb responded: "We are
withholding judgement on that question pending what kind of answers
you get in your hearings tomorrow and the day after." He then added, "I
think the final judgement is going to be rendered after some years of per-
formance."[8]

Although the specific source of the environmental community's apprehensions was Ruckelshaus's recent record, environmentalists recognized that Burford had been a symptom of the problem, not the cause.
As a spokesman for the Natural Resources Defense Council suggested:
"President Reagan has charged in the past that Mrs. Burford was chased
out of office for doing no more than carrying out his policies. If that is so,
it is time to change his policies because EPA's actions over the past two
years flout both the requirements of law and the will of the American
people."[9] Environmentalists wanted nothing less than a clear statement
of Ruckelshaus's intention to reverse the administration's previous policies. Although he did not provide that statement, Ruckelshaus did explain: "The environmental laws of this country were passed by Congress
and were meant to be taken seriously by the administering authorities. I
do take the Congressional charge seriously, and if I am confirmed, EPA
will take that charge seriously."[10] This sentiment, in combination with
his pledge to restore public confidence in EPA, led to Ruckelshaus's
unanimous confirmation on May 17.

Another encouraging sign for environmentalists came a month later,
when Watt announced the end of the Asset Management Program and
thereby the demise of the privatization initiative. This event was followed by Watt's resignation under fire on October 9. However, if
Reagan's choice of Ruckelshaus seemed to be a conciliatory maneuver,
his choice of William Clark to replace Watt moved in the opposite direction. In fact, the day after Reagan announced Clark's nomination, Edwin
Meese explained: "The policies of this Administration inaugurated by
Jim Watt and approved by President Reagan will be the policies that continue under the stewardship of Bill Clark."[11] This explanation seemed to
affirm the assertion made by the president of Friends of the Earth, Rafe
Pomerance: "You can't change Ronald Reagan by changing James Watt.
The policies will remain but the Lip will be gone."[12]

Clark's confirmation hearings did little to allay the fears of the environmental community. Senator Howard Metzenbaum (D-Ohio) set the tone of the hearings in his opening remarks: "We must view the Clark nomination in the context of President Reagan's environmental program and specifically within the context of Watt's tenure at the Department of Interior."[13] The implication was clear: these hearings were to be as much a repudiation of Watt as an assessment of Clark's ability. However, Clark proved to be a formidable opponent. He seemed to create distance between himself and Watt by suggesting: "President Reagan's mandate to me, if confirmed, is to independently review what he calls the three P's: policy, personnel, and process."[14] Furthermore, he steadfastly refused to comment on Watt's tenure. At one point Senator Dale Bumpers (D-Ark.) asked bluntly, "Can you name one policy of James Watt's that you disagree with?" To which Clark replied:

> I have not thus far in my appraisal weighed out whether I disagree or agree with what Mr. Watt has done with respect to policy, its implementation, or in explanation of that policy, anymore than I have looked at Secretary Andrus', Hathaway's, or others. I may get to that at some point when I confront specific issues . . . and am able to hammer out these issues with experts in the Department and with many of you.[15]

Exchanges such as these led Senator Paul Tsongas (D-Mass.) to conclude that Clark's "approach to his new chores is simply that of a James Watt who took the Dale Carnegie course in civil behavior."[16]

Whereas environmental groups had adopted a "wait and see" stance with Ruckelshaus, there was no doubt about their position with Clark. Only the National Wildlife Federation and Audubon Society declined to express formal opposition, but the pessimistic tone of their statements clearly reflected their belief that a Republican-controlled Senate would not block Clark's nomination. Although Clark secured the endorsement of the Energy and Natural Resource Committee, Senate Democrats tried to delay the nomination vote until after consideration of a resolution denouncing Watt's policies. That effort failed, and Clark was confirmed on November 18 by a vote of 71 to 18. All the opposition votes were cast by Democrats.[17]

The environmental community was ambivalent about these events. As Sierra Club Political Director Carl Pope suggested: "Watt, Anne Gorsuch [Burford], and the architects of many other Reagan environmental programs are gone, and officials of a far more moderate bent or manner have taken their place."[18] It was unclear though, whether the administration's moderation indicated a change in direction, or merely an attempt to defuse the controversy until after the 1984 elections. In Pope's opinion, at least, the prognosis for Reagan's second term was not promising: "The entire ideological thrust of Ronald Reagan's presidency makes it unlikely that he will continue the present tempo of moderation; rather, there is every reason to believe the Watt-Gorsuch agenda is the *real* Reagan agenda, to which he (and his appointees) will return if reelected."[19](emphasis in the original). One way to avoid a return to the "real Reagan agenda" was to bring a premature end to the Reagan era. The question was whether or not environmentalists were prepared to take the bold step of openly opposing Reagan in the 1984 presidential election.

Several factors argued in favor of this move. Troublesome as Watt's baiting may have been, it revitalized environmental politics to levels not seen since the heady times surrounding Earth Day 1970. A profusion of opinion polls showed strong public support for environmental protection policies,[20] and all the major environmental groups experienced dramatic increases in memberships and funding. Moreover, the environmental community's success during the 1982 elections provided both evidence that environmental issues could influence elections and a cadre of environmentalists trained in the techniques of electoral politics. Finally, the resignations of Watt and Burford, combined with the administration's apparent moderation, seemed to represent a tacit admission that earlier, confrontational stances had constituted a tactical error.

But there were other issues to consider. For example, one of the more salient criticisms raised by the environmental community was that the Reagan administration's ideological posture violated a long standing tradition of bipartisan support for environmental concerns. Indeed, environmentalists frequently reminded the administration of the crucial role played by Richard Nixon, a Republican president, in galvanizing modern concern for environmental protection. Furthermore, environmentalists had carefully buttressed their bipartisan posture by endorsing Republican and Democratic candidates during the 1982 elections. Taking sides in a presidential contest would require adopting a distinctively partisan posture.

In addition, endorsing presidential candidates was a more risky proposition than endorsing congressional candidates. The fact that roughly 60 percent of the candidates endorsed by the environmental community won seats in 1982 could be portrayed as a victory that affirmed public support for the environmental movement. Presidential contests, in contrast, are not open to percentage interpretations. Openly endorsing a presidential candidate was equivalent to calling for a national referendum on environmentalism. Losing such a referendum, especially to Reagan, would threaten the environmental community's claim that it represented the true sentiment of the American public.

Gallup polls conducted in the spring of 1983 looked encouraging for the environmental community. Only 41 percent of the respondents expressed approval of Reagan's job as president, and 50 percent of the respondents expressed disapproval of the way Reagan was handling environmental issues.[21] Yet by November, Reagan's overall approval rating had jumped to 53 percent.[22] Equally important, the environment did not appear on a list of responses given to the question: "What do you think is the most important problem facing this country today?"[23] Therefore, the possibility that Reagan's environmental record might be a decisive campaign issue looked less promising at the end of 1983 than it had earlier.

Nevertheless, the first sign that some members of the environmental community were prepared to challenge Reagan came in February 1984, when several prominent environmental leaders formed Environmentalists for Mondale.[24] Since this was an independent organization, it allowed environmentalists to enter the presidential contest without violating the bipartisan posture of established environmental groups. And while former Vice President Walter Mondale was not the strongest environmental candidate among the Democratic hopefuls (in fact, the League of Conservation Voters rated Alan Cranston and Gary Hart higher than Mondale[25]), his record was better than Reagan's. More important, Mondale appeared to be the only candidate in the Democratic field capable of defeating Reagan.

There were a few clashes during the ensuing months. In June, for example, Reagan used an address to the National Geographic Society as an occasion to defend his environmental record and to dismiss criticisms of his administration as "ignorant attacks on the entrepreneurs who help the economy grow."[26] This speech provoked six environmental groups (Sierra Club, National Audubon Society, Friends of the Earth, Natural Resources Defense Council, League of Conservation Voters, and Environmental Policy Institute) to label Reagan's overall environmental record as "dismal."[27] A month later, the administration announced that Anne Burford had been selected to head a national advisory group, which precipitated more fire from the environmental community.[28]

Despite these flareups, it seemed that Philip Shabecoff's assertion was correct: the "optimal timing for partisan exploitation of [environmental issues] may have passed."[29] Indeed, a Gallup poll conducted in August asked whether Reagan or Mondale would do a better job of "improving the environment and dealing with environmental issues'—47 percent of the respondents picked Mondale, 31 percent picked Reagan.[30] However, 53 percent of the respondents in the same poll indicated that they would vote for Reagan.[31] Yet the environmental community was not ready to concede.

In September the Sierra Club created a major media event by announcing that it was breaking with its 92 year tradition and joining the Friends of the Earth in formally endorsing Mondale's candidacy. In a letter to Mondale, the club's Board of Directors noted: "The Sierra Club is a bipartisan organization—and will remain so." However, "confronted by a President whose first-term actions contain so blatant and tragically consistent a record of opposition to the environmental interests of the people of the United States," the Board had little recourse. "We are urging our members and the American people to vote for their environment—by voting for Walter Mondale and Geraldine Ferraro."[32]

As it turned out, of course, not only did Reagan win reelection, but he carried every state except Minnesota, Mondale's home state. Thus, the environmental community's gamble on the 1984 elections failed to pay off. But the loss was not complete. To the extent that the environmentalists had demonstrated widespread public opposition to the Watt/Burford era, it seemed unlikely that the administration would use the election outcome as a mandate for a return to its earlier confrontational posture—a small consolation, but an important one, since Ruckelshaus had announced his intent to leave EPA and Clark was expected to leave the Interior Department.

At the end of Reagan's first term, then, it was not clear whether or not environmentalists had improved their position within the policy arena. The intensity that characterized earlier confrontations had certainly waned, but there was little evidence to suggest that the root arguments had been resolved. What directions would the administration and the environmental community take during Reagan's second term? In the next section, we attempt to sketch out an answer to this question.

A NEW MANAGEMENT PHASE

In his letter of resignation, James Watt suggested: "It is time for a new phase of management, one to consolidate the gains we have made."[33] Coming from an official forced from office, this statement seemed arrogant, but it also demonstrated how formidable an adversary Watt had been: even shrouded in public disgrace, Watt claimed victory. As was so often the case with Watt, his boast carried more validity than environmentalists cared to admit.

Ruckelshaus had quieted the controversy created by Burford, but he was unable to convince the administration to restore the deep budget and personnel cuts EPA had sustained during the first part of Reagan's term. Moreover, as Russell Peterson of the National Audubon Society argued, Clark's tenure as Interior secretary represented a "sharp contrast to the hostile, antienvironmental crusade of Mr. Watt," but Clark was "certainly no champion of environmental protection."[34] From the environmental community's perspective, then, the change brought about by Ruckelshaus and Clark was primarily one of style. Given Reagan's decisive victory, there was little reason to expect anything but a continuation of this pattern.

Reagan's choice of Lee M. Thomas to head EPA affirmed that the general direction established by Ruckelshaus would carry through into Reagan's second term. Thomas had moved from the Federal Emergency Management Agency to EPA in 1983 as part of the personnel changes following Burford's resignation. Despite his short track record, Thomas won enthusiastic praise from the environmental community. At his confirmation hearings, for example, representatives of the National Audubon Society described Thomas as "dedicated, intelligent, accessible and open minded. He is a man of integrity and commitment."[35] Similar sentiments were expressed in statements submitted by the Sierra Club, National Wildlife Federation, and Environmental Defense Fund.

However, environmentalists made it clear that support for Thomas should not be interpreted as support for the administration. As Sierra Club spokesperson Blakeman Early noted, the environmental community still had an axe to grind regarding the administration's handling of EPA's budget:

> The Committee is considering the wrong man for EPA Administrator. As we learned with the unveiling of the President's budget, Mr. Thomas' hands have already been effectively bound, making the true czar of America's environmental programs the Director of the Office of Management and Budget. David Stockman, not Lee Thomas, deserves to be interviewed by the Committee and, ultimately, to be held responsible for the implementation of Congressionally mandated programs to protect the environment.[36]

Nevertheless, Thomas's hearings went smoothly and he was confirmed unanimously.

Reagan's choice of Donald Hodel for secretary of Interior elicited a different, albeit predictable, response from the environmental community. Hodel served as under secretary to Watt before he became head of the Department of Energy in 1982. Like Watt, Hodel was an advocate of prodevelopment policies, especially increased domestic energy production. However, like Clark, Hodel exhibited little proclivity for confrontational politics, so his confirmation hearings were nearly identical to Clark's.

Most environmental groups opposed Hodel's nomination on the familiar grounds that he represented an extension of the Watt legacy. The exceptions, once again, were the National Audubon Society and the National Wildlife Federation. As Clark had done, Hodel pledged to rebuild a consensus on Interior policies, but refused to repudiate Watt's policies.[37] The similarity between the two hearings was itself an important statement. It transmitted a clear signal that the administration intended to pursue a nonconfrontational articulation of the Watt legacy. It seemed that the Administration had in fact embarked on a new management phase directed at consolidating its position within the policy arena.

At the same time, the environmental movement also seemed to be entering a new management phase. Writing in the December 27, 1984, edition of the *Los Angeles Times*, Robert Jones reported: "Over the next year most of the nation's major conservation groups, from the Sierra Club to the National Audubon Society, will see their top executives resign or substantially alter their roles to make way for a new generation of leaders."[38] Joining the above groups in leadership shifts were the Wilderness Society, the Environmental Defense Fund, and Friends of the Earth. "These groups," Jones noted, "form the constellation of the present environmental movement in this country."[39]

Although environmental leaders insisted these changes were coincidental, a "series of isolated occurrences," there did seem to be an underlying pattern. As Rochelle Stanfield suggested: "While different circumstances triggered the exodus of individual leaders, a common thread ties the organizations' search for new executives—an emphasis on managerial skills and a pragmatic approach to environmental advocacy."[40] Indeed, events during the 1980s created a need for a new generation of professional managers at the helm of environmental groups.

As noted earlier, one of the beneficial aspects of Watt's confrontational approach was a dramatic increase in membership and funding among environmental groups. Moreover, many of the major environmental organizations had come to resemble full-fledged corporate entities that published books, magazines, and newsletters; ran mail order catalogue services; offered vacation packages; and conducted fund-raising campaigns in addition to their lobbying efforts. The demands of these activities, as outgoing Sierra Club director Michael McCloskey suggested, were significant: "I spent most of last year developing a budget and finally realized I did not want to be in this movement to crunch numbers."[41] In consequence, finding managers trained in the skills necessary for running large organizations appeared to be a practical move for maintaining the vitality of environmental groups.

Even though the new management phase was motivated by practical concerns, the change raised other questions. "In the rush toward professional management," one observer asked, "is it possible that some of the passion will be lost in the organizations that, in the beginning, were founded by volunteers like John Muir, who cared deeply about the natural world and never much thought about career tracks or marketing strategies?"[42] A spokesperson for the Wilderness Society expressed the belief that this kind of change was needed: "Movements do not go on forever, and we are now entering a new stage of environmental protection. The question is whether the organization will be run by well-paid professionals or whether we will cling to the bleeding hearts concept. If we continue with the latter, I believe we are doomed."[43] Jay Hair of the National Wildlife Federation offered a similar view: "Moderate voices that try to achieve consensus on very, very difficult issues in the long haul are going to be more effective than kamikaze environmentalists. . . . If you are really sincere about protecting the environment, you've got to be a player at the table. You've got to work with the forces in our society and be at the table where the decisions are being made."[44] A more tangible indication of the environmental community's shifting posture is provided by comparing two documents published three years apart: *Ronald Reagan and the American Environment* (1982), and *An Environmental Agenda for the Future* (1985).[45]

In the former, subtitled "An Indictment," environmental leaders wasted little time in drawing the battle lines.

> President Reagan has broken faith with the American people on environmental protection. . . . We have watched for a year as the Administration took or proposed scores of actions that veered radically away from the broad bipartisan consensus in support of environmental protection that has existed for many years. . . . It is difficult to read [the Reagan environmental record] without sorrow, anger, and real concern for our future.[46]

Moreover, they accused the Reagan administration of "making a mockery of the multiple use/sustained yield concept" while attempting to satisfy "some of the demands of the 'Sagebrush Rebels' by dropping conservation goals in managing western lands."[47]

In the *Agenda*, many of the same groups adopted a far more moderate voice.[48] Indeed, the project was portrayed as the result of a "suggestion that [environmental leaders] step back and think about where the environmental movement should be going and what goals it should be pursuing."[49] It also "recognized that solutions to emerging environmental problems require a public dialogue on the nature and dimensions of the challenges, and that . . . a successful strategy for the future must appeal to the broadest spectrum of the American people."[50] Even the discussion of the public lands reflected a tone of moderation.

Many of the recommendations contained familiar themes. For example, one recommendation identified a need for planning "to insure truly balanced multiple use of the lands so that timber production, mining, oil and coal exploitation and grazing do not overshadow conservation values."[51] Another called for a "coordinated program to rehabilitate the millions of acres of public lands that have been damaged by overgrazing, inappropriate mineral exploration and development, logging, or intensive recreational use."[52] But the *Agenda* contained no references to either the Reagan Administration or the *Indictment*—curious omissions given the fact that environmentalists had insisted, especially at Hodel's confirmation hearings, that Reagan's second term represented a continuation of the Watt legacy.

Why did the environmental community believe that a more pragmatic public image was needed? Part of the answer to this question had to do with the confusing political undertow created by events between 1982 and 1985. The apparent demise of the Sagebrush Rebellion, defeat of the privatization initiative, and resignations of Watt and Burford seemed to vindicate the environmental community's stance and thereby reinforce its political clout. However, Reagan's decisive victory, even in the face of documented public opposition to his environmental record, suggested that the environmental community's political clout had definite limits. Furthermore, Reagan's choice of Hodel gave clear warning that future negotiations would more likely take place in the Interior secretary's office than on the front pages of newspapers. Thus, as Geoffrey Wandesforde-Smith observed:

> any realistic assessment of strategic political choice making by the leadership of the environmental movement would have to recognize that a stubborn refusal to bring their thinking into line with that of an incumbent Administration and its allies runs the risk of exclusion from decision making. The practical question, then, is not whether they should adapt to changing political circumstances but how they should do it.[53]

A shift to more pragmatic phrasing of the environmental community's position did offer a way to bring the movement more in line with the administration.

Equally important, the emphasis on a "future strategy" contained in the *Agenda* also fit political realities. Reagan's second term was, after all, his last term, so there was little to be gained by continuing the earlier anti-Reagan posture. However, by using the final years of the Reagan era to reaffirm the movement's bipartisan foundation, environmentalists had a better chance of making environmental issues an influential factor in the 1988 presidential elections. Yet this view leaves some unanswered questions. Wandesforde-Smith notes, for example, that it was not altogether clear "why the leaders of the major environmental groups thought they had to issue a national agenda . . . in order to get the Administration's attention and be taken seriously as actors in national environmental politics."[54] Moreover, since most of the groups involved with the *Indictment* project were also involved in the *Agenda* project, and these groups represented the backbone of the environmental movement, it was not immediately apparent who Jay Hair had in mind with his reference to "kamikaze environmentalists."

Robert Gottlieb and Helen Ingram suggest a possible answer to these questions: "While the mainstream environmental organizations were becoming more bureaucratized (or, as some of their leaders like to say, "professionalized"), a more militant, direct-action wing of environmentalism began to take shape."[55] Indeed, Kirkpatrick Sale argued that this movement emerged from "within the very ranks of the environmental movement and among those who have been its most ardent champions."[56]

Although a full account of the emerging tensions within the environmental movement falls beyond the scope of this project,[57] there is one facet of it that has direct bearing on our story: the radical group, Earth First!. It might be more accurate to categorize Earth First! as a nongroup, since it has no formal leadership, no membership rosters, and it does not collect dues. Nevertheless, Earth First! was frequently identified as one of the groups in the vanguard of growing protest against the environmental establishment.

A brief sketch of Earth First! serves our purposes for several reasons. First, whereas much of the emerging environmental militancy centered on hazardous waste issues, giving rise to the NIMBY (Not In My Backyard) syndrome, Earth First! has focused its activities almost exclusively on federal land issues. Second, the extremist posture of Earth First!—as typified by its early rallying cry, "No Compromise in Defense of Mother Earth"—offers a sharp contrast to the moderating stance of the national environmental groups. Finally, the origins of Earth First!, as explained by its cofounder Dave Foreman, provide insights about both the tensions within the environmental community and the connection between those tensions and the Sagebrush Rebellion.

"NO COMPROMISE IN
THE DEFENSE OF MOTHER EARTH"

Earth First! made its public debut in March 1981 by draping a 300-foot piece of black plastic—a symbolic crack—down the face of the Glen Canyon Dam on the Colorado River. In July 1982, Earth First!ers gathered near Yellowstone National Park, "vowing to prevent—by almost any means—oil drilling" on a federal lease issued to Getty Oil Company.[58] The following summer, Earth First!ers staged a series of protests in the Siskiyou National Forest in Oregon as part of an effort to halt construction of a logging road in an area adjacent to the Kalmiopsis Wilderness Area.[59]

At one level, then, Earth First! seemed to have adapted 1960s antiwar protest techniques to federal land policy battles. Though such tactics clearly deviated from the lobbying and legal efforts favored by traditional environmental groups, the ultimate goal of Earth First! was the same as the environmental establishment: to protect wilderness and other environmental values from the alleged abuses of commodity development. Nevertheless, Earth First! has been criticized by the environmental establishment almost since its founding.

In 1982, for example, *Environmental Ethics* editor Eugene Hargrove suggested: "Perhaps if [Earth First!] is really able to engage in civil disobedience . . . there will be no cause for alarm."[60] Hargrove was unconvinced that this would be the case, however. Earth First! was inspired by Edward Abbey's novel, *The Monkey Wrench Gang*. This novel followed the fictional account of a band of "ecoterrorists" bent on using whatever means at their disposal to eliminate all development activities on the federal estate. The connection between Abbey's novel and Earth First! led Hargrove to argue: "The activities in Abbey's book . . . are criminal, not civil, in nature, and it is hard to imagine a group of people enthusiastically inspired by Abbey's book foregoing the acts described in it indefinitely. Indeed, it seems hard to imagine the ecological sabotage of the book having anything to do with civil disobedience at all."[61] More important, Hargrove viewed ecological sabotage as having the potential to "create a terrible backlash," thereby "undoing all the good that has been done and preventing future accomplishments" in the environmental cause.[62]

Earth First! cofounder Dave Foreman was asked whether or not the group's activities might be "counterproductive to the environmental cause" during a 1985 interview. Admitting that the risk of a backlash was "worth considering," Foreman went on to suggest: "The situation today is that the establishment environmental movement is *not* saving natural diversity. Species are going under every day. Old growth forests are disappearing. Overgrazing continues to ruin our western public lands. Off-road vehicles are cutting up the countryside everywhere. Poisons are continually and increasingly being injected into the environment. . . . In short, the environment is *losing*"[63](emphasis in the original). Foreman's view here is especially important because, in 1985, he published the first edition of *Ecodefense: A Field Guide to Monkeywrenching*. And just as Hargrove had predicted, *Ecodefense* read very much like a sequel to Abbey's novel.

"It is time," Foreman declared, "for women and men, individually and in small groups, to act heroically and admittedly illegally in defense of the wild." Among various "defensive" tactics explained in the book were tree spiking, road spiking, fence cutting, and methods for "disabling motor vehicles of all kinds." Though such monkeywrenching activities were illegal and potentially dangerous, Foreman remained convinced that they could be "effective in stopping timber cutting, road building, overgrazing, oil and gas exploration, mining, dam building, powerline construction, off-road vehicle use, trapping, ski area development and other forms of destruction of the wilderness, as well as cancerous suburban sprawl."[64] In short, monkeywrenching offered a way for people to become "engaged in the most moral of all actions: protecting life, defending the Earth."[65]

There are, of course, multiple issues raised by *Ecodefense*. But for our purposes, the central questions are how the philosophy espoused in *Ecodefense* affected the political landscape; and why Earth First!ers felt compelled to use civil disobedience and illegal actions in pursuing their claims. These questions are surprisingly similar to those we have considered regarding another outbreak of civil disobedience—the Sagebrush Rebellion.

Several factors suggest that the approach advocated in *Ecodefense* struck a resonant chord within the environmental community. The first edition of *Ecodefense* went through two printings, and sold over five thousand copies in less than a year and a half;[66] by the mid 1980s Earth First! chapters had been organized in most states;[67] and a rash of monkeywrenching incidents had occurred throughout the federal lands in the West, a situation that helped place ecoterrorism on the Federal Bureau of Investigation's list of monitored domestic subversive activities.[68] Yet, there is no evidence of the movement's "success" as measured by traditional policy indicators.

Nevertheless, Earth First! had become a prominent feature in the public land policy arena and posed problems for the national groups trying to refocus the image of the environmental movement. Virtually every aspect of Earth First! seemed purposely designed to counter the moves of the environmental establishment. Whereas national leaders called for professionalism and pragmatism, Earth First! advocated a return to the movement's volunteer activism roots. Whereas the national groups' *Agenda* emphasized a "truly balanced multiple use" program for the federal lands, *Ecodefense* was "aimed at keeping 'industrial' civilization out of natural areas and causing its retreat from areas that should be wild."[69]

Even the structure of Earth First! offered a sharp contrast to the national groups. It had no formal leadership, no membership roster, no dues, and consequently no need for professional managers.

The contrasts created by Earth First! were not coincidental. As Foreman explains, the founders of Earth First! "set out to be radical in style, positions, philosophy, and organization in order to be effective and to avoid the pitfalls of co-option and moderation which [they] had already experienced."[70] This comment brings us to the question of why Earth First!ers felt compelled to adopt a radical posture.

Generalizations are always a risky business, and given the character of Earth First!, they are even more so. However, Foreman's account of his own move to radicalism is useful for several reasons. First, though not a "leader" of Earth First!, Foreman quickly became a leading spokesperson for the movement. Second, Foreman's motivations were not atypical of the views expressed by other Earth First!ers.[71] Finally, and perhaps most important, Foreman's story provides insights that help establish connections between the conflict in the environmental community and the Sagebrush Rebellion.

Writing in the October 1981 edition of *The Progressive*, Foreman explained that he had begun his "career" as a volunteer for the Wilderness Society. In 1973 he became the society's representative for the Southwest, and subsequently joined the society's national staff as issues coordinator. During this time, Foreman subscribed to the view that environmentalists "could inculcate conservation in the Establishment by using rational, economic arguments. The last thing we needed was somebody running amok. We needed to present a unified front."[72] However, a series of events, beginning in 1979, led to a "major crack in [his] personal moderation."

In January 1979 the Carter administration announced its decision to recommend wilderness designation for 15 million acres, out of a possible 60 million acres, of Forest Service land under the auspices of the Roadless Area Review Evaluation (RARE II) process. Although Foreman was unhappy with the small size of the proposed wilderness area, he was all the more frustrated by the decision because:

> Jimmy Carter, supposedly a great friend of wilderness, was President . . . [and] M. Rupert Cutler, a former assistant executive director of the Wilderness Society, was assistant secretary of agriculture over the Forest Service . . . had conceived the RARE II program. . . . Moreover, damn it, we—the conservationists—had been moderate. The anti-environmental side had been extreme, radical, emotional. Their arguments had been easily shot full of holes. We had been factual, rational. . . . But we had lost.[73]

As a result of this event, Foreman became increasingly disenchanted with a national environmental establishment populated by people who "saw jobs in the environmental organizations in the same light as jobs in government or industry" and were therefore "less part of a cause and more part of a profession." This situation, he argued, contributed to a pattern in which the "national groups—Sierra Club, Friends of the Earth, Audubon Society, Wilderness Society, and the rest—took almost identical middle-of-the-road positions on most issues. And then those half-a-loaf demands were readily compromised further."[74] In consequence, Foreman returned to New Mexico and his earlier post as representative for the Wilderness Society in the Southwest.

What Foreman experienced there was a barrage of personal threats and "the howling, impassioned, extreme stand set forth by off-road-vehicle zealots, many ranchers, local boosters, loggers, and miners." But for Foreman, the last straw was the July 4 celebration in Moab, Utah.

> There the local county commission sent a flag-flying bulldozer into an area the Bureau of Land Management had identified as a possible study area for wilderness review. The bulldozer incursion was an opening salvo for the so-called Sagebrush Rebellion, a move by chambers of commerce, ranchers, and right-wing fanatics in the West to claim all Federal public lands for the states and eventual transfer to private hands.[75]

This incident, followed by Reagan's election and Watt's appointment, led Foreman and a handful of other discontented members from national environmental groups to decide that "it was time for a new joker in the deck: a militant, uncompromising group unafraid to say what needed to be said or to back it up with stronger actions than the established organizations were willing to take."[76] Thus Earth First! was born.

It appears, then, that at least in the federal land policy arena, the controversy precipitated by the Sagebrush Rebellion exacted a heavier toll on the environmental community than commonly assumed. To be sure, environmentalists were relatively successful in blocking the administration's more radical overtures and in affirming public support for environmental goals. But part of the price for this success was growing dissent within the environmental movement.

The national leaders of the environmental movement found themselves caught in an uncomfortable bind. On the one hand, growing organizational complexities and the administration's changing posture made the move to professionalism and moderation seem a practical necessity as well as an appropriate political strategy. On the other hand, these attempts to adapt to the changing landscape seemed to fuel criticism like that of Earth First! cofounder Mike Rosselle: "Mainstream environmentalists are out of touch. . . . Most of them are in D.C. doing lunch in their designer khakis and working out their retirement bennies. The problem is, the environment isn't a calling anymore, its a job."[77] Moreover, the willingness of Earth First!ers to combine their radical rhetoric with equally radical actions simply tightened the bind. As Jay Hair complained: "People hear about Earth First! and tend to lump us [national groups] right into the same category of ecoterrorism. . . . In the public eye, that greatly diminishes all the good we've done. We're a nation of laws. Terrorism has no place in changing public policy—I see no fundamental difference between destroying a river and destroying a bulldozer."[78] Hair's concern may have been public confusion, but it might also have been a fear that the administration would be unable, or unwilling, to distinguish between the agendas of the national groups and that of Earth First!.

There is another more intriguing aspect of the turmoil within the environmental community that warrants attention. Earlier we noted that a key point of contention between James Watt and the environmental community was the issue of extremism. Watt charged that criticism of his agenda was orchestrated by "environmental extremists," while environmentalists countered that Watt's extremism, not their own, had created the conflict. It is curious, then, that in the wake of Watt's departure the environmental community would find itself embroiled in an internal argument that appeared to pit forces of moderation against "environmental extremists" and "kamikaze environmentalists."

It could be that the controversy surrounding the Sagebrush Rebellion and Watt was a catalyst for the tensions within the environmental community rather than their cause. After all, Foreman identified the Carter administration's decision on RARE II as the event that led him to reassess his posture. But catalyst or a cause, the Sagebrush Rebellion was clearly an important ingredient in the overall controversy. The emergence of Earth First! simply provided further evidence of how thoroughly disrupted the public land policy arena had become. Viewed in this light, the consequences of the Sagebrush Rebellion appear more far-reaching than commonly assumed.

THE SIGNIFICANCE OF THE SAGEBRUSH REBELLION

If we follow the dictates of traditional policy analysis, we would find little tangible evidence that the controversy spawned by the Sagebrush Rebellion produced any lasting consequences. The public lands remain in federal ownership and continue to be managed under the mandates adopted in the 1960s and 1970s. However, the argument advanced in this study is that the broader significance of the Sagebrush Rebellion lies within the less tangible context of political influence. In this context, there are several reasons to conclude that the Sagebrush Rebellion left an identifiable mark on the policy landscape.

At base, the Sagebrush Rebellion represented a protest against the growing influence of the environmental community. The measure of environmentalist influence, in turn, was the proliferation of regulations during the 1970s that exhibited a distinct bias in favor of environmental protection values. The question confronting Sagebrush Rebels, therefore, was how to curtail the environmental community's influence and thereby stem the tide of regulations. Initially, the call for conveyance of federal lands to the states seemed to provide an appropriate strategy. But after the 1980 elections, new possibilities emerged.

Although the Reagan administration did not effect a wholesale dismantling of environmental regulations, it did establish a policy tilt that paid renewed attention to the demands raised by the Sagebrush Rebels. At the same time, the administration's willingness to openly challenge the environmental movement revealed an important lesson about the character of environmentalist influence in the policy arena. As Walter Rosenbaum observed:

> The environmental movement prospered [during the 1970s] in a benign political climate assured by a succession of White House occupants tolerant, if not always sympathetic, to its objectives. . . . All this changed with the Reagan administration. . . . The Reagan years severely tested the foundations of the environmental movement. While the foundations held, little was done to advance the implementation of existing policy or to address new and urgent environmental problems.[79]

In short, the Reagan administration produced a stalemate in the public land policy arena.[80]

Lacking sufficient support to eliminate objectionable environmental policies, the administration was able to slow the environmental movement's momentum. Conversely, the environmental community could not eliminate the threat posed by the administration, but it did block implementation of most of Reagan's environmental agenda. Whether or not this stalemate warrants classifying the Sagebrush Rebellion as a success, it does indicate that the relative influence of Sagebrush Rebels and environmentalists was approaching parity in the mid 1980s. Moreover, the fact that the administration remained committed to a prodevelopment posture after the 1984 election, even in the face of environmental protests and public opposition, indicated that the policy arena was undergoing a fundamental change.

It is the character of this change that points to the broader significance of the Sagebrush Rebellion. The controversy surrounding the Sagebrush Rebellion served to transform the underlying structure of the policy dialogue and thereby insure that the arguments of the 1980s would not be resolved in the immediate future. Furthermore, despite some initial indications to the contrary, the transition from the Reagan administration to the Bush administration seemed to confirm that public land policy discussions would continue to follow the basic themes established in the 1980s. It is with an exploration of these issues that we conclude our story of the Sagebrush Rebellion.

We began this study by arguing that the meaning attached to conservation in the policy dialogue provided insights regarding the patterns of influence within the policy arena. Once again, throughout the first half of the twentieth century, the resource production emphasis of traditional conservation established a policy dialogue more attentive to development interests than to preservation interests. In the 1950s, the dominance of traditional conservation began to wane, and by the 1960s, it had been replaced by new conservation. New conservation's emphasis on preservation and restoration of environmental values, in turn, created a policy dialogue more supportive of environmental interests than commodity users.

The controversy spawned by the Sagebrush Rebellion introduced a new twist by bringing the traditional and the new definitions of conservation into direct conflict. Sagebrush Rebels, and more particularly James Watt, attempted to reclaim traditional conservation as a way to reopen negotiations about the relative balance between development and preservation in land use decisions. This move forced environmentalists to defend new conservation in order to protect the advances they had made during the 1970s. Although neither side prevailed, the argument offered a graphic reminder that conservation is a term with multiple, and not necessarily consistent, meanings. More important, it seems unlikely that future public land policy discussions will be able to assume that there is a widely accepted definition for conservation. In consequence, it also seems unlikely that either Sagebrush Rebels or environmentalists will be able to exert the dominant influence over the public land policy agenda they both once enjoyed.

The intervention of privatization and radical environmentalism illustrated the altered structure of the policy dialogue even more clearly than the argument over conservation. Indeed, the convention of portraying public land disputes as confrontations between development interests and preservation interests simply failed to capture the complexity of conflicts involving Sagebrush Rebels, privatization advocates, radical environmentalists, and the environmental establishment. And though privatization advocates retreated to academia after their brief stint in the Reagan administration, radical environmentalism remained a prominent feature in the policy arena.

The policy landscape of the 1980s was certainly not what the Sagebrush Rebels had in mind when they launched their movement. Nevertheless, the Reagan administration's ongoing commitment to a prodevelopment agenda, in combination with the growing schism within the environmental community, seemed to preclude a return to the policy arena of the 1970s. However, there was no escaping the fact that the changes resulted more from the Reagan administration's actions than from the Sagebrush Rebels' efforts. Thus, there was a distinct possibility that the end of the Reagan administration might signal a resurgence of environmental influence within the policy arena.

For a brief moment during the 1988 presidential election, it seemed that such might be the case. On August 31, Republican presidential candidate George Bush made a surprise move by pledging to be an "environmental president," if elected.[81] Although expressing relief that the open antienvironmentalism of the Reagan years might have ended, environmentalists remained wary of Bush's sincerity. As Sierra Club spokesperson Larry Williams noted: "Anyone who is familiar with Bush's career . . . knows that there is nothing in his history to suggest that he will live up to his campaign pledges."[82]

Yet there were reasons for suspecting that history might not be a reliable predictor. First, several events in 1988 brought environmental issues back to the center of national attention. A major drought and record-breaking heat wave affected large portions of the nation. The drought not only created serious economic losses in the agricultural sector, but also contributed to massive forest fires throughout the West. One of the more notable of these fires occurred in Yellowstone National Park, which experienced its worst fire in over three hundred years. The environmental community, in turn, seized upon the heat wave and drought as evidence of what life would be like if global warming occurred. A few observers even went so far as to suggest that climatic conditions of 1988 demonstrated that global warming had already begun. In addition, the discovery of raw sewage and medical wastes on the beaches of New Jersey and New York brought renewed concern about the dual problems of waste disposal and ocean pollution. Although these and other situations would have captured national attention at any time, it was especially fortuitous for environmentalists that they came during the election year that marked the end of the Reagan era. Second, given the arguments within the environmental community, it was not at all clear what it meant to be an environmental president. From a radical environmental perspective, neither Bush nor his Democratic opponent, Michael Dukakis, were acceptable candidates. From a moderate environmental perspective, however, both candidates were a significant improvement over Reagan. Moreover, Bush's environmental philosophy seemed to have been borrowed from *An Environmental Agenda for the Future*.

Writing in *Sierra*, Bush explained:

> I am a businessman by background and a conservative by inclination. But I do not believe that being either one of these is inconsistent with being an environmentalist. In fact, one goal of a Bush presidency would be to lead America toward a greater "conservation ethic"—a greater understanding that a clean and protected environment is essential to our public health, to our continued enjoyment of the outdoors, to our economic development, and ultimately to our quality of life.[83]

Bush's statement was obviously parallel to a key assertion in the *Agenda*: "Concern for the environment at a deeply personal level has joined with concern for economic well-being and the two have become integrated into a quality-of-life goal shared by Americans from all regions and in all economic groups."[84] Furthermore, there was reason to suspect that this parallel was more than a coincidence. Among Bush's environmental advisors were Nathaniel Reed and Russell Train—both prominent members of the environmental establishment that endorsed the *Agenda*.[85]

Finally, unlike the 1980 elections, there was no Sagebrush Rebellion and consequently no national controversy on which to base a push for continuation of Reagan's policies. Representatives from many of the interests that had populated the Sagebrush Rebellion convened in Reno, Nevada, in August 1988 to attend a national Multiple Use Strategy conference. This conference marked the beginning of the Wise Use Movement which, as we will see below, quickly became a prominent feature on the policy landscape. However, these developments received little attention during the presidential campaign.

In short, there was ample reason for an attitude of guarded optimism in 1988 about a new environmental era taking shape. Once Bush was elected, however, earlier skepticism regarding his sincerity quickly returned. On the one hand, Bush's choice of William Reilly to head the EPA won widespread praise from the environmental community. As a former staff member for the Council on Environmental Quality and president of the World Wildlife Fund–U.S./Conservation Fund, Reilly represented, in Jay Hair's words, "a world-class environmental leader and

. . . the first professional environmentalist ever to be named the EPA Administrator."[86] But environmentalists also used the Reilly nomination hearings to recount the budget cuts and regulatory constraints that served as a lasting reminder of the Reagan administration's attacks on EPA. Unless those restrictions were removed, warned Environmental Policy Institute president Michael Clark, "the appointment of Mr. Reilly will only be a hollow gesture from the Bush Administration."[87]

Bush's choice for Interior secretary, on the other hand, won no praise from the environmental community. Manuel Lujan, a Republican congressman representing New Mexico from 1968 to 1988, had been named as a possible replacement for both Watt and Clark during the Reagan administration. And though Lujan's official biography suggested that he had been actively involved in "numerous pieces of legislation to create Wilderness Areas, to designate Wild and Scenic Rivers, and to establish National Trails," as well as cosponsoring "seven major environmental protection bills,"[88] a detailed analysis of his voting record by the League of Conservation Voters (LCV) offered a contrasting view. "Lujan's overall average vote rating since 1973 . . . [was] only 18 on a scale of 100," a record indicating that Lujan had "voted against the environment more than four out of every five times."[89]

Lujan's statement of goals did little to allay environmentalist opposition. Promising to "bring a spirit of harmony to [policy] discussions through a process of consultation, cooperation, and coordination . . . among competing interests," Lujan also explained: "President Bush and I are committed to protecting and enhancing the Nation's natural resources, as well as proceeding with their environmentally sound development. We believe that development of our most promising domestic resources is called for, because continued development is essential to the national security and economic well-being of the United States."[90] It seemed, therefore, that Lujan was simply reading from the script crafted by Watt and refined by Clark and Hodel.

Despite his campaign pledge, then, the Bush administration looked less like the beginning of a new environmental era than a continuation of the Reagan era. Indeed, Bush's choices of Reilly and Lujan followed the basic pattern established by Reagan after the resignations of Watt and Burford: offering concessions to the environmental community at the EPA (Ruckelshaus, Thomas) while remaining committed to a moderate prodevelopment stance at Interior (Clark, Hodel). It seemed, therefore, that the changes in the policy arena formulated by the Reagan administration had survived the transition to the Bush administration.

There were other signs that the arguments spawned by the Sagebrush Rebellion had not been resolved. As noted above, a national Multiple Use Strategy Conference was held in Reno, Nevada during August

1988. Sponsored by the Center for the Defense of Free Enterprise (CDFE), an organization founded by Alan Gottlieb, an active participant in the New Right movement,[91] this conference gave birth to the Wise Use Movement. The conference participants were described as neither "single-minded preservationists" nor "single-minded apologists for industrial development," but rather "representatives of a new balance, of a middle way between extreme environmentalism and extreme industrialism."[92] Yet the groups populating the Wise Use Movement fell into familiar categories: off-road-vehicle users, mining, grazing, timbering, and farming interests.[93]

Ron Arnold, executive vice-president of CDFE and the driving force behind the Wise Use Movement, claims that the inspiration for the movement's name came from Gifford Pinchot's insistence that conservation meant the "wise use of resources."[94] Arnold resists characterizations that portray the Wise Use Movement as the "Sagebrush Rebellion in a new suit of clothes," because in his view, the movement "is much broader and deeper than a temper tantrum over public lands thrown by a handful of Nevada cowboys."[95] *The Wise Use Agenda*, which defines the unifying philosophy of the movement, outlines a far more diverse and sophisticated set of demands than the Sagebrush Rebels' call for conveyance of federal lands to the states.[96]

Nevertheless, the parallels between the two movements are too obvious to be ignored. Arnold's invocation of Pinchot gives clear evidence that the Wise Use Movement is a continuation of the effort to reclaim traditional conservation. As mentioned above, the interests represented in the Wise Use Movement are virtually identical to those that populated the Sagebrush Rebellion. Finally, though the twenty-five goals identified by the Wise Use Movement are certainly more diverse than the call for conveyance, they nonetheless address most of the underlying issues raised by the Sagebrush Rebels. Thus, Arnold's protests notwithstanding, it seems safe to conclude that the Wise Use Movement is an extension of the effort begun by the Sagebrush Rebels.[97]

One indication that the environmental community viewed the developments after the 1988 election as a continuation of earlier battles is provided by a fund-raising letter sent out by the Sierra Club in the early 1990s. The letter, mailed in an envelope with Watt's picture captioned "He's Back!," contained the following 1989 quote attributed to Watt. "The most important thing a man leaves behind are people and policies. And it's a tremendous compliment to see that during the years, the five years since I've been gone, that 'my people' continue in positions. And I've had conversations with [Interior] Secretary Lujan and I would expect that those policies and people, in a good degree, will stay." The letter went on to alert potential new members of the vital need for additional funds in order to fight an "alliance of 250 right-wing groups in what is cleverly called the *'Wise-Use Movement.'* "[98]

But the Wise Use Movement was not the only problem facing the environmental community. Buoyed by the increased attention to environmental issues and a twentieth anniversary of Earth Day that rivaled the early 1970s in demonstrating a groundswell of public support, environmentalists launched another foray into electoral politics. Using the initiative process, environmentalists succeeded in placing wide-reaching measures on state ballots in the 1990 elections. Initially it seemed that a resurgence of environmentalism had indeed occurred. As *Sierra* associate editor Paul Rauber noted: "So strong was the apparent green tide that even many traditional opponents accepted it as inevitable and set about honing post-election legal challenges."[99] When the votes were in, however, virtually every initiative had been defeated.

At the same time, the schism within the environmental movement developed interesting new twists. Although radical environmentalists continued their attacks on the environmental establishment,[100] the radical camp began exhibiting tensions of its own. At the risk of oversimplifying a far more complicated debate, the primary argument among radical environmentalists pitted "deep ecology" advocates against "social ecology" advocates. Generally speaking, deep ecologists argue that environmentally destructive practices result from the human-centered (anthropocentric) values underpinning western civilization.[101] In contrast, social ecologists portray environmental deterioration as another facet of the broader problems created by political and economic institutions that produce an unequal distribution of resources and power in society.[102] Although a more detailed discussion of the debate among radical environmentalists falls beyond the scope of this project,[103] this brief account suggests that the policy dialogue has continued to follow curious directions.

It seems obvious, therefore, that the policy arena of the 1990s contains a far more diverse set of claims and more diffuse patterns of influence than the arena of the 1970s. Thus, the contemporary arena is far less likely to develop the kinds of rules and regulations that produced the Sagebrush Rebellion. Nevertheless, the underlying arguments about public land use decisions have certainly not been resolved. Indeed, the September 30, 1991, edition of *Newsweek* carried a cover story entitled "The War for the West." Except for the details (names, locations, and the like), this story could be mistaken for our discussion in Chapter 3.

In one regard, all public land disputes evoke a sense of *déjà vu*. As we have seen, the Sagebrush Rebellion echoed the Stanfield and McCarran controversies. Moreover, the Sagebrush Rebellion has itself already become a recognized reference point for public land policy analysis.[104] However, our study suggests the possibility for viewing the

Sagebrush Rebellion as something more than just another episode in a long train of public land policy disputes.

The Sagebrush Rebellion marked the beginning of a period in which virtually every assumption about federal land policy underwent challenge and reconsideration. To be sure, the major assumptions—that public lands should remain in federal ownership and that they should be managed under the mandates enacted in the 1960s and 1970s—were reaffirmed by this process. But other assumptions did not fair so well. It is no longer possible, for example, to talk about conservation as if it possessed a widely accepted meaning. In a similar fashion, references to environmentalism must take into account both the moderate/radical distinction, and the differentiation among radical environmental postures. And since these shifts in the dialogue represent arguments that will not be resolved in the near future, there is reason to suspect that the controversy surrounding the Sagebrush Rebellion transformed the structure of the policy dialogue.

On this basis, then, it is possible to conclude that the Sagebrush Rebellion deserves to be listed with the conservation movement and the environmental movement as pivotal events in shaping the history of U.S. federal land policy. What unites these movements is that each marked the beginning of an episode in which the established patterns of influence within the policy arena gave way to new, or at least different, arrangements. Where the discussions in the aftermath of the Sagebrush Rebellion may lead is a question to be answered by future analysts. However, it is clear that the language of those discussions will carry an indelible reminder of the controversy launched by the state of Nevada in 1979.

NOTES

PREFACE

1. Tim Wirth, "What Bill Clinton Means for the West," *High Country News*, November 16, 1992, p. 11.

CHAPTER ONE. INTRODUCTION

1. Walt Whitman, *Leaves of Grass* (New York: Aventine Press, 1931), p. 9.
2. Alexander Hamilton, James Madison, John Jay, *The Federalist Papers*, Clinton Rossiter, ed. (New York: New American Library, 1961), p. 117.
3. Rochelle L. Stanfield, "Environmental Lobby's Changing of the Guard Is Part of the Movement's Evolution," *National Journal* June 8, 1985, p. 1350.
4. U.S. Congress, Senate, Subcommittee on Parks, Recreation, and Renewable Resources, *Bureau of Land Management Grazing Program, Hearings*, 96th Cong., 1st sess., 1979, p. 162.
5. Except as otherwise noted, the following discussion is derived from accounts published in the *Times-Independent* (Moab, Utah), *High Country News*, the *Salt Lake City Tribune*, and documents provided by the Grand County Commission and the Moab District Office of the BLM.
6. John L. Harmer, "A LASER Foundation Editorial," *LASER Beam*, August 1980, p. 3.
7. Henry Campbell Black, *Black's Law Dictionary*, 5th ed. (St. Paul: West Publishing, 1979), p. 223.
8. Roger W. Cobb and Charles D. Elder, *Participation in American Politics: The Dynamics of Agenda-Building*, 2d. ed. (Baltimore: Johns Hopkins University Press, 1983), p. 11.
9. Deborah A. Stone, *Policy Paradox and Political Reason* (Glenview, Ill.: Scott, Foresman, 1988), p. 109.

CHAPTER TWO. CONSERVATION: THE CHANGING STORY

1. Ronald Reagan, "Our Environment Crisis," *Nation's Business*, 58, 2 (February 1970): 25, 26.
2. Denis Hayes, "The Beginning," in Steven Cotton, ed., *Earth Day—The Beginning* (New York: Bantam Books, 1970), p. xiii.
3. Samuel P. Hays, *Conservation and the Gospel of Efficiency: The Progressive Conservation Movement, 1890–1920* (New York: Atheneum, 1975), p. 5.
4. Sally K. Fairfax, "Interstate Bargaining over Revenue Sharing and Payments in Lieu of Taxes: Federalism as if States Mattered," in Phillip O. Foss, ed., *Federal Land Policy* (New York: Greenwood Press, 1987).

5. Hays, *Conservation and the Gospel of Efficiency*, p. 3.

6. Gifford Pinchot, *The Fight for Conservation* (Seattle: University of Washington Press, 1967), pp. 42–44. This is a new edition of Pinchot's book, which was originally published in 1910.

7. Ibid., p. 50.

8. Roderick Nash, *Wilderness and the American Mind*, 3d ed. (New Haven, Conn.: Yale University Press, 1982), p. 129.

9. Ibid., pp. 161–181.

10. Douglas H. Strong, *The Conservationists* (Menlo Park, Calif.: Addison-Wesley Publishing, 1971), pp. 110–38.

11. Henry P. Caulfield, Jr., "Policy Goals and Values in Historical Perspective," in Dean F. Peterson and A. Berry Crawford, eds., *Values and Choices in the Development of the Colorado River Basin* (Tucson: University of Arizona Press, 1978), p. 116.

12. Elmo Richardson, *Dams, Parks and Politics* (Lexington: University Press of Kentucky, 1973), pp. 129–53.

13. Grant McConnell, "The Conservation Movement—Past and Present," *Western Political Quarterly*, 7, 3 (September 1954): 468.

14. Harold K. Steen, *The U.S. Forest Service: A History* (Seattle: University of Washington Press, 1976), pp. 278–07.

15. It should be noted that the wilderness language in MUSY referred to areas established administratively by the Forest Service. With the enactment of the Wilderness Act of 1964, wilderness management became a legally mandated use of the national forests.

16. 74 Stat. 215 (1960).

17. U.S. Congress, House, Committee on Agriculture, *National Forests—Multiple Use and Sustained Yield. Hearings*, 86th Cong., 2d sess., 1960, p. 39.

18. J. Michael McCloskey, "Natural Resources—National Forests—The Multiple Use–Sustained Yield Act of 1960," *Oregon Law Review*, 41, 1 (December 1961): 49–79.

19. See the collection of comments in "The Multiple Use Bill Advances," *Living Wilderness*, 25, 72 (1960): 40–42; and also Steen, *U.S. Forest Service*, pp. 308–17.

20. John F. Kennedy, "Special Message to Congress on Natural Resources," *Public Papers of the Presidents of the United States: John F. Kennedy, 1961* (Washington, D.C.: Government Printing Office, 1962), p. 119.

21. Marion Clawson, *The Western Livestock Industry* (New York: McGraw-Hill, 1950), p. 381.

22. U.S. Department of Interior, Bureau of Land Management, *Proceedings: National Advisory Board Council 21st Annual Meeting, March 14–16, 1961* (Washington, D.C.: Government Printing Office, 1961), p. 8.

23. Ibid., p. 23.

24. Phillip O. Foss, *Politics and Grass* (Seattle: University of Washington Press, 1960), p. 136.

25. Ibid., p. 139.

26. U.S. Department of Interior, Bureau of Land Management, *Proceedings: NABC, 1961*, p. 34.

27. Ibid., p. 38.

28. U.S. Department of Interior, Bureau of Land Management, *Proceedings: National Advisory Board Council 23rd Annual Meeting, March 11–13, 1963* (Washington, D.C.: Government Printing Office, 1963), p. 4.

29. U.S. Congress, Outdoor Recreation Resources Review Commission, *Outdoor Recreation for America* (Washington, D.C.: Government Printing Office, 1962), p. 21.

30. Ibid., p. 132.

31. Ibid., p. 113.

32. Pinchot, *Fight for Conservation*, p. 42.

33. Stewart Udall, *The Quiet Crisis* (New York: Avon Books, 1963), p. 120.

34. *Proceedings: White House Conference on Conservation* (Washington, D.C.: Government Printing Office, 1962), p. 2.

35. Udall, *Quiet Crisis*, p. viii.

36. Ibid., pp. 192–93.

37. U.S. Congress, House, Committee on Interior and Insular Affairs, *Public Land Law Review Commission: Background and Need*, Committee Print no. 39, 88 Cong., 2nd sess., 1964, p. 17.

38. *White House Conference*, p. 61.

39. Ibid., p. 62.

40. Ibid., p. 65.

41. *PLLRC: Background and Need*, p. 119.

42. John F. Kennedy, "Letter to Representative Aspinall Concerning Revision of the Public Land Laws," *Public Papers of the Presidents of the United States: John F. Kennedy, 1963* (Washington, D.C.: Government Printing Office, 1964), pp. 100–102.

43. 78 Stat. 890 (1964).

44. 78 Stat. 982 (1964).

45. 78 Stat. 986 (1964).

46. 78 Stat. 988 (1964).

47. Lyndon B. Johnson, "Special Message to Congress on Conservation and Restoration of Natural Beauty," *Public Papers of the Presidents of the United States: Lyndon B. Johnson, 1965, vol. 1* (Washington, D.C.: Government Printing Office, 1966), p. 156.

48. Ibid.

49. Ibid., p. 157.

50. See Samuel P. Hays, *Beauty, Health and Permanence: Environmental Politics in the United States, 1955–1985* (Cambridge, Eng.: Cambridge University Press, 1987).

51. Thomas Kimball, "Wilderness and Public Lands," *The Living Wilderness* 30, 95 (Winter 1966/67): 16.

52. "The Audubon View," *Audubon* 70, 2 (March/April, 1968): 4.

53. U.S. Congress, Senate, Committee on Interior and Insular Affairs, *National Land Use Policy. Hearings*, 91st Cong., 2d sess., 1970, p. 775.

54. U.S. Congress, Senate, Committee on Interior and Insular Affairs, *Surface Mining Regulation. Hearings*, 90th Cong., 2d sess., 1968, p. 361.

55. Ron Arnold, *At the Eye of the Storm: James Watt and the Environmentalists* (Chicago: Regner Gateway, 1982), p. 13.

56. Quoted in Roderick Nash, *The American Environment: Readings in the History of Conservation* (Menlo Park, Calif.: Addison-Wesley Publishing, 1976), p. 300.

57. Richard M. Nixon, "Remarks to Employees at the Department of Interior," *Public Papers of the Presidents of the United States: Richard M. Nixon, 1969* (Washington, D.C.: Government Printing Office, 1971), p. 119.

58. Richard M. Nixon, "Statement Announcing the Creation of the Envi-

ronmental Quality Council and the Citizens Advisory Committee on Environmental Quality," ibid., p. 422. The title of the agency was subsequently changed to the Council on Environmental Quality.

59. Quoted in Nash, *The American Environment*, p. 340.

60. Richard M. Nixon, "Special Message to Congress on the Environment," *Public Papers of the Presidents of the United States: Richard M. Nixon, 1971* (Washington, D.C.: Government Printing Office, 1973), p. 97.

61. Ibid., pp. 108–9.

62. Paul Brooks, "Notes on the Conservation Revolution," in John G. Mitchell, ed., *Ecotactics: The Sierra Club Handbook for Environment Activists* (New York: Pocket Books, 1970), p. 42.

63. Hays, *Conservation and the Gospel of Efficiency*, p. 265.

64. "Highlights of the September Board Meeting," *Sierra Club Bulletin* 55, 10 (October 1970): 17.

CHAPTER THREE. MULTIPLE USE—
MULTIPLE FRUSTRATION

1. U.S. Congress, House, Committee on Interior and Insular Affairs, *Sagebrush Rebellion: Impacts on Energy and Minerals. Oversight Hearings*, 96th Cong., 2d sess., 1980, p. 69.

2. Bernard Shanks, *This Land Is Your Land: The Struggle to Save America's Public Lands* (San Fransisco: Sierra Club Books, 1984), p. 265.

3. Public Land Law Review Commission (PLLRC), *One Third of the Nation's Lands* (Washington, D.C.: Government Printing Office, 1970), p. 1.

4. Ibid., p. 5.

5. Ibid., p. 45.

6. Ibid., p. 199.

7. Michael Frome, "The Environment and Timber Resources," in Hamilton K. Pyles, ed., *What's Ahead for Our Public Lands?* (Washington D.C.: Natural Resources Council of America, 1970), pp. 25–26.

8. PLLRC, *One Third*, p. 51.

9. Phillip Berry, "An Analysis: The PLLRC Report," *Sierra Club Bulletin* 55, 10 (October 1970): 19.

10. U.S. Congress, Senate, Committee on Interior and Insular Affairs, *Legislation to Revise the Public Land Laws. Hearings*, 92d Cong., 1st sess., 1971, p. 7.

11. Ibid., p. 11.

12. U.S. Congress, House, Committee on Interior and Insular Affairs, *Public Land Policy Act of 1971. Hearings*, 92d Cong., 1st sess., 1971, p. 42.

13. U.S. Congress, House, Committee on Interior and Insular Affairs, *BLM Organic Act: Part I. Hearings*, 93d Cong., 1st sess., 1973, p. 176.

14. Ibid., p. 177.

15. Ibid., p. 826.

16. U.S. Congress, House, Committee on Interior and Insular Affairs, *BLM Organic Act: Part II. Hearings*, 93d Cong., 2d sess., 1974, p. 1161.

17. 90 Stat. 2745 (1976).

18. 90 Stat. 2746 (1976).

19. Robert Dahl, *Pluralist Democracy in the United States: Conflict and Consent* (Chicago: Rand McNally, 1967), p. 24.

20. Roger W. Cobb and Charles D. Elder, *Participation in American Politics: The*

Dynamics of Agenda-Building, 2d ed. (Baltimore: Johns Hopkins University Press, 1983), p. 5.

21. Marion Clawson, "The Federal Land Policy and Management Act in a Broad Historical View," *Arizona Law Review* 21(1979): 596.

22. U.S. Congress, Senate, Committee on Interior and Insular Affairs, *The Proposed Nomination of Governor Cecil D. Andrus to Be Secretary of Interior. Hearings*, 95th Cong., 1st sess., 1977, p. 9.

23. David Speights, "Profile: Cecil D. Andrus," *Congressional Quarterly Weekly Reports* 34, 52 (December 1976): 3355.

24. John C. Hendee, George H. Stankey, and Robert C. Lucas, *Wilderness Management*, 2d ed. (Golden, Colo.: North American Press, 1990), pp. 160–61.

25. William Tucker, *Progress and Privilege: America in the Age of Environmentalism* (Garden City, N. Y.: Anchor Press/Doubleday, 1982), p. 131.

26. *Parker v. United States* 309 F. Supp. 593 (D. Colo. 1970).

27. For more detailed discussions of this case see Michael Frome, *Battle for the Wilderness* (New York: Praeger Publishers, 1974), pp. 159–162; Glen O. Robinson, *The Forest Service* (Baltimore: The Johns Hopkins University Press, 1975), pp. 168–170; and Craig W. Allin, *The Politics of Wilderness Preservation* (Westport, Conn.: Greenwood Press, 1982), 154–155.

28. Frome, *Battle for Wilderness*, p. 162.

29. Robinson, *Forest Service*, p. 163.

30. Hendee, et al.,*Wilderness Management*, p. 128.

31. For a discussion of the RARE processes see Hendee et al., *Wilderness Management*, pp. 129–39.

32. Samuel Trask Dana and Sally K. Fairfax, *Forest and Range Policy: Its Development in the United States* (New York: McGraw-Hill, 1980), p. 229.

33. U.S. Congress, House, Committee on Interior and Insular Affairs, *Wilderness Preservation System. Hearings*, 87th Cong., 2d sess., 1962, p. 1162.

34. "Memorandum to the PLLRC," in Hamilton K. Pyles, ed., *What's Ahead for Our Public Lands?* (Washington, D.C.: Natural Resources Council of America, 1970), p. 324.

35. 90 Stat. 2785 (1975).

36. The BLM did establish a small number of "primitive areas" under the auspices of the Multiple Use and Classification Act of 1964. See John C. Hendee, George H. Stankey, and Robert C. Lucas, *Wilderness Management* (Washington, D.C.: Government Printing Office, 1978), pp. 126–27.

37. Phillip O. Foss, *Politics and Grass* (Seattle: University of Washington Press, 1960), p. 35.

38. U.S. Department of Interior, Bureau of Land Management, *Range Condition Report* (Washington, D.C.: Government Printing Office, 1975), pp. v–1.

39. *Natural Resources Defense Council, Inc., et al. v. Rodgers C. B. Morton, et al.* (DC DC) 388 F. Supp. 829 (1974).

40. Robert H. Nelson, "NRDC v. Morton: The Role of Judicial Policy Making in Public Rangeland Management," *Policy Studies Journal* 14, 2 (December 1985): 257.

41. U.S. Department of Interior, Bureau of Land Management, *Managing the Public Rangelands* (Washington, D.C.: Government Printing Office, 1979), p. 15.

42. U.S. Department of Interior, Bureau of Land Management, "Interim Management Policy and Guidelines for Lands under Wilderness Review," December 12, 1979, p. 23.

43. *NRDC v. Morton*, 388 F. Supp. 840; U.S. Department of the Interior, Bu-

reau of Land Management, *Effects of Livestock Grazing on Wildlife, Watershed, Recreation, and Other Resource Values in Nevada* (Washington, D.C.: Government Printing Office, 1974).

44. Quoted in Nelson, "NRDC v. Morton," p. 259.

45. General Acounting Office, *Public Rangelands Continue to Deteriorate*, p. i.

46. General Accounting Office, *Learning to Look Ahead: The Need for a National Materials Policy and Planning Process* (Washington, D.C.: Government Printing Office, 1979), p. 7.

47. Hans H. Landsberg, Leonard L. Fischman, and Joseph L. Fisher, *Resources in America's Future* (Baltimore: Johns Hopkins University Press, 1963), p. 427.

48. Wildlands Research Center, *Wilderness and Recreation: A Report on Resources, Values and Problems* (Washington, D.C.: Government Printing Office, 1962), pp. 109–10.

49. Ibid.

50. For a more detailed discussion of the controversy surrounding mineral development and the Wilderness Act, see R. McGreggor Cawley, "Biodiversity: Lessons from the U.S. Wilderness Act," *Society and Natural Resources* 1, 2 (1988): 205–14.

51. U.S. Congress, House, Committee on Interior and Insular Affairs, *National Mining and Minerals Policy. Hearings*, 91st Cong., 1969–1970, p. 10.

52. PLLRC, *One Third*, p. 121.

53. 84 Stat. 1876 (1970).

54. U.S. Department of Interior, *Final Report on the Task Force on the Availability of Federally Owned Mineral Lands*, vol. 1 (Washington, D.C.: Government Printing Office, 1978), p. 50.

55. Ibid.

56. U.S. Department of Interior, *Final Report on the Task Force on the Availability of Federally Owned Mineral Lands*, vol. 2 (Washington, D.C.: Government Printing Office, 1978), pp. A-11, A-12.

57. Ibid., pp. A-18, A-19.

58. 90 Stat. 2746 (1976).

59. 90 Stat. 2785 (1976).

60. General Accounting Office, *Interior Programs for Assessing Mineral Resources on Federal Land Need Improvements* (Washington, D.C.: Government Printing Office, 1978), pp. 8–9.

61. Ibid.

62. Ibid.

63. *Rocky Mountain Oil and Gas Association v. Andrus*, 500 F. Supp. 1347 (1980).

64. "Interior Releases 33 Million Acres of Public Land from Wilderness Review," *Environment Reporter* 11 (1980): 1046.

65. U.S. Congress, House, Committee on Interior and Insular Affairs, *U.S. Minerals Vulnerability: National Policy Implications*, Committee Print no. 9, 96th Cong., 2d sess., 1980, p. 59.

66. David Sheridan, *Off-Road Vehicles on Public Lands* (Washington, D.C.: Government Printing Office, 1979), p. 7.

67. PLLRC, *One Third*, pp. 207–8.

68. *National Wildlife Federation v. Rogers C. B. Morton, et al.*, 393 F. Supp. 1286 (1974).

69. Ibid. at 1292.

70. Sheridan, *Off-Road Vehicles*, p. 69.

71. Alice J. Lamberson, "Excessively Restrictive Federal Land Use Policies and Their Adverse Effects on the Family," *Agenda for the 80's: A New Federal Land Policy. Proceedings* (Salt Lake City: League for the Advancement of States' Equal Rights, 1981), p. 376.

72. Frank J. Popper, *The Politics of Land Use* (Madison: University of Wisconsin Press, 1981), p. 3.

73. U.S. Congress, Senate, Subcommittee on Parks, Recreation, and Renewable Resources, *Bureau of Land Management Grazing Program. Hearings*, 96th Cong., 1st sess., 1979, p. 169.

74. James Santini, "The Sagebrush Rebellion," *MacNeil/Lehrer Report*, transcript, May 12, 1980, p. 6.

75. Alberta Sbragia, "Washington as Landlord: Federalism, Land-Use, and State Politics," paper presented at the Annual Conference of the Western Political Science Association, March 16–18, 1978, p. 33.

76. Sally K. Fairfax, "Beyond the Sagebrush Rebellion: The BLM as Neighbor and Manager in the Western States," in John G. Francis and Richard Ganzel, eds., *Western Public Lands: The Management of Natural Resources in a Time of Declining Federalism* (Totowa, N.J.: Rowman & Allanheld Publishers, 1984), p. 89.

77. *Ventura County v. Gulf Oil Corporation*, 601 F. Supp. 1080.

78. Brief provided by the Western Governors' Policy Office, p. 3.

79. Ibid., p. 9.

80. Richard D. Lamm and Michael McCarthy, *The Angry West: A Vulnerable Land and Its Future* (Boston: Houghton Mifflin, 1982), pp. 241–42.

81. Richard McArdle, quoted in Phillip O. Foss, *Recreation* (New York: Chelsea House Publishers, 1971), p. 401.

82. Samuel P. Hays, *Beauty, Health, and Permanence: Environmental Politics in the United States, 1955–1985* (Cambridge, Eng.: Cambridge University Press, 1987), pp. 529–30.

CHAPTER FOUR. WESTERN ANGER AND THE SAGEBRUSH REBELLION

1. Frederick Jackson Turner, *The Significance of Sections in American History* (New York: Henry Holt, 1932), p. 252.

2. Richard D. Lamm and Michael McCarthy, *The Angry West: A Vulnerable Land and Its Future* (Boston: Houghton Mifflin, 1982), p. 2.

3. Advisory Commission on Intergovernmental Relations, *Changing Public Attitudes on Governments and Taxes: 1979* (Washington, D.C.: Government Printing Office, 1979), p. 11.

4. Jimmy Carter, "Energy and National Goals," *Public Papers of the Presidents of the United States of America: Jimmy Carter, 1979*, vol. 2 (Washington, D.C.: Government Printing Office, 1980), pp. 1235, 1237.

5. Ibid., p. 1237.

6. Ibid., p. 1238.

7. Tom Mathews, Gerald C. Lubenow, Martin Kasindorf, and Gloria Borger, "The Angry West vs. the Rest," *Newsweek*, September 17, 1979, pp. 31–32.

8. Richard E. Blakemore, "Sagebrush Rebellion: Nevada's View," *State Government News* 22, 10 (November 1979): 4.

9. Samuel Trask Dana, *Forest and Range Policy* (New York: McGraw-Hill, 1956), p. 230.

10. U.S. Congress, Senate, Committee on the Public Lands and Surveys, *Granting Remaining Unreserved Public Lands to States. Hearings*, 72d Cong., 1st sess., 1932, p. 30.

11. Phillip O. Foss, *Politics and Grass* (Seattle: University of Washington Press, 1960), p. 176.

12. Ibid., p. 137.

13. A. F. Gustafson, C. H. Guise, W. J. Hamiliton, Jr., and H. Ries, *Conservation in the United States*, 3d ed. (Ithaca, N. Y.: Comstock, 1949), p. 327.

14. Ibid., p. 325.

15. Richard Lamm, "Some Reflections on the Balkanization of America," keynote address for the First Annual Meeting of the Western Governors' Policy Office, Vail, Colorado, August 18, 1978.

16. "Special Report: The Second War between the States," *Business Week*, May 17, 1976, p. 97.

17. Joel Haveman and Rochelle L. Stanfield, "Federal Spending: The North's Loss Is the Sunbelt's Gain," *National Journal*, June 26, 1976, pp. 878–91.

18. Compiled from reports in *Keystone Coal Industry Manual* (New York: Mc-Graw-Hill, 1972–1982).

19. Quoted in Lynton Hayes, *Energy, Economic Growth, and Regionalism in the West* (Albuquerque: University of New Mexico Press, 1978), p. 102.

20. Ibid., pp. 97–98.

21. James J. Lopach, "The Supreme Court and Resource Federalism," in John G. Francis and Richard Ganzel, eds., *Western Public Lands: The Management of Natural Resources in a Time of Declining Federalism* (Totowa, N.J.: Rowman & Allanheld Publishers, 1984), p. 283.

22. U.S. Department of Commerce, *State Government Tax Collections* (Washington, D.C.: Government Printing Office, 1979).

23. Quoted in R. McGreggor Cawley and Kenyon N. Griffin, "Regional Equity: The Politics of Severance Taxation," in Richard Ganzel, ed., *Resource Conflicts in the West* (Reno: Nevada Public Affairs Institute, 1983), p. 86.

24. Jimmy Carter, "Water Resource Projects," *Public Papers of the Presidents of the United States: Jimmy Carter, 1977*, vol. 2 (Washington, D.C.: Government Printing Office, 1977), p. 207.

25. Energy Policy Project of the Ford Foundation, *A Time to Choose* (Cambridge, Mass.: Ballinger, 1974), p. 273.

26. For a more thorough discussion of Carter's opposition to water projects see Marc Reisner, *Cadillac Desert: The American West and Its Disappearing Water* (New York: Viking Penguin, 1986), pp. 317–43.

27. Jimmy Carter, "The Environment," *Public Papers, 1977*, vol. 2, pp. 974–75.

28. Ibid., p. 979.

29. "Carter Acts to Preserve Alaskan Wilderness," *Congressional Quarterly Almanac*, vol. 34 (Washington, D.C.: Congressional Quarterly, 1978), p. 18.

30. Stewart McBride, "The Battle for Alaska Land," *Atlantic* 243, 5 (May 1979): p. 81. Emphasis in the original.

31. Ibid.

32. Edgar Wayburn, "Alaska: President Carter to the Rescue," *Sierra*, 64, 1 (January/February 1979): 22.

33. Robert Cahn, "Perspective: Jimmy Carter, Anti-Environmentalist?" *Audubon*, 8, 5 (September 1979): 7.

34. Carter, "Energy and National Goals," p. 1240.

35. Ibid., p. 1239.

36. Council on Environmental Quality, *Environmental Quality: Tenth Annual Report of the Council on Environmental Quality* (Washington, D.C.: Government Printing Office, 1979), p. 357.

37. Carter, "Energy and National Goals," p. 1240.

38. U.S. Congress, House, Interior and Insular Affairs Committee, *The MX Missile System. Oversight Hearings*, 96th Cong., 1st and 2d sess., 1979, 1980, p. 422.

39. U.S. Department of the Air Force, "IV Basing Mode Evaluation," *Final Environmental Impact Statement, MX: Milestone II* (Washington, D.C.: Government Printing Office, 1980), pp. iv-193–iv-213.

40. Paul J.Culhane, "Heading 'Em Off at the Pass: Mx and the Public Lands Subgovernment," in Phillip O. Foss, ed., *Federal Lands Policy* (New York: Greenwood Press, 1987), p. 97.

41. Richard D. Lamm and Michael McCarthy, *The Angry West: A Vulnerable Land and Its Future* (Boston: Houghton Mifflin, 1982), p. 241.

42. E.E. Schattschneider, *The Semisovereign People: A Realist's View of Democracy in America* (New York: Holt, Rinehart and Winston, 1960), pp. 3, 17.

CHAPTER FIVE. THE SAGEBRUSH REBELLION:
ISSUES AND TACTICS

1. Alexander Hamilton, James Madison, John Jay, *The Federalist Papers*, Clinton Rossiter, ed. (New York: New American Library, 1961), p. 117.

2. Orrin G. Hatch, "The Stewardship of the Public Domain," in *Agenda for the '80s: A New Federal Land Policy. Proceedings* (Salt Lake City, Utah: League for the Advancement of States' Equal Rights, 1981), p. 17.

3. Hatch, "Stewardship of Public Domain," p. 16.

4. U.S. Congress, House, Subcommittee on Mines and Mining, *Sagebrush Rebellion: Impacts on Energy and Minerals. Hearings*, 96th Cong., 2d sess., 1980, p. 10.

5. Ibid.

6. Hatch, "Stewardship of Public Domain," p. 16.

7. *Agenda for the '80s*, p. 4.

8. Richard Blakemore, "Sagebrush Rebellion: Nevada's View," *State Government News*, November 1979, p. 3.

9. E. E. Schattschneider, *The Semisovereign People: A Realist's View of Democracy in America* (Hinsdale, Ill.: Dryden Press, 1975), p. 60.

10. The text of both acts can be found in U.S. Congress, House, *Documents Illustrative of the Formation of the Union of the American States*, H. Doc. 398, 69th Cong., 1st sess., 1927.

11. William F. Swindler, ed., *Sources and Documents of United States Constitutions*, vol. 1–10 (Dobbs Ferry, N.Y.: Oceana Publications, 1973).

12. *Stearns v. Minnesota* 179 U.S. 242–243 (1900).

13. *Coyle v. Oklahoma* 221 U.S. 559 (1911).

14. Robert List, *Equal Footing Doctrine and Its Application by Congress and the Courts* (Carson City: Office of the Nevada Attorney General, 1977), p. 29.

15. *United States v. Texas* 339 U.S. 707 (1950).

16. Louis W. Koenig, ed., *The Truman Administration* (New York: New York University Press, 1956), p. 147.

17. U.S. Congress, Senate, *Western Lands Distribution and Regional Equalization Act of 1979*, S. 1680, 95th Cong., 1st sess., 1979, p. 13.

18. Charles Callison, "'Sagebrush Rebellion' Is Just Another Name for a Public Land Heist," *National Parks & Conservation Magazine: The Environmental Journal* 54, 3 (March 1980): pp. 11–12.

19. Samuel Hays, *Beauty, Health, and Permanence: Environmental Politics in the United States, 1955–1985* (Cambridge, Eng.: Cambridge University Press, 1987), pp. 40–41.

20. John G. Francis, "Environmental Values, Intergovernmental Politics, and the Sagebrush Rebellion," in John G. Francis and Richard Ganzel, eds., *Western Public Lands: The Management of Natural Resources in a Time of Declining Federalism* (Totowa, N. J.: Rowman & Allenheld, 1984), p. 42.

21. Jon Grand, "Environmental Management: Emerging Issues," *Book of the States* (Lexington, Ky.: Council of State Governments, 1985), p. 454.

22. Calculated from figures in James P. Lester, "State Budgetary Commitments to Environmental Quality under Austerity," in Francis and Ganzel, eds., *Western Public Lands*, pp. 201–2.

23. Cecil D. Andrus, "The Attack on Federal Lands," *Wall Street Journal*, December 5, 1979, p. 22.

24. William C. Patric, *Trust Land Administration in the Western States* (Denver: Public Lands Institute, 1981), p. 7.

25. See, for example, Alan Berlow, "National Taxpayers Union: Group Wants to Balance Nation's Checkbook," *Congressional Quarterly Weekly Reports* 37, 6 (February 10, 1979): 277–79.

26. Leonard H. Johnson, "Comparison of BLM Management Costs and State Land Management Agency Costs," a study prepared for the American Farm Bureau Federation in December 1979.

27. Except where noted, the following revenue estimates were calculated using figures from the U.S. Department of Interior, Bureau of Land Management, *Public Land Statistics* (Washington, D.C.: Government Printing Office, 1978).

28. Sally K. Fairfax and Carolyn E. Yale, *Federal Lands: A Guide to Planning, Management, and State Revenues* (Washington, D.C.: Island Press, 1987), p. 160.

29. Ibid., p. 156.

30. Utah Agricultural Experiment Station, "An Economic Evaluation of the Transfer of Federal Lands in Utah to State Ownership," pp. 47–48; University of Wyoming, College of Agriculture, "Bureau of Land Management and Forest Service Lands in Wyoming," p. 4.

31. U.S. Department of Agriculture, National Forest Service, *Report of the Forest Service* (Washington, D.C.: Government Printing Office, 1981), pp. 68–69.

32. "Election Day—November 4, 1980," *Coalition Comments*, 2, 4 (November 1980): 12.

33. "Mountain States Legal Foundation," Ibid.

34. Personal interview with Dean Rhoads at the LASER conference.

35. William Voigt, *Public Grazing Lands* (New Brunswick, N. J.: Rutgers University Press, 1976), p. 8.

36. "Watt's Up," *Wall Street Journal*, December 26, 1980, p. 4.

37. Sanford Ungar, "Washington: The 'New Conservatives,'" *Atlantic Monthly* 243, 2 (February 1979): 23.

38. "James G. Watt: Secretary of Interior," *Congressional Quarterly Weekly Report* 38, 50 (December 13, 1980): 3650.

39. Ibid.

40. "Watt Calls for 'Reasonable' Energy-Source Development," *Rocky Mountain News*, December 23, 1980, pp. 8, 138.

41. U.S. Congress, Senate, Committee on Energy and Natural Resources, *Proposed Nomination of James G. Watt to Be Secretary of Interior. Hearings*, 97th Cong., 1st sess., 1981, p. 163.

42. Ibid., p. 30.

43. See Chapter 2 for references to Aspinall comment.

44. Gifford Pinchot, *The Fight for Conservation* (Seattle: University of Washington Press, 1967), p. 42.

45. See Chapter 2 for references to Udall comment.

46. Watt's confirmation hearings, p. 59.

47. For more detailed discussions of the regulatory strategy employed by Watt and the Reagan administration see Donald C. Menzel, "Redirecting the Implementation of a Law: The Reagan Administration and Coal Surface Mining Regulation," *Public Administration Review* 43, 5 (September/October 1983): 411–20; and Robert F. Durant, "Toward Assessing the Administrative Presidency: Public Lands, the BLM, and the Reagan Administration," *Public Administration Review* 47, 2 (March/April 1987): 180–89.

48. Philip Shabecoff, "Watt and Foes Are the Best of Enemies," *New York Times*, November 11, 1981, p. A22.

49. Schattschneider, *Semisovereign People*, p. 60.

50. Walter Isaacson and Gary Lee, "A Watt That Produces Steam," *Time*, August 31, 1981, p. 15.

51. "Sagebrush Leader Outlines Accomplishments of the Rebellion," *Coalition Comments* 4, 1 (January 1982): 6.

52. "Nevada Develops Resolutions on Public Lands," *Coalition Comments* 4, 3 (July 1982): 5.

53. Ronald Reagan, "Message to Congress Transmitting the Fiscal Year 1983 Budget," *Public Papers of the Presidents of the United States: Ronald Reagan, 1982* (Washington, D.C.: Government Printing Office, 1982), p. 130.

54. U.S. Congress, House, Subcommittee on Public Lands and National Parks, *Public Land Sales and Transfers. Oversight Hearings*, 97th Cong., 2d sess., 1982, p. 226.

55. Watt's nomination hearings, p. 107.

CHAPTER SIX. PRIVATIZATION: A FLANK ATTACK

1. Steve Hanke, "Watt Never Did Believe in Privatizing U.S. Lands," *Wall Street Journal*, August 5, 1983, p. 20.

2. James G. Watt, *The Courage of a Conservative* (New York: Simon and Schuster, 1985), p. 203.

3. Christopher K. Leman, "How the Privatization Revolution Failed, and Why Public Land Management Needs Reform Anyway," in John G. Francis and Richard Ganzel, eds., *Western Public Lands: The Management of Natural Resources in a Time of Declining Federalism* (Totowa, N. J.: Rowman & Allanheld Publishers, 1984), p. 113.

4. E. E. Schattschneider, *The Semisovereign People: A Realist's View of Democracy in America* (Hinsdale, Ill.: Dryden Press, 1975), p. 66.

5. Peter Stoler and Gary Lee, "Land Sale of the Century," *Time*, August 23, 1982, p. 16.

6. U.S. Senate, Committee on Energy and Natural Resources, *Inventory, Management, and Disposal of Federal Real Property. Hearings*, 97th Cong., 2d sess., 1982, p. 74.

7. U.S. Congress, House, Subcommittee on Public Lands and National Parks, *Public Land Sales and Transfers. Oversight Hearings*, 97th Cong., 2d sess., 1982, p. 239.

8. Steve Hanke, "Wise Use of Federal Lands," *New York Times*, May 6, 1983, p. A31.

9. "Memorandum to Western Governors," July 18, 1983, provided by the Wyoming Governor's Office.

10. Philip Shabecoff, "Watt Removes Agency's Land from Sale Plan," *New York Times*, July 28, 1983, p. 1.

11. Ibid., p. A17.

12. Steve Hanke, "Watt Never Did Believe in Privatizing," p. 20.

13. George H. Nash, *The Conservative Intellectual Movement in America Since 1945* (New York: Basic Books, 1976), p. 131.

14. What actually constitutes the public interest is, of course, open to much debate. Here and in the following discussion, however, the point is to explain the conservative posture, not to engage in a debate about the definition of the public interest.

15. Ibid., p. 82.

16. Ibid., p. xi.

17. Phillips quoted in Richard A. Viguerie, *The New Right: We're Ready to Lead* (Falls Church, Va.: Viguerie Company, 1980), p. 63.

18. Ibid., p. 13.

19. Ronald Reagan, "Inaugural Address," *Public Papers of the Presidents of the United States: Ronald Reagan, 1981* (Washington, D.C.: Government Printing Office, 1983), p. 2.

20. Ibid.

21. Ibid.

22. Ron Arnold, *At the Eye of the Storm: James Watt and the Environmentalists* (Chicago: Regnery Gateway, 1982), p. 22.

23. Ibid., p. 52.

24. Viguerie, *New Right*, p.105.

25. James Watt, "Ours Is the Earth," *Saturday Evening Post* 254, 1 (January/February 1982): 75.

26. Gifford Pinchot, *The Fight for Conservation* (Seattle: University of Washington Press, 1967), p. 43.

27. Ibid., p. 20.

28. Watt, "Ours Is the Earth," pp. 75, 104.

29. Ibid., p. 75.

30. Samuel Hays, *Conservation and the Gospel of Efficiency* (New York: Atheneum, 1975), p. 265.

31. U.S. Congress, House, Subcommittee on Public Lands and National Parks, *Public Land Sales and Transfers. Oversight Hearings*, 97th Cong., 2d sess., 1982, p. 406.

32. *Federal Land Policy and Management Act* 90 Stat. 2744 (1976).

33. 90 Stat. 2750.

34. Hanke quoted in Ann Crittenden, "Exodus of the Supply Siders," *New York Times*, July 25, 1982, p. F6.

35. Steve Hanke, "Watt's Liberal Sins," *New York Times*, July 3, 1983, p. E12.

36. Watt quoted in Robert SanGeorge, "Watt Unleashes a Barb at Indian Reservations," *Washington Post*, January 19, 1983, p. A7.

37. "Secretary Watt Fires Back at His Critics," *Business Week*, January 24, 1983, p. 86.

38. "Environmentalists: More of a Political Force," *Business Week*, January 24, 1983, p. 85.

39. Dale Russakoff, "Watt's Off-the-Cuff Remark Sparks Storm of Criticism," *Washington Post*, September 22, 1983, p. A1.

40. Dole quoted in *Congressional Quarterly Almanac* (Washington, D.C.: Congressional Quarterly, 1983), p. 327.

41. U.S. Congress, House, Subcommittee on Public Lands and National Parks, *Administration's Asset Management Program and Its Impact on Federal Land Management and Recreation Programs. Oversight Hearings*, 98th Cong., 1st sess., 1983, p. 185.

42. Richard M. Nixon, "Special Message to Congress on the Environment," *Public Papers of the Presidents of the United States: Richard Nixon, 1971* (Washington, D.C.: Government Printing Office, 1973), p. 106.

43. "Public land" refers to the lands administered by the BLM. Other portions of the federal estate, most notably the national parks, have virtually no history of disposal efforts.

44. Milton Friedman, *Capitalism and Freedom* (Chicago: University of Chicago Press, 1962), p. 15.

45. Ibid., p. 31.

46. Garrett Hardin, "The Tragedy of the Commons," *Science* 162 (1968): 1244.

47. Ibid., p. 1245.

48. Ibid.

49. Ibid., p. 1247.

50. Robert K. Davis, Steve H. Hanke, and Frank Mitchell, "Conventional and Unconventional Approaches to Wildlife Exploitation," in *Transactions of the 38th North American Wildlife and Natural Resources Conference* (Washington, D.C.: Wildlife Management Institute, 1973), pp. 75–87.

51. Richard Stroup and John Baden, "Externality, Property Rights, and the Management of Our National Forests," *Journal of Law and Economics* 16, 2 (October 1973): 305.

52. Ibid., p. 310.

53. Ibid.

54. Garrett Hardin and John Baden, eds., *Managing the Commons* (San Francisco, Calif.: W.H. Freeman, 1977), p. xii.

55. Ibid., pp. 137–38.

56. John Baden, *Earth Day Reconsidered* (Washington, D.C.: Heritage Foundation, 1980), p. 3.

57. Ibid., p. 95.

58. John Baden, "The Sagebrush Rebellion and the Environmental Decade: An Introduction," in *Agenda for the '80s: A New Federal Land Policy. Proceedings* (Salt Lake City, Utah: League for the Advancement of States' Equal Rights, 1981), p. xi–xii.

59. Ibid., p. xiii.

60. John Baden, "Introductory Remarks," *Agenda for the '80s*, p. 176.

CHAPTER SEVEN. THE AFTERMATH

1. James G. Watt, "Text of Resignation by Watt and Its Acceptance by Reagan," *New York Times*, October 10, 1983, p. D10.

2. Jay Hair of the National Wildlife Federation quoted in Rochelle L. Stanfield, "Environmental Lobby's Changing of the Guard Is Part of Movement's Evolution," *National Journal*, June 6, 1985, p. 1350.

3. Russell Peterson, "The Audubon View: No Common Ground," *Audubon* 84, 2 (March 1982): 107.

4. Kenneth T. Walsh, "Lobby Tables Turned: Environment War Gets New Arena," *Denver Post*, July 12, 1982, p. 1B.

5. Ibid., p. 7B.

6. "Environmentalists: More of a Political Force," *Business Week*, January 24, 1983, p. 86.

7. U.S. Congress, Senate, Committee on Environment and Public Works, *Nomination of William D. Ruckelshaus. Hearings*, 98th Cong., 1st sess., 1983, p. 9.

8. Ibid.

9. Ibid., p. 19.

10. Ibid., p. 191.

11. U.S. Congress, Senate, Committee on Energy and Natural Resources, *Nomination of William P. Clark. Hearings*, 98th Cong., 1st sess. (1983), p. 56.

12. Steven R. Weisman, "Watt Quits Post; President Accepts with Reluctance," *New York Times*, October 10, 1983, p. D10.

13. *Nomination of William P. Clark. Hearings*, p. 3.

14. Ibid., p. 52.

15. Ibid., p. 86.

16. Ibid., p. 15.

17. "Clark Replaces Watt at Interior Department," *1983 Congressional Quarterly Almanac* (Washington, D.C.: Congressional Quarterly, 1983), pp. 327–31.

18. Carl Pope, "Ronald Reagan and the Limits of Responsibility," *Sierra* 69, 3 (May/June 1984): 52.

19. Ibid.

20. Robert Cameron Mitchell, "Public Opinion and Environmental Politics in the 1970s and 1980s," in Norman J. Vig and Michael E. Kraft, eds., *Environmental Policy in the 1980s: Reagan's New Agenda* (Washington, D.C.: Congressional Quarterly, 1985), pp. 51–74.

21. George Gallup, Jr., *The Gallup Poll: Public Opinion 1983* (Wilmington, Del.: Scholarly Resources, 1984), pp. 90, 107.

22. Ibid., p. 261.

23. Ibid., p. 260.

24. "Environmental Group Endorses Mondale," *New York Times*, February 22, 1984, p. A16.

25. "Conservationists Grade Candidates on the Issues," *New York Times*, February 25, 1984, p. 8.

26. Francis X. Clines, "Reagan Hails Environmental Record," *New York Times*, June 20, 1984, p. 22.

27. "President Draws Fire from Conservationists," *New York Times*, June 26, 1984, p. B6.

28. Philip Shabecoff, "Environment Shrinks as Political Issue," *New York Times*, July 8, 1984, p. 4E.

29. Ibid.

30. George Gallup, Jr., *The Gallup Poll: Public Opinion 1984* (Wilmington, Del.: Scholarly Resources, 1985), p. 146.

31. Ibid.

32. "Sierra Club Endorses Mondale/Ferraro: Staff Report," *Sierra* 69, 5 (September/October 1984): 39.

33. James G. Watt, "Text of Resignation by Watt," p. D10.

34. Philip Shabecoff, "Clark to Stay on for 2 or 3 Months," *New York Times*, January 3, 1985, p. A19.

35. U.S. Congress, Senate, Committee on Environment and Public Works, *Nomination of Lee M. Thomas. Hearings*, 99th Cong., 1st sess., February 1985, p. 375.

36. Ibid., p. 361.

37. U.S. Congress, Senate, Committee on Energy and Natural Resources, *Nomination of Donald Paul Hodel. Hearings*, 99th Cong., 1st sess., 1985.

38. Robert A. Jones, "Environmental Movement—Wholesale Changes at the Top," *Los Angeles Times*, December 27, 1984, p. 3.

39. Ibid.

40. Stanfield, "Environmental Lobby's Changing of the Guard," p. 1350.

41. Jones, "Environmental Movement," p. 3.

42. Ibid., p. 21.

43. Ibid., p. 3.

44. Stanfield, "Environmental Lobby's Changing of the Guard,"pp. 1350, 1353.

45. Friends of the Earth, et al., *Ronald Reagan and the American Environment: An Indictment, Alternative Budget Proposal, and Citizen's Guide to Action* (Andover, Mass.: Brick House Publishing, 1982), hereafter cited as *Indictment*; Robert Cahn, ed., *An Environmental Agenda for the Future* (Washington, D.C.: Island Press, 1985), hereafter cited as *Agenda*.

46. *Indictment*, p. 6.

47. Ibid., pp. 7, 19.

48. The list of groups involved in both publications includes: Friends of the Earth, Natural Resources Defense Council, Wilderness Society, Sierra Club, National Audubon Society, Environmental Defense Fund, Izaak Walton League, National Parks and Conservation Association, and National Wildlife Federation.

49. *Agenda*, p. 1.

50. Ibid.

51. Ibid., p. 19.

52. Ibid.

53. Geoffrey Wandesforde-Smith, "Learning from Experience, Planning for the Future: Beyond the Parable (and Paradox?) of Environmentalists as Pin-Striped Pantheists," *Ecology Law Quarterly* 13 (1986): 745.

54. Ibid., footnote 225, p. 755.

55. Robert Gottlieb and Helen Ingram, "The New Environmentalists," *The Progressive* 52, 8 (August 1988): 14.

56. Kirkpatrick Sale, "The Forest for the Trees: Can Today's Environmentalists Tell the Difference," *Mother Jones* 11, 7 (November 1986): 25.

57. For discussions of this phenomenon see Peter Borrelli, ed., *Crossroads: Environmental Priorities for the Future* (Washington, D.C.: Island Press, 1988); Robert Gottlieb and Helen Ingram, "Which Way Environmentalism? Toward a New Democratic Movement," in Marcus Raskin and Chester Hartman, eds., *Winning America: Ideas and Leadership for the 1990s* (Boston: South End Press and the Institute for Policy Studies, 1988), pp. 371–84; Gary E. Machlis, "The Tension between Local and National Conservation Groups in the Democratic Regime," *Society and Natural Resources* 3, 3 (1990), pp. 267–79; Roderick Nash, *The Rights of Nature: A History of Environmental Ethics* (Madison: University of Wisconsin Press, 1989), pp. 161–98; and Roderick Nash, *American Environmentalism: Readings in Conservation History*, 3d ed. (New York: McGraw-Hill, 1990), pp. 225–348.

58. "The Ecological Green Berets," *Newsweek*, July 19, 1982, pp. 25–26.

59. The Plowboy Interview, "Dave Foreman: No Compromise in Defense of Mother Earth," *Mother Earth News* 91 (January/February, 1985): 18–19 (hereafter cited as Plowboy).

60. Eugene Hargrove, "Ecological Sabotage: Pranks or Terrorism?" *Environmental Ethics* 4, 4 (Winter 1982): 291.

61. Ibid., p. 291–92.

62. Ibid., p. 292.

63. Plowboy, p. 22.

64. Dave Foreman and Bill Haywood, *Ecodefense: A Field Guide to Monkeywrenching*, 2d. ed. (Tucson, Ariz.: Nedd Ludd Books, 1987), p. 14 (hereafter cited as *Ecodefense*).

65. Ibid., p. 17.

66. Ibid., p. 3.

67. Joe Kane, "Mother Nature's Army: Guerrilla Warfare Comes to the American Forest," *Esquire* 107, 2 (February 1987): 102.

68. Indeed, Dave Foreman and several other people were arrested by the FBI in 1989 in connection with monkeywrenching activity in Arizona. They subsequently pleaded guilty to charges stemming from the incident.

69. *Ecodefense*, p. 16.

70. Dave Foreman, "Earth First!: Move Out the People and Cars, Reclaim the Roads and Plowed Land, Free Shackled Rivers," *The Progressive* 45, 10 (October 1981): 40.

71. See, for example, Christoph Manes, *Green Rage: Radical Environmentalism and the Unmaking of Civilization* (Boston: Little, Brown, 1990); John Davis, ed., *Earth First! Reader: Ten Years of Radical Environmentalism* (Layton, Utah: Peregrine Smith, 1991); and Howie Wolke, *Wilderness on the Rocks* (Tucson, Ariz.: Nedd Ludd Books, 1991).

72. Foreman, *Earth First!*, p. 40.

73. Ibid., p. 39.

74. Ibid., p. 40.

75. Ibid.

76. Ibid.

77. Kane, p. 98.

78. Kane, "Mother Nature's Army," p. 102.

79. Walter A. Rosenbaum, *Environmental Politics and Policy*, 2d. ed. (Washington, D.C.: Congressional Quarterly Press, 1991), pp. 4–5.

80. Samuel Hays arrives at a similar conclusion in *Beauty, Health, and Permanence: Environmental Politics in the United States, 1955–1985* (Cambridge, Eng.: Cambridge University Press, 1987), p. 525.

81. Eliot Marshall, "Campaigning on the Environment," *Science*, September 23, 1988, pp. 1589–90; Mark D. Valentine, "Election Year Environmentalism," *Bioscience* 38, 10 (November 1988): 668.

82. Marshall, "Campaigning on the Environment," p. 1590.

83. George Bush, "Promises to Keep," *Sierra* 73, 6 (November/December 1988): 62.

84. *Agenda*, p. 5.

85. Ibid., pp. 1589–90.

86. U.S. Congress, Senate, Committee on Environment and Public Works, *Nomination of William K. Reilly. Hearings*, 100th Cong., 1st sess., 1989, p. 295.

87. Ibid., p. 275.

88. U.S. Congress, Senate, Committee on Energy and Natural Resources, *Manuel Lujan, Jr., Nomination. Hearings*, 100th Cong., 1st sess., 1989, p. 129.

89. Ibid., p. 85.

90. Ibid., pp. 38–39.

91. Richard Viguerie, *The New Right: We're Ready to Lead* (Falls Church, Va.: Viguerie Company, 1980), p. 66.

92. Alan M. Gottlieb, ed., *The Wise Use Agenda: The Citizen's Policy Guide to Environmental Resource Issues* (Bellevue, Wash.: Free Enterprise Press, 1989), p. ix.

93. Ibid., pp. 157–66.

94. Jon Krakauer, "Brown Fellas," *Outside* 16, 12 (December 1991): 71.

95. Ibid., p. 72.

96. In addition to *The Wise Use Agenda*, cited above, two books by Arnold help establish a background for understanding the philosophy behind the Wise Use Movement: *At the Eye of the Storm: James Watt and the Environmentalists* (Chicago, Ill.: Regnery Gateway, 1982); and *Ecology Wars: Environmentalism As If People Mattered* (Bellevue, Wash.: Free Enterprise Press, 1987).

97. For additional discussions of the Wise Use Movement and related issues see Margaret L. Knox, "The Wise Use Guys," *Buzzworm*, 2, 6 (November/December 1990): 30–36; Dan Baum, "Wise Guise," *Sierra* 76, 3 (May/June 1991): 71–93; Margaret Knox, "Meet the Anti-Greens," *The Progressive* 55, 10 (October 1991): 21–23; Charles P. Alexander, "Gunning for the Greens," *Time*, February 3, 1992, pp. 50–52; and Florance Williams, "Sagebrush Rebellion II," *High Country News*, February 24, 1992, pp. 1–11.

98. Undated Sierra Club mailing.

99. Paul Rauber, "Losing the Initiative?" *Sierra* 76, 3 (May/June 1991): 20.

100. Jay Letto, "One Hundred Years of Compromise," *Buzzworm* 4, 3 (March/April 1992): 26–32.

101. For further clarification of deep ecology concepts see Bill Deval and George Sessions, *Deep Ecology: Living As If Nature Mattered* (Layton, Utah: Peregrine Smith, 1985).

102. For further clarification of social ecology concepts, see Murray Bookchin, *The Philosophy of Social Ecology: Essays on Dialectical Naturalism* (Montreal: Black Rose Books, 1990); and Murray Bookchin, *Ecology of Freedom: The Emergence and Dissolution of Hierarchy* (Palto Alto, Calif.: Cheshire Books, 1982).

103. For discussions of the arguments among radical ecologists see Rik Scarce, *Eco-Warriors: Understanding the Radical Environmental Movement* (Chicago: Noble Press, 1990); Steve Chase, ed., *Defending the Earth: A Dialogue between Murray Bookchin and Dave Foreman* (Boston: South End Press, 1991); and Dave Foreman, *Confessions of an Eco-Warrior* (New York: Harmony Books, 1991).

104. For instance, William Graf has used the Sagebrush Rebellion as a focus for reconsidering public land history in his book, *Wilderness Preservation and the Sagebrush Rebellions* (Savage, Md.: Rowman & Littlefield, 1990).

INDEX